For Ri Gardiner—
Who knew Lower Manhattan
was important before "9/11".
With admiration +
affection.   *[signature]* 9/25/06

Hilary Lewis
Román Viñoly

THINK NEW YORK
A Ground Zero Diary

images
Publishing

congress / clinton /

The Challenge

In the case of rebuilding the World Trade Center site in New York, hindsight may provide some insight but hardly all the answers. Several years have gone by since we realized that big ideas, implementation and financial support were needed to repair Lower Manhattan. During that time, plenty of suggestions and decisions have been made, sufficient funding appeared to be available and work has begun, but the final outcome is still unclear. With so much at stake, this complicated but critical process continues to be an enormously challenging one.

To begin with, how do you embark on a large-scale urban planning project on some of Manhattan's most valuable land and balance the needs, rights and hopes of the many constituencies involved? Do you have a small, select group make decisions? Do you leave it solely to those who have legal control of the property? Do you open it up to an international competition? Do you accept that your current public agencies are not structured to tackle this type of problem? Where do you start? In a city where it is rare to get one acre of land to develop, there were now 16 contiguous acres crying out for transformation. The traditional New York fabric, where developers frequently build slender towers on the sites of former parking lots, was not present here. Big thinking was needed for a very large design problem.

Almost immediately following the events of September 11, 2001, two strains emerged in speaking about the city and its rebuilding. The first was a real estate story. How should space be used and remade and, most of all, paid for? The second was an architectural challenge separate from the more practical elements. This was a debate about remaking the image of the city, of symbolically tackling the memory of great loss and coming to terms with crafting a future.

In fairness to architects, all good ones understand that they cannot divorce themselves from the realities of real estate. The best architectural solutions bring together artistic and utilitarian aspects, acknowledging the constraints of client, program, political climate and, not least of all, finances. But, it bears noting that prior to addressing all of those practical parameters, which were simply not defined in the fall of 2001, architects tended to focus on form, or perhaps it is more true to say, the idea of what to build next.

Today, the site has been cleared. Plans have been drawn, changed, and doubtlessly will change again. The process that began in September 2001 is ongoing, despite the decisions that were made with apparent finality in February 2003, when the agency charged with selecting a designer for the master plan declared its winner.

What has stopped though is any serious consideration of what could have been created if issues of ownership had been addressed differently. What was essentially taken as a given was the primacy of the Port Authority's claim over the land and therefore that of its lessee, Larry Silverstein. Yes, ideas were floated about trading the World Trade Center site for alternative land at Kennedy Airport, but that deal got shot down quite quickly. The ability of government to take over the land and start from scratch using eminent domain surely should have been seen as a serious option.

However, the need for immediate funding in the form of a private developer appeared to trump that possibility, which gave great importance to the participation of Mr. Silverstein. The one sure thing therefore became the need to replace the majority of the lost square footage of office space, which the developer's insurance money was thought to be adequate to fund. That assumption was and is significant for all involved in the project.

Given those fixed constraints, much is still to be determined. A review of what really happened during that tortuous time when designers first addressed how to rebuild, the LMDC requested ideas, then specific plans from a selected group of designers and eventually crafted and selected a master plan, should give us some insight into how we can now best proceed.

For the moment, let's go back even earlier. Prior to September 11, 2001, the Twin Towers were an important part of the skyline, but did not resonate with New Yorkers as their memory does today. The truth was their form and the underused plaza between them never engendered widespread affection among Manhattanites. Big and blocky, they anchored the city's southern skyline, which seems so bare today. But, from the start in 1977, when the Twin Towers were completed, their imagery never matched that of New York's other great skyscrapers. Impressive for their height, the towers never obtained the same status as the Empire State Building and the Chrysler Building. Like so many things following the attacks on New York in September 2001, that status changed. The imagery of the World Trade Center has taken on an entirely different meaning in the post-9/11 world. Its hulking modern form now seems to represent a more optimistic time to which many would be happy to return.

An example of what did not work at the Trade Center was the windswept plaza that was once at the base of architect Minoru Yamasaki's gargantuan, rectangular skyscrapers. Distinct from other popular New York gathering places, from the outdoor room formed by the main buildings at Lincoln Center to the dramatic sunken space at Rockefeller Center, the plaza at the base of the World Trade Center rarely attracted large crowds. How many films show New Yorkers gathering in the shadow of those 110-story skyscrapers as opposed to in Central Park, Washington Square or the monumental plaza at the crossroads of 59th Street and Fifth Avenue?

Those who may have derided the complex's architecture and overall planning as antithetical to New York's traditional urbanism are confronted by a sea change in public attitude about the site. In polls taken after the destruction of the towers, a high number of New Yorkers felt that the correct course was simply to rebuild the towers just as they were, despite any earlier objections to their architectural inadequacies.

Another stumbling block post-9/11 was detailed by the press who suggested the great height of the Twin Towers made those buildings a magnet for both tourists and terrorists. The conclusion seemed clear: build high and risk much. Questions about the safety and desirability of tall buildings ensued. Other tall landmarks in New York however did not experience mass departures of their tenants despite concerns over safety. Nonetheless, there was talk that in the future New York buildings should not reach skyward at record heights.

Although there were those in New York that embraced the idea of replacing the Trade Center complex with identical structures, most eventually came to agree that a better course to follow was to rethink the entire area and in doing so produce a fitting memorial to those lost and a monument to the city's rebirth following 9/11—replacing the 10 million square feet of office space, of course.

That is a tough environment in which to propose new designs, especially for towers that could fill in the missing section of skyline. Throw in the powerful and emotional atmosphere surrounding the buildings' destruction and you increase the difficulty many times over of developing acceptable plans of widespread acceptance. Yet, that was precisely what was asked of the designers and public officials who shouldered the mantle of repairing the damaged portion of New York post-9/11.

In 2001, the city was not organized in such a way to mount a major rebuilding process on its own, therefore an agency incorporating city, state and federal representatives was formed. The public body that assumed the responsibility was the Lower Manhattan Development Corporation. With no history of building, this agency made great strides to assemble ideas and specific proposals on how to remake the 16 acres that were now so much in the forefront of the public's mind.

That assignment would have been a tough one even for a seasoned institution, but for a brand-new agency the work at hand must have been daunting, especially when its mandate was ambiguous from the start. Was the LMDC really the client? How could it be if it did not control the project's financing or the site itself? After all, this land was owned by a strange political animal, the Port Authority of New York and New Jersey, the product of two states, yet nonetheless semi-autonomous. No single official, mayor or governor, could easily take the project over fully. To complicate matters further, the Port Authority was now answerable to real estate investor and developer, Larry Silverstein, who as described above, now had the right to oversee partly the redevelopment of the land.

It was no simple hurdle to determine who should make decisions let alone how to make those decisions. Without a clarified client other elements were hard to pin down, in particular the program and budget, the components of any project that normally guide the work of architects and planners.

Another complicating factor was the form of the city itself. New York's urbanism is one of the city's most powerful characteristics. Based on the grid and filled with some of America's most distinct landmarks, the texture of the city is both gritty and grand. Unmistakably recognizable as New Amsterdam, Gotham or any of the many names New York is known by, the place is hard to confuse with any other metropolis, long shot and close-up included.

New Yorkers take the unique aspects of their city seriously, and are hard-pressed to accept quietly changes to its form. The introduction of new urban interventions, from parks to mega-structures, has usually been met with resistance and critical concern, even when well intended and designed. Ironic for a city that has prospered from population growth and real estate development, New York has nonetheless had a long tradition of skepticism when it comes to large-scale urban planning, especially in the postwar period. Preparing a master plan for any significant section of New York is a tricky business.

How can anyone be expected to develop coherent and consistent urban plans for such a place that despite its fairly strict street-grid is actually a concrete celebration of individual variety? Pity anyone who tries. No matter how beautiful or brilliant the proposal, be prepared for objections from a host of sources. Rockefeller Center and Battery Park City notwithstanding, the basic look of New York defies large-scale planning. For many, this is precisely why the original World Trade Center was not consistent with New York urbanism. Based on a super block, the gargantuan towers paid no respect to the streetscape and imposed a single vision of dominant, late modernism.

This may in part explain why the extraordinary challenge of developing design solutions for Lower Manhattan in the wake of the tragic events of 9/11 produced such drama. New Yorkers are not neutral when it comes to their local environment. They may not be able to control it directly or fully, but they passionately care about it, and if asked, would like to express an opinion or two about how it should be maintained or expanded. Give people a forum for this and they will show up—often in large numbers.

In a nutshell, that explains the first chapter of the story of New York's attempt to rebuild its southern portion. The community wanted a say in the city's attempt to heal and renew the urban wound left by the loss of the two tallest structures on this important island. New York could not prevent the disaster of September 11, 2001, but it could help affect the aftermath. Residents made their feelings known—loud and clear—when the city initially presented its proposals for rebuilding in July 2002. Thousands crowded into Manhattan's Jacob Javits Convention Center to reject resoundingly what they felt was an inadequate response to the World Trade Center site's complexity and the community's needs.

Faced with so many issues of remembrance, respect and renewal, the redevelopment of this site merited not only the attention of the locals, but of people around the country and the globe. Negotiating the many suggestions, proposals and criticisms would not be a simple task for even a well-established civic institution. What about a newly formed and untested organization that would be honored and burdened with the responsibility of making sense of the constituencies and challenges inevitably involved with the remaking of New York's downtown? The Lower Manhattan Development Corporation was in rough waters from day one. And that was just from the perspective of average citizens. The combination of financial interests, political pressures, concerns of victims' families and input of the design community only complicated matters further.

What ensued was an extraordinary period of debate, reflection and struggle, which continues today. Despite the importance of decisions still to come, the period that began September 2001 and ended in February 2003 with the selection of a master plan defines the scope of this book, because it was during this timeframe that the greatest range of design concepts were proposed. This was in part due to spontaneous actions by individuals, but also because of structured oversight by public authorities. The process that followed is a rich and important lesson of how a major city can tackle the challenge of large-scale building, when budget, client and program are all ambiguous.

In particular, the purpose of this book is to show the work of one group of architects who in the year-and-a-half following the destruction of the World Trade Center assembled a broad series of concepts and proposals for remaking Ground Zero. Four designers: Shigeru Ban, Frederic Schwartz, Ken Smith and Rafael Viñoly began thinking about the problems of this site before they ever joined forces. However, the synthesis of their work as an ensemble, what became THINK, is evidence of not only the power of collaboration, but of a historic time for the design community. In a pressure cooker of media exposure, political oversight and worldwide attention, THINK developed a process for coordinating the many requirements of this site and its evolving program and was eventually selected as one of two finalist design teams considered for the master plan.

An architect supported by a royal patron or an all-powerful state, would surely not have endured the trials required of the designers who worked with the city and state agencies involved in New York's rebuilding. City planning by fiat may occur in modern China, but is nearly impossible in today's New York. Like most American cities, New York relies not only on government and the public's voice to form its cities, but also on economic forces. These could not be ignored, which meant that those entities that brought money to the table did not just get to sit there, they would get the best seats.

So where do you begin to develop physical solutions for downtown New York? With a great amount of respect for the many lives lost and affected as well as with an eye toward the current and future denizens of Manhattan, architects began to draw. Those early sketches show a wide variety of responses to the problem of remaking Lower Manhattan. While some architects spoke of leaving a vast open space at what was now termed Ground Zero, many responded by focusing on one of New York's most salient architectural features: height.

Like so many other architects around the world, the principals of THINK responded quickly to the fall of the World Trade Center. From focusing on the making of a memorial, as in the case of Tokyo-based Shigeru Ban, or to addressing the damaged urban connections at street level, as in Ken Smith's landscapes, the individuals who would form THINK did not wait to be asked to produce visual answers for New York's damaged downtown.

The earliest responses to the needs of Lower Manhattan from both Frederic Schwartz and Rafael Viñoly were primarily architectural and related to the making of distinctive, tall structures. Both Viñoly and Schwartz initially considered structures that could repair the New York skyline. Viñoly sketched a massive flagpole and Schwartz drew DNA-inspired towers. Both approaches focused more on symbolism and artistry than urban infrastructure, which contrasts with THINK's later emphasis on the fine details of developing a master plan.

The fact that most architects seemed attracted to addressing the skyline as opposed to the streetscape is hardly surprising. After all, buildings are at the center of the practice of architecture, but the impulse of designers to consider the loss of twin hundred-plus story buildings emerges from something even stronger: the power of symbolism, of an architectural idea. That's what can transform a plan into a great architectural work.

In the section that follows, there are examples of the early ideas of THINK's principals. These were not meant to be proposals, but early artistic responses. Elements of some of these designs would reappear in various forms throughout the later work of THINK. Given this, the diary format is extremely useful here. In the pages of the following sections the reader gets a taste of the vicissitudes of navigating a rough road of public opinion, political power and the internal struggles of design. But here in the early stages of reflection on Ground Zero, one gets a pure view into a creative process untrammeled by the constraints that would surely come.

For starters, architect Shigeru Ban begins with one of the most basic forms in the history of architecture for sacred building, the circular structure. His design is reminiscent of Rome's ancient Temple of Vesta, whose form derives from a circular colonnade and a pitched roof very similar to Ban's. A gentle and comforting image, one could imagine a well-visited place of remembrance built using this highly recognized shape for a place of worship and contemplation.

Ken Smith produced a memorial landscape that is also an urban connection, replete with a reflecting pool and a wall commemorating the lives of those lost on 9/11. This design was in keeping with Smith's longstanding commitment to landscape architecture, integrating the built and natural environments. His Sky Memorial meaningfully addressed the relationship between earth and sky in an urban context.

Immediately following the events of September 2001, Frederic Schwartz put pen to paper. From his office he has a direct view to the World Trade Center site and is reminded daily of all that transpired on 9/11. His initial response was to think big and remember. His sketches show quick strokes and a dose of sadness resulting from Schwartz's contact with the day's disturbing events. Deeply affected by the loss of life, Schwartz embraced the building block of life as inspiration. DNA strands permeate his towers.

Rafael Viñoly began his thinking by considering great urban monuments, from Paris's Eiffel Tower to the more recent London Eye. In a series of drawings done in several different sketchbooks, Viñoly experimented with formal solutions to New York's need for a tall replacement for the lost towers. Additionally, Viñoly incorporated his belief in the advantage of adding public participation and experience within such large structures. Like the famed European monuments mentioned above, some of Viñoly's imagined structures include a way for a visitor to scale the building using a ride of some sort. He clearly wanted to offer the public a way to experience the new structure at all levels, something that is rarely proffered by privately held skyscrapers.

These early concepts were not intended to be complete solutions, but they are important and interesting records of the way in which talented designers create their far more complex final products. Unlike Athena emerging from the head of Zeus, design does not spring fully formed from the first sketches of the architect. That said, the early ideas that would resonate in later work are detailed in the pages of this book.

Serious design is the result of a process that incorporates the requirements of the client, environment and a host of other factors. A successful designer, or design team, has to negotiate and digest these various elements and adjust the design accordingly. This book is evidence of that process, one where political curveballs, changing budgets and a shifting crew of decision-makers affected the work of the architects, often on a weekly basis. While in many ways this project and its conditions were unique, its history also contains a blueprint of how to shape a city, in this case, how to THINK about New York.

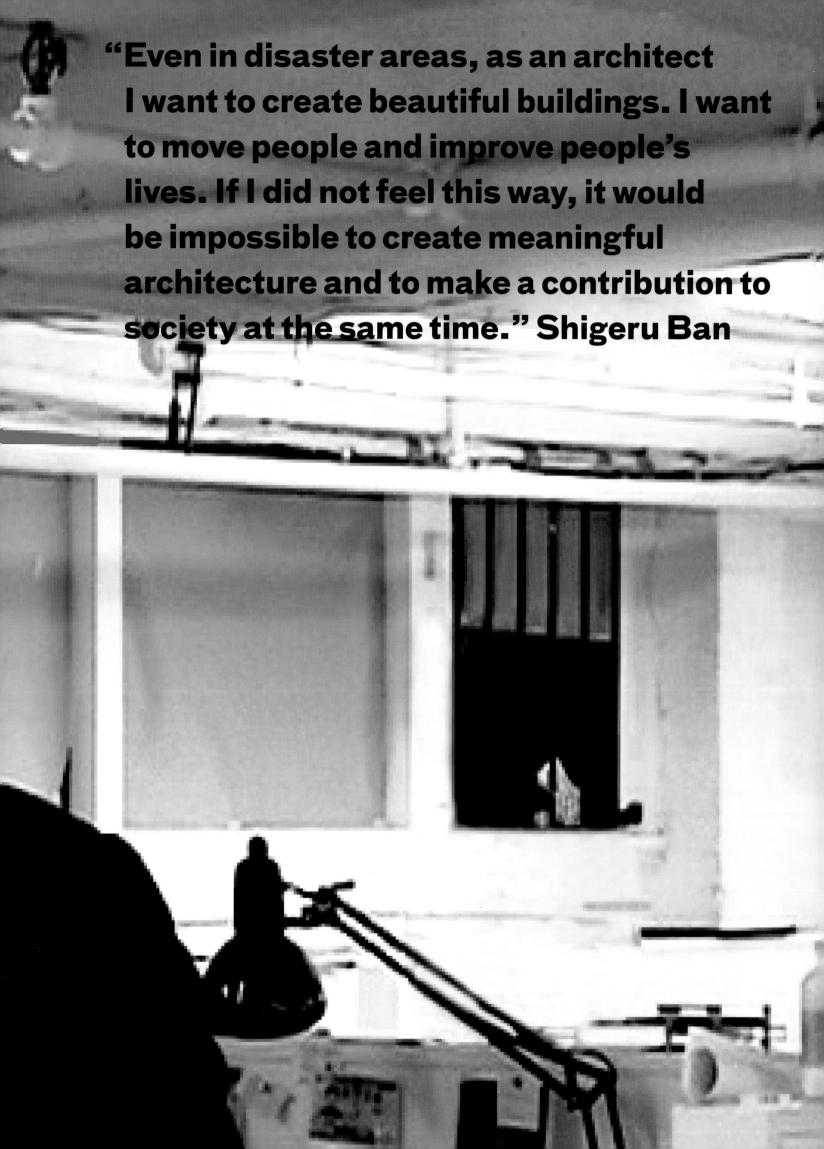

"Even in disaster areas, as an architect I want to create beautiful buildings. I want to move people and improve people's lives. If I did not feel this way, it would be impossible to create meaningful architecture and to make a contribution to society at the same time." Shigeru Ban

WTC Memorial for New York   16/09/01

skylight

Membrane

Pn

Rubles
Steel Plates

Shigeru Ban's early proposal for a design response to September 11 was a circular pavilion topped with a conical roof. Ban's elegant structure reaches back to the history of architecture in its direct reference to Rome's ancient Temple of Vesta. Here, he uses a double colonnade in a circular plan, which harkens back to the long tradition of centrally planned structures dedicated to sacred space, from baptisteries to temples. Ban introduces a layer of fabric between the two colonnades, creating a tent-like effect, which softens the design and lends an air of mystery and transience to the structure.

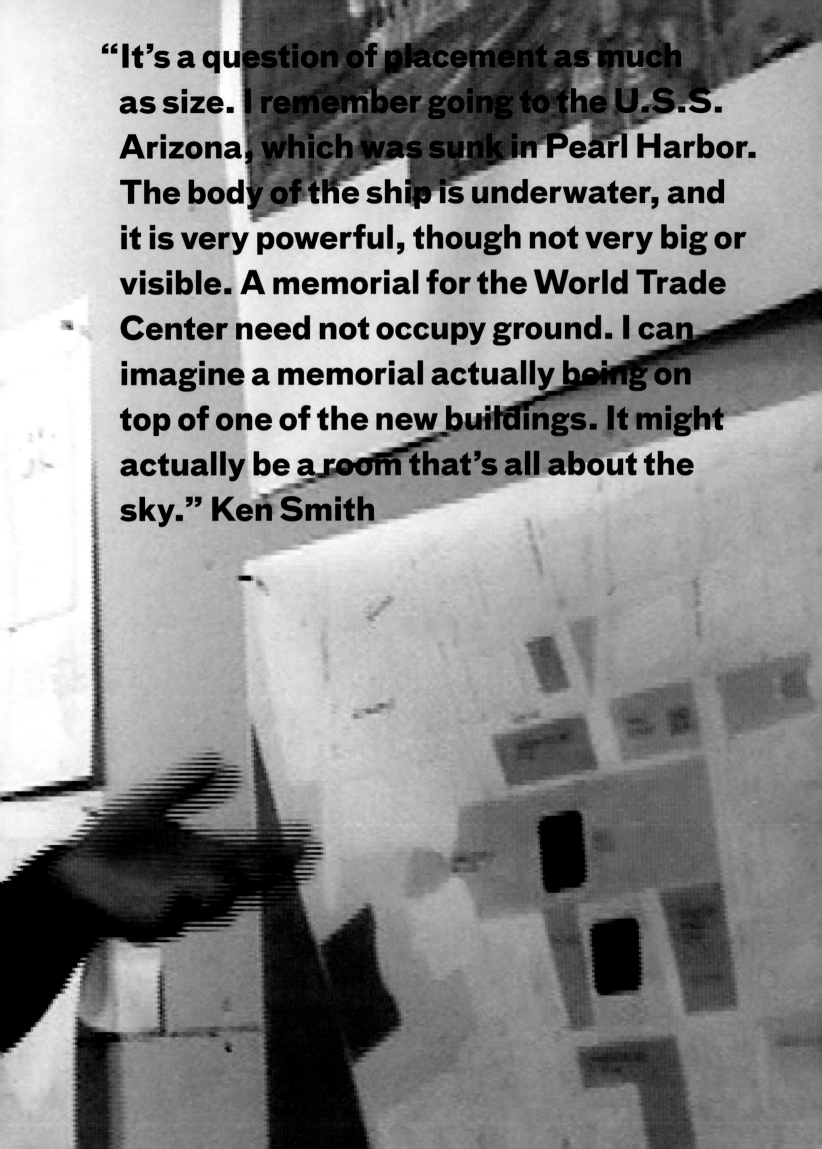

"It's a question of placement as much as size. I remember going to the U.S.S. Arizona, which was sunk in Pearl Harbor. The body of the ship is underwater, and it is very powerful, though not very big or visible. A memorial for the World Trade Center need not occupy ground. I can imagine a memorial actually being on top of one of the new buildings. It might actually be a room that's all about the sky." Ken Smith

Subject: Re: Hope you are OK
Date: 11 Sep 2001 12:37:39
From: Ken Smith
To: Lissa Thompson

Lissa

Thanks for the e-mail. I am ok as is everyone in the office. My wife Priscilla is uptown and ok. My office is six blocks form the World Trade Center so I saw and experienced first hand much of what happened which is truly horrible. One of my employees saw people jumping from the tower to sure death soon before it collapsed. Crowds of people were fleeing. My office building shook severely and the electricity flickered. The dust ball was incredible. I couldn't see the building accross the street and now everything is covered with a thick layer of dust. My house is located between the office and the Trade Center. I have contacted people in the building and know that our building is safe but this entire area is being evacuated. Since I can't go home I'm sitting tight here at the office for now.

This is the closest thing to war that I've ever experienced.

Ken

——-Lissa Thompson wrote:——-

Ken,

Still at home watching the morning news. Don't know where you are...but hope you and yours are O.K. Hopefully, not too many were at work in those buildings already.

I watched the second World Trade Center get hit by the large plane. Am stunned. Can't be any other explanation than terrorism. It will be a mess on the ground and in the area for some time to come.

How will they reconstruct?

Be careful.

Lissa

Subject: RE: found business card
Date: 1 Oct 2001 13:26:04
From: Nedunuri, Rajeev [IT]
To: Ken Smith

Ken,
I am fine. Thank you for your concern and support. I was one of the lucky ones who escaped this terrible disaster unharmed.

Thank You again,
Rajeev

——-Original Message——-
From: Ken Smith
Sent: Sunday, September 30, 2001 5:23 PM
To: Nedunuri, Rajeev [IT]
Subject: found business card

To Rajeev Nedunuri,
Solomon Smith Barney
From: Ken Smith,
80 Warren Street

Dear Rajeev

I found your business card in the debris on my window sill three blocks north of Seven World Trade Center.

Are you OK?

Subject: WORKSHOP
Date: 20 September , 2001
To: All
From: Ken Smith

WE ARE OPEN FOR BUSINESS
Ken Smith Landscape Architect

Please note that we are back in business following the recent tragedy at the World Trade Center.

Verizon is forwarding our regular phone service to an emergency cell phone so we can now receive your calls and voice mail.

We are not able to receive faxes or e-mail at this time. Also our mail delivery has been affected.

Please bear with us. We hope that all services will return to normal as quickly as possible.

79 Chambers Street 2nd Fl. New York, N.Y. 10007
212-791-3595 p/f e-mail: KSLA@earthlink.net

Subject: Re: WTC Sketches
Date: 30 October, 2001
From: Ken Smith
To: Janet Froelich,
New York Times Magazine
From: Ken Smith

Enclosed is a rough sketch / montage of the sky memorial idea.

I always associated the trade towers with looking up toward the sky. On sunny days they would shimmer and on overcast days they would dissolve into the clouds, it seems that the sky is an appropriate metaphor for the memorial.

My idea is that the changing sky and light conditions would be registered and reflected in the etched faces on the glass wall set against the sky. The space would have a phenomenological quality; an ever changing sense of awe and serenity.

Let me know if you want any specific changes to the image. I would like to try out a couple of other sky conditions to explore the concept of the memorial.

Subject: Re: Additional WTC Sketches
Date: 30 October, 2001
From: Ken Smith
To: Janet Froelich,
New York Times Magazine
From: Ken Smith

I have given more thought to my sketch idea for the sky memorial.

The temporary memorials that have sprung up around the city seem to be the true memorials because they are so real and immediate. The missing persons, often shown in casual snapshots, are powerful in their normality. These everyday images are effective in bringing the reality of the horrible event to a very personal level. The permanent memorial should try to capture the emotion of these interim memorials.

For the sky memorial, the glass walls will be etched with snapshots of the victims, much like the hand made posters on the impromptu walls. The photo images with short memorial messages will be set against the backdrop of the sky. The faces will register the ephemerality of the changing sky and light conditions.

I am preparing a second sketch to illustrate this memorial concept and I am making some refinements to my original sketch. I will send both images to you on compact disc. Please let me know if you need anything else.

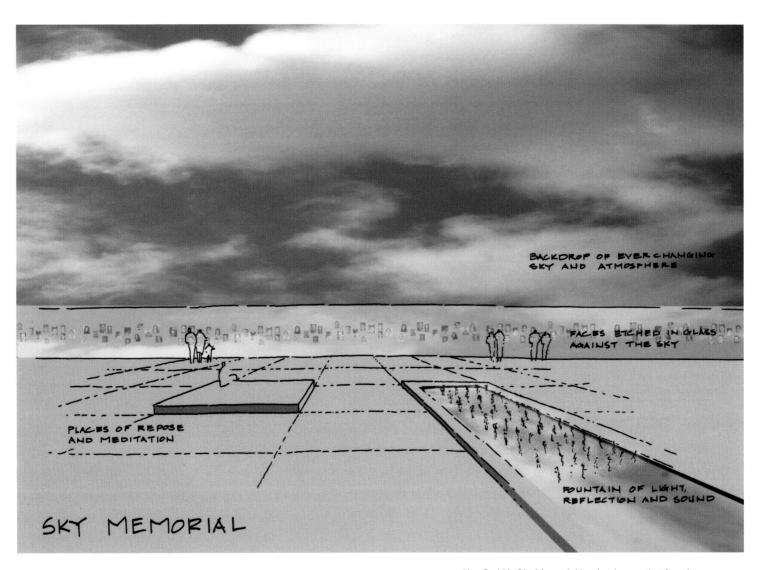

BACKDROP OF EVER-CHANGING SKY AND ATMOSPHERE

FACES ETCHED IN GLASS AGAINST THE SKY

PLACES OF REPOSE AND MEDITATION

FOUNTAIN OF LIGHT, REFLECTION AND SOUND

SKY MEMORIAL

Ken Smith's Sky Memorial is a landscape that functions as a memorial. The scheme includes a reflecting pool and a wall commemorating the lives of those lost on September 11. Known for his dedication to mediating the relationship between built and natural environments, Smith's Sky Memorial uses air and light to examine the connection between earth and sky in an urban context.

"I started drawing immediately in an effort to remember but not yet rebuild. I drew the horrible things I witnessed that day; trying to imagine ways to help my city heal." Frederic Schwartz

REALISTIC
PRAGMATIC
CONSTRAINTS
CONED EXAMPLE

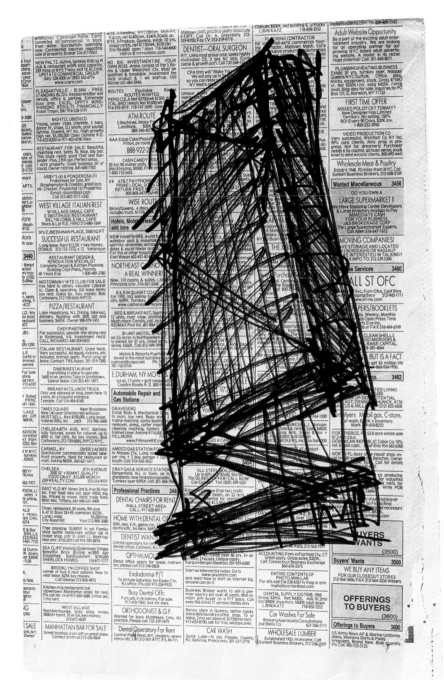

Frederic Schwartz's earliest sketches made in response to 9/11 reflected two of the architect's interests: the need for tall structures to replace the World Trade Center's presence on the New York skyline and the importance of imbuing such structures with symbolism relating to renewal and life. In particular, Schwartz referenced the imagery of DNA strands both here and in later, more refined drawings. Rafael Viñoly also made early sketches based on DNA helixes, which underscores the shared vision between these two architects.

In these very preliminary designs, Schwartz also explores the possibility of interconnections between tall structures; this foreshadows the design of THINK's **World Cultural Center**. Also, one of the images bears resemblance to Schwartz's housing solution, which he contributed to *The New York Times Magazine*.

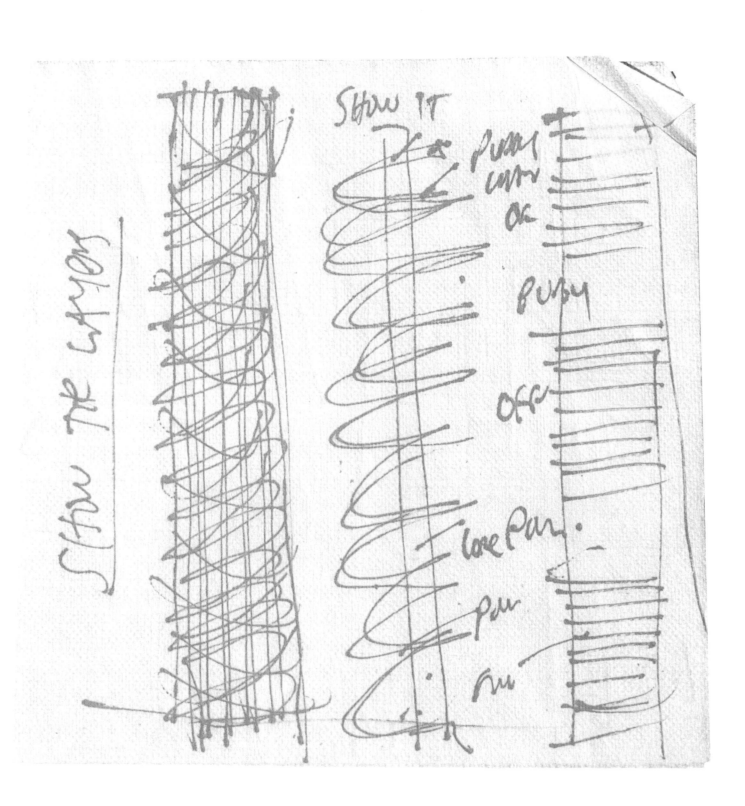

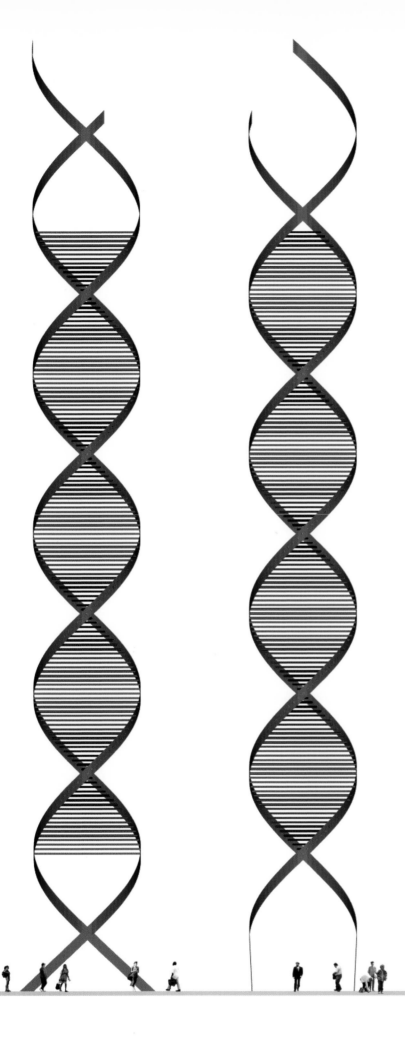

Schwartz describes his conversations with Dr. Mark Philips, a professor of medicine and cell biology at New York University, as an important reason for his focus on DNA as appropriate imagery for a memorial or other structures at Ground Zero. These images contrast the energy of quick sketches with a more developed illustration of DNA structure.

"If you open up your design process to the client and the community for whom you work, you benefit from it—there is a lot of learning. You miss a lot of value in terms of other people's ideas if you insulate yourself." Rafael Viñoly

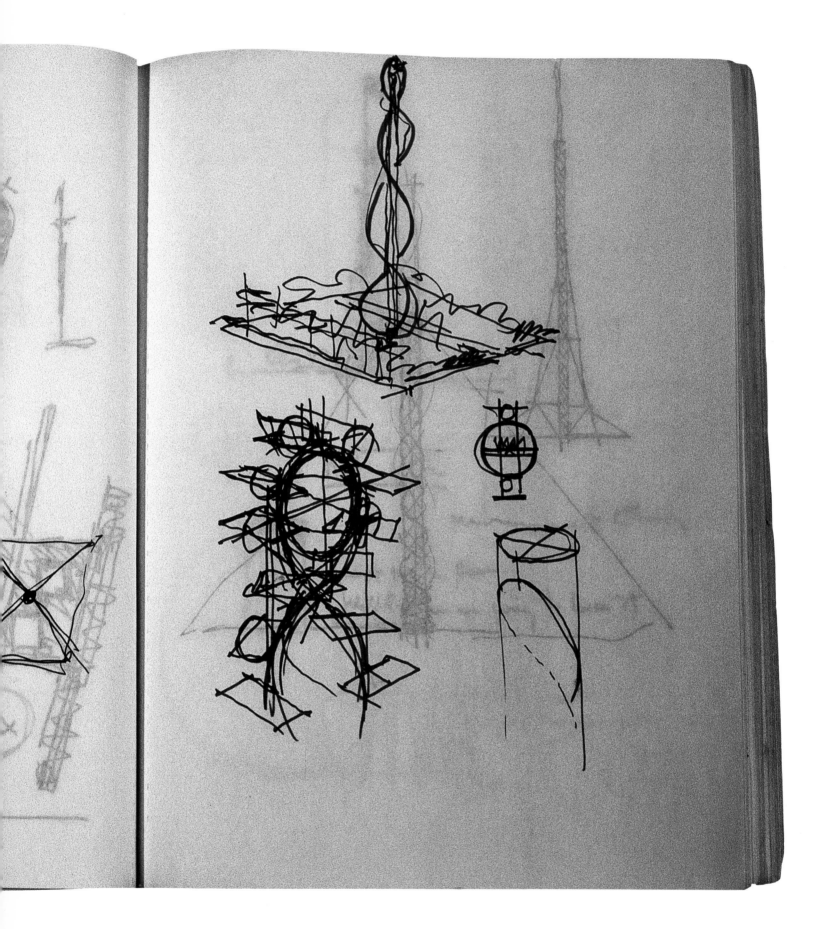

The images shown here are loose sketches of the London Eye, the towering Ferris wheel structure in London that commemorated the Millennium, which Viñoly recognized as a valuable example of a popular monument. Viñoly was clearly struck by the London Eye's dynamic viewing platform and transformed it through his sketches into something distinct for New York. The sketches combine the concept of a ride, with Viñoly's interest in a DNA helix.

While a ride may seem frivolous—an amusement on a hallowed site—it was surely not meant to be. Viñoly recognized the power of opening up the experience of great height to the general public, for in New York most high floors in tall buildings are the exclusive aerie of private owners. To give the public the chance to observe the city while riding from base to summit is something no New York structure now offers and would lend a sense of public ownership to the skyline.

Viñoly began sketching general ideas for Ground Zero the day following September 11, most of which examined the issue of height. The first image he produced was of a pyramidal form of structures topped by an extremely tall flagpole, which can be seen earlier in this section. Early on, he recognized that beyond all else, a tall monument—visible from great distances and therefore with a regional presence—made sense as a starting point.

Producing this modern Eiffel Tower-like image, Viñoly even echoed the elevator system on Paris's great symbol, which is used as an experiential ride up the Tower, but in the Viñoly version there is a twist, literally. The visitor can ride up the structure along a corkscrew track. What Viñoly was after was the chance to offer visitors the experience of moving around and up a great structure—on the outside. At this point Viñoly did not focus on inhabitable structures, just ones that could be mounted and traversed—not ones to be lived in or used for offices. That would come later.

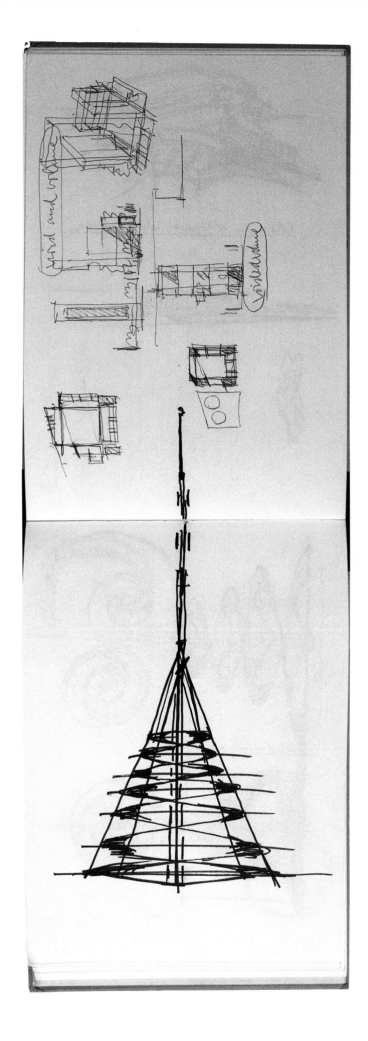

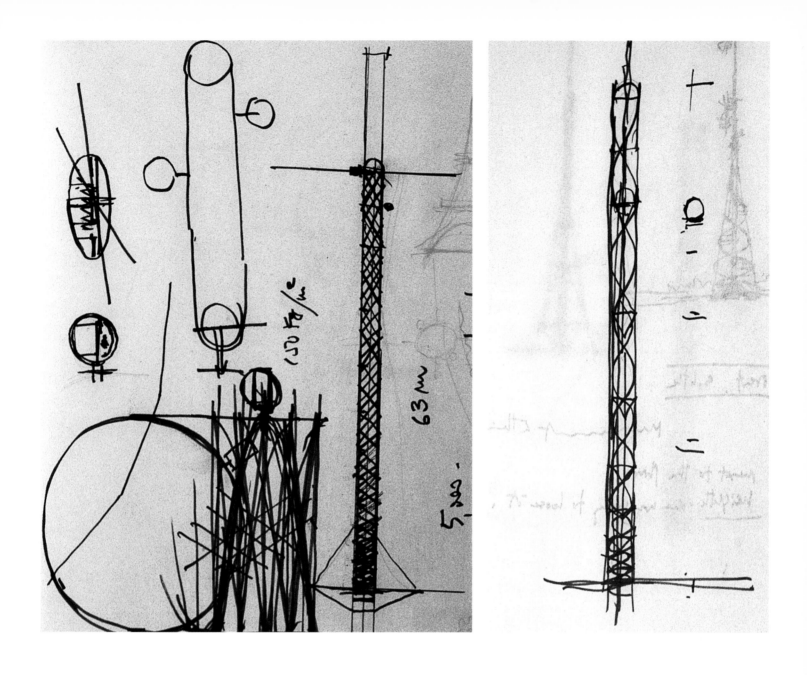

63 m

Rafael Viñoly

The planning process at Ground Zero, as flawed as it was fascinating, showed, perhaps better than any other project in recent times, the lamentably diminished role the architectural profession plays in the development process. It also demonstrated that our potential as the shapers of urban life is lost on the general public and convinced me that political manipulation and conservative ideology are the fundamental characteristics of America's zeitgeist today. An experimental search for a broadly acceptable solution to the problem of Ground Zero—the kind of leap of faith in Democracy that was occasioned by the Great Depression—was only feigned by the people in control of the process. As a result, education, always the happy byproduct of any "new" or exploratory exercise, was not a significant part of the process.

The facts:

1   The official reconstruction process started as a "secret" negotiation between the LMDC and those with a financial or real estate stake in the project: leaseholders, Larry Silverstein and Westfield America and owner, the Port Authority of New York and New Jersey. The LMDC, locked in an unwanted partnership with the Port Authority and saddled with the separate mandates of the Metropolitan Transit Authority and City Hall, struggled for design control and budget allocation, contributing to a climate of confusion and opportunism that made the process barely manageable.

2   *The New York Times* pulled off a daring, but ineffective, attempt to put architecture in the limelight through the presentation in its magazine of Fred Schwartz's elegant West Street planning idea. Unfortunately, the plan lost the clarity that made it so compelling when it was represented by a series of images, without any logic or substance, produced by "brand name" architects motivated in part by the desire for publicity, myself included.

3   Public uproar over the blandness of the six schemes negotiated under the original process and presented in the second Listening to the City event at the Jacob Javits Convention Center in July 2002, was compounded by the already highly charged, emotional reaction to the tragedy in addition to the LMDC's awareness of the *New York Times* initiative. This finally forced the LMDC to undertake a "public" search for "one or more consultants" to "help" develop a master plan. As is clearly stated in the Request for Proposal (RFP), this was "not a design competition."

4   Once the LMDC completed the hurried selection of another group of designers, which seemed arbitrary, and apparently had enough federal funds promised at the time to implement a drastic solution to the basic problems that the World Trade Center created in the first place, the agency made a fateful move. It immediately took Fred's West Street concept off the table and limited the scope of the Innovative Design Study to the site itself. The best of all possible solutions, the West Street plan had been the organizing principle behind *The New York Times* effort and was notable for its suggestion that development on the World Trade Center site be frozen until a reasonable time for healing could transpire. Later, Ground Zero's memorial function and the option of depressing West Street to recreate the typical Manhattan grid could be permanently addressed. But these effects clearly did not benefit the interests of the developer, Mr. Silverstein, and the "secessionist" climate of the Battery Park City residential community, which wanted to preserve its physical isolation from the rest of Lower Manhattan.

5   In keeping with the characteristic state of delusion of today's architectural culture, the short-listed architects—some of them in a clear ethical breach given their pre-existing involvement with the LMDC and/or Larry Silverstein—interpreted that process as an exercise in megalomaniac architectural fantasy, rather than as a complex planning problem and infrastructural puzzle. All but two teams, ours and Petersen-Littenberg's, represented their buildings, not as generic illustrations (as was done by the LMDC's first team of planners, Beyer Blinder Belle), but as defined pieces of architecture to be constructed without any regard to program, phasing, market conditions or technical feasibility.

6   As organizers, the LMDC's failure to reorient the work during the review process, or to discard it all together, became the source of political jockeying around preferred "solutions" once the images were in the public domain.

7   The choice of two "finalists" corresponded to a very clear opposition of approaches. Whereas the Libeskind scheme did not demand the up-front commitment of public funds for cultural programs and placed the making of the skyline element within the purview of the private developer, the THINK proposal made reestablishing the skyline the main focus of its plan and therefore, made non-negotiable the construction of the vertical infrastructure for the cultural components.

8   In a surprising moment of magical alignment, THINK was chosen by the Site Planning Committee of the LMDC, a spirited group of well-intended New Yorkers selected by the Governor for that function.

9   Inexplicably, Governor Pataki unilaterally overruled his own selection committee.

To me, the master plan was always political, where opportunities were always counterbalanced by inherent failures, but nevertheless worthwhile due to the civic nature of the project. Fatalism is not a practical attitude in this profession; neither is daydreaming about the power of ideas.

This was a rare opportunity to transform the city, not just the site. The belief that everything was possible in the extraordinary climate of support the city enjoyed in the aftermath of the attacks, created the backdrop for an exercise in utopia, which, although making many critics happy, served to obscure the real mechanisms through which public space is appropriated and, more importantly, how funds are allocated.

The dynamics of the "client group" revealed the conflict between private ownership and civic projects, a historic problem for planning and development agencies. The inability of government institutions to manage private ownership as a creative force, rather than as an opposing interlocutor that would in any case prevail, is an essential part of the story. There was also pure and legitimate confusion due to the complexity of the project.

Since the initial mandate of the "Innovative Design Study" was to "select a consultant to collaborate with the LMDC in defining the Master Plan," our initial approach was not to produce a design *per se*, but to demonstrate through the creation of alternatives, the need to allocate the appropriate level of investment in the component of the project devoted to the public realm. We did not want to rely on the customary method of charging the developer to produce this essential public space; we requested real, public investment in accessible space and structures that could generate a sense of civic pride.

In spite of regular progress meetings with all the participating designers, the LMDC again failed to focus on planning issues (perhaps believing that on this particular issue it did not need "help" or had already reached a conclusion) and therefore allowed the process to become a popularity contest in the public's perception—a competition between words and architectural image, as opposed to the more substantive issues surrounding the redevelopment of a literally embattled portion of the city.

We wanted to test the proposition that you could reestablish the connection between the actual conditions (emotional loss, political manipulation, public money, and technical feasibility) and collective pride (the energy of urban life). For a limited but diverse group of people that participated in the effort and for whom our work resonated, we achieved our goals.

All in all, I regret not having had the chance to interact even more intently with my partners, and more importantly, missing the opportunity to listen to the real client: the people of New York City, in a less oppressive situation, with more time and better memories.

The public representation of culture remains the unfulfilled project of our generation and, I am afraid will remain so for some time to come.

"Rebuild the towers bigger & better than before...
Paid for by an asset management firm which would be
honored to relocate into the new buildings."

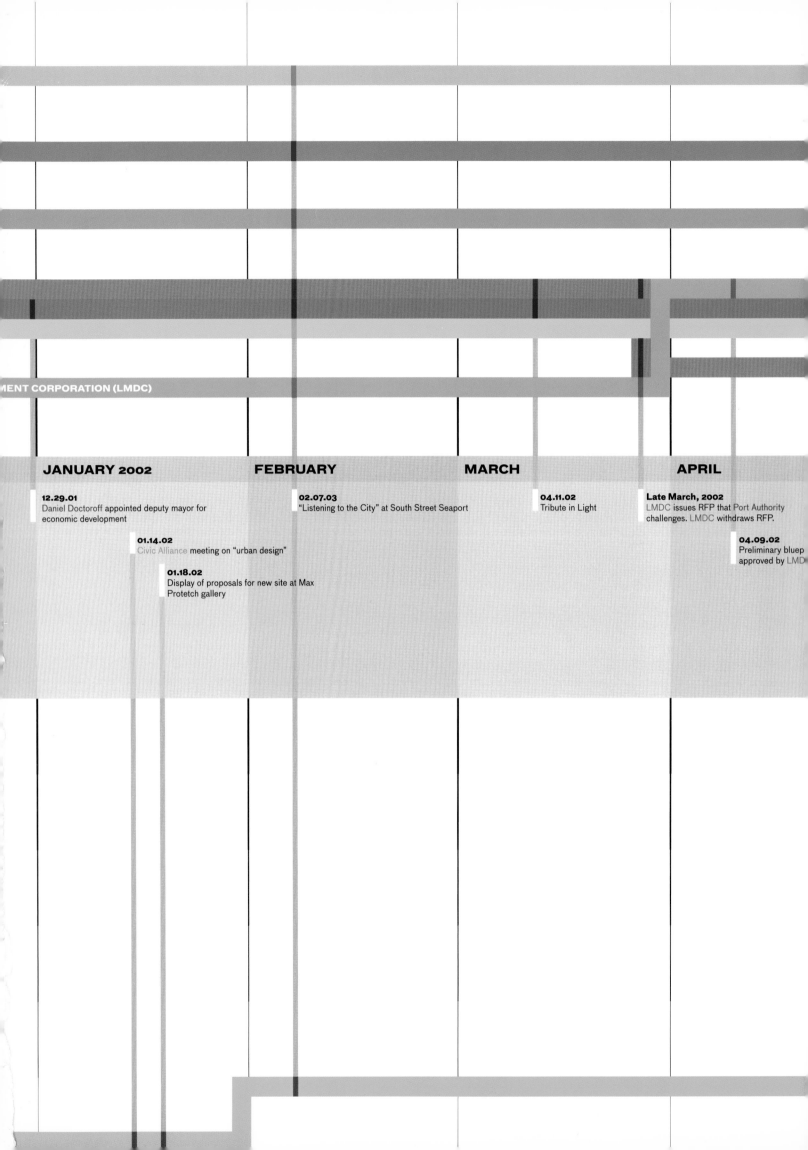

ENT CORPORATION (LMDC)

JANUARY 2002　　　　　　FEBRUARY　　　　　　MARCH　　　　　　APRIL

12.29.01
Daniel Doctoroff appointed deputy mayor for
economic development

02.07.03
"Listening to the City" at South Street Seaport

04.11.02
Tribute in Light

Late March, 2002
LMDC issues RFP that Port Authority
challenges. LMDC withdraws RFP.

01.14.02
Civic Alliance meeting on "urban design"

01.18.02
Display of proposals for new site at Max
Protetch gallery

04.09.02
Preliminary bluep
approved by LMD

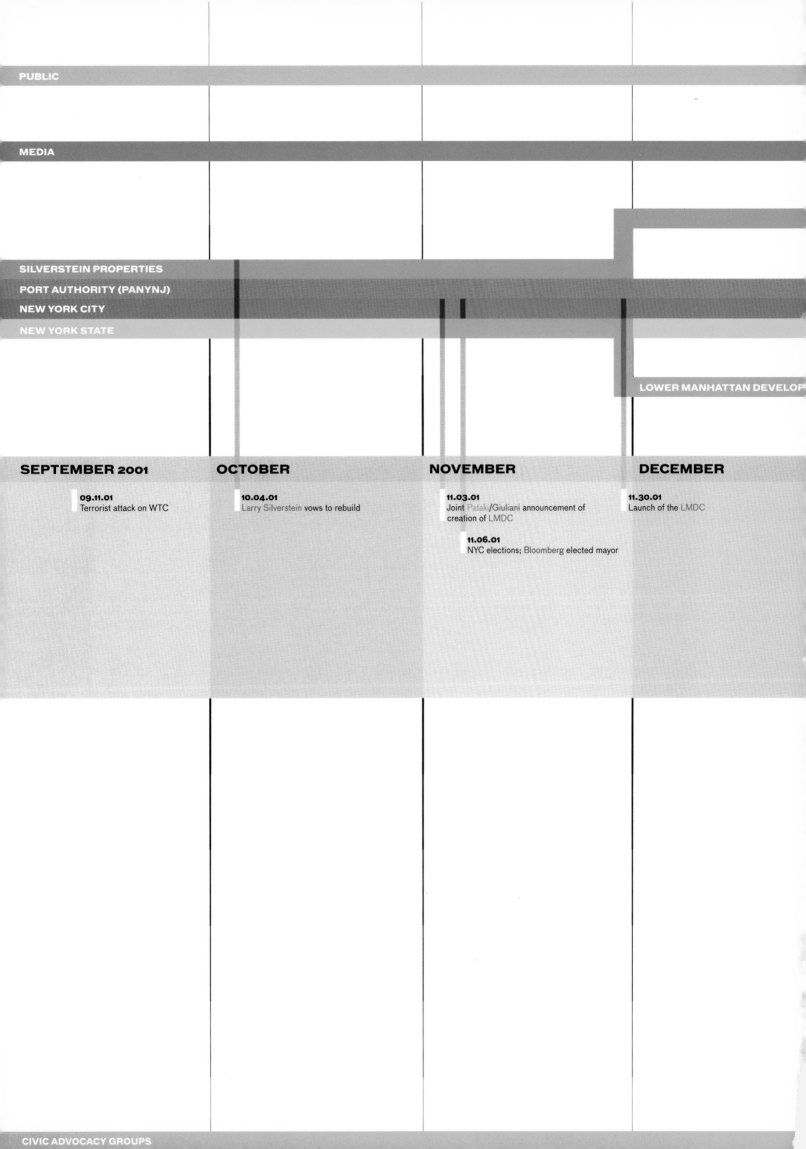

PUBLIC

MEDIA

SILVERSTEIN PROPERTIES
PORT AUTHORITY (PANYNJ)
NEW YORK CITY
NEW YORK STATE

LOWER MANHATTAN DEVELOP

SEPTEMBER 2001

09.11.01
Terrorist attack on WTC

OCTOBER

10.04.01
Larry Silverstein vows to rebuild

NOVEMBER

11.03.01
Joint Pataki/Giuliani announcement of
creation of LMDC

11.06.01
NYC elections; Bloomberg elected mayor

DECEMBER

11.30.01
Launch of the LMDC

CIVIC ADVOCACY GROUPS

Timeline

This timeline covers the period between September 11, 2001, when the World Trade Center was attacked, and February 27, 2003, when a master plan for guiding the site's reconstruction was officially announced. The timeline identifies the key players in the process—the design community below the centerline with the political and public context found above—and plots the relative influence of each over the decision-making process. Key events in the chronology are overlaid to illustrate their influences on the players' trajectories—the closer to the dividing line, the more influence over the future of the site. This timeline is our version of events and should serve to contextualize broadly the contents of this book.

AUGUST

SE

07.15.02
Herbert Muschamp of *The New York Times* gathers architects to rethink development of Lower Manhattan

07.16.02
LMDC and PANYNJ unveil the six BBB proposals for the WTC site

07.20–22.02
Public forum at Javits Center, a second "Listening to the City," leads to uniformly negative response to proposals

08.14.02
LMDC launches new global design s

08.15.02
LMDC and NY New Visions annou members of panel to select archite

̄EMBER

OCTOBER

RFQ for
al teams

09.26.02
Six architectural teams selected for design
competition

10.11.02
Innovative Design Study b

10.12.02
First **THINK** meeting
Viñoly Architects

10.20.
Second

Design Alliances

If 2001 was a time for architects concerned about New York to conceive of monumental ideas for the World Trade Center site, 2002 marked a year when designers were motivated to develop urban planning concepts independently, without the commission of a client. From re-examining the street grid and rethinking Manhattan housing to creating new forms for a transportation hub, architects came together to suggest an array of solutions. Individual designers gathered in groups, small and large, to brainstorm over how to re-imagine Ground Zero, at a time when there was no client, no budget and no specific time frame under which to work. There wasn't anyone to pay the bills—other than the architects themselves—proving that scores of architects, planners and professionals involved in city affairs are willing to focus with gusto on urban problems, even when no compensation is guaranteed.

From the Civic Alliance to New York New Visions, talented professionals of different ages, levels and temperament, made strides first to analyze the site's problems and potential; and second, to propose a variety of responses. These organizations paralleled those of other politically engaged groups such as those formed by residents of Lower Manhattan who had been directly affected by the destruction of the towers and victims' families who assiduously worked to assure that the memory of their loved ones would be respected as decisions were made to rebuild the area. The introduction of the LMDC in late 2001 marked the acknowledgment by the government that an official agency was needed to oversee the development process, while the formation of nongovernmental civic groups was evidence of the need for citizens to have structures for their discourse over how to rebuild.

For architects, this would mean some unlikely alliances. Committees within organizations such as New York New Visions brought together designers who might never have had reason before to join forces. In fact, plenty of these individuals would normally be in competition with one another rather than in a position to collaborate. Nonetheless, from well-recognized names to young, untested newcomers, a wide range of talent agreed to share ideas and proposals in an open and organized *charrette*, or intense period of study and design development.

Frederic Schwartz, who had spent the past 25 years working in the public realm, became active in New York New Visions soon after its inception. In very little time, he became convinced that the essential problem planners should face was the redistribution of development, not just within the confines of the 16 acres of Ground Zero itself, but in the surrounding areas, especially the West Street Corridor and the southern area of Greenwich Street. Schwartz was no novice when it came to Lower Manhattan. His projects include the Whitehall Ferry Terminal, home of the Staten Island Ferry at the tip of Manhattan, and the proposed 100-acre state park on the Hudson River and the related reconfiguration and suppression of the Westside Highway in the 1980s, known as Westway. SoHo, Tribeca, Wall Street and the Battery were extremely familiar design territory to him.

One of the early questions under consideration by all designers tackling the problem of Ground Zero was where to put the significant amount of square footage of new development that would be required. With the loss of the towers, ten million square feet of office space was gone. It seemed safe to assume that much of this would have to be replaced. Or would it? Some people suggested turning the entire zone into a massive park or memorial free of development. There were even editorials that proposed leaving the site untouched as a powerful historic record of the events of 9/11. But keen observers recognized that the economic value of the area was too great to be ignored. You could not let acres of prime land lie fallow, at least in economic terms. Savvy designers foresaw the likelihood that the site would be, at least in part, the centerpiece of major development.

Schwartz looked at this challenge and saw a particular solution that made more and more sense to him, but was not obvious to others. Based on his familiarity with the layout and texture of Lower Manhattan he saw a way of bringing together these two directions of design thinking. Yes, lots of new space would be needed, but did it really have to be located directly on the site?

In his work with several subcommittees for New York New Visions including the Memorial Process, Connections and Uses and Design Strategies, Schwartz was exposed to a wide range of debate on how to address the memorial function, remake the skyline and reintegrate the site with its surroundings. He became convinced that his initial reaction was on track and would go to the heart of not only repairing Ground Zero and the surrounding community, but would improve the area so that it would be far better off than it was on September 10, 2001. Why not take advantage of the lack of development along West Street, a broad thoroughfare that cuts off Battery

Park City and the World Financial Center from the World Trade Center site and the rest of Lower Manhattan? (This is the same road so unfriendly to pedestrians it can be best traversed by bridge, not at street level.) Years earlier, planners had considered depressing this wide expanse of road in order to build above it. Schwartz was prepared to revisit this idea and take it to a new level.

He got to work examining how to move ten million-plus square feet to West Street, using a number of low-rise and mid-rise buildings with various programs. There could be housing, office, retailing, cultural and mixed-use projects along this reconceived boulevard. What Schwartz saw was a win-win situation; this development would repair the physical breach caused by West Street and create a pleasant neighborhood of buildings in keeping with the New York tradition of structures arranged along the street edge. The West Street solution would also allow a complete rethinking of the Ground Zero site. This land could then be used for a memorial or any other use considered appropriate. It could even be left alone until the many constituencies could find agreement. Schwartz would take this idea with him to his New York New Visions committee meetings.

When asked to join a group of prominent architectural figures meeting at the New York offices of Richard Meier, he maintained his belief that this was the appropriate solution on which to base a master plan for Ground Zero. Meeting during the summer of 2002, architects including Meier, Charles Gwathmey, David Rockwell, Peter Eisenman, Steven Holl, and others (including Schwartz and Rafael Viñoly), met with *The New York Times*'s architecture critic, Herbert Muschamp to discuss creative possibilities for the site. Their efforts, along with those of some other invited guests, would eventually develop into an extraordinary 14-page section in *The New York Times Magazine*, published on September 8, 2002, under the title "The Masters' Plan." The full feature, "Thinking Big: A Plan for Ground Zero and Beyond," would garner great public attention for its innovative and bold thinking concerning not only the 16-acre site, but also the adjacent areas of Lower Manhattan. Following the publication, it seemed unacceptable not to think ambitiously and creatively about Ground Zero.

What the magazine presented was a series of projects for housing, transportation, recreation and, yes, office space, without the usual constraints of a specific client. The architects and designers were free to break the mold of traditional corporate and developer architecture. The results were visually stunning. Schwartz would not only contribute the underlying plan along the West Street corridor, his office, along with FACE, a young firm based in Brooklyn, would produce a striking housing design for the issue.

Viñoly would work on a transportation hub for downtown, using the opportunity to explore not only intermodal, but also urban connections. The result of Viñoly's efforts was a dramatic form that would rise above street level and offer extraordinary visual experiences for its users.

With an appreciation of Schwartz's West Street plan, Viñoly openly considered a number of possibilities for the site. His sketchbooks reveal a variety of approaches. Somewhat torn between the requirement to rebuild with the need to take time and reflect on what could work best on the site, Viñoly deliberated between "all or nothing." Yes, you could build tall, but you could also leave the space open for the memorial or public use. His sketches also show his consideration of known monuments for inspiration, from the 19th-century Eiffel Tower to the 21st-century London Eye. Viñoly's sketchbooks are evidence of how large-scale this designer's thinking was from the start. His concern was the utilization of the site, not architecture *per se*.

However, for the purposes of the design study curated by Muschamp, Viñoly returned his focus to architecture. Using the complex system of transportation pathways, Viñoly conceived a structure that would reveal these below-grade passages via transparent surfaces. Blurring the line between above and below-grade, Viñoly generated an elegant form. Using a variety of colors reminiscent of those used in New York City transit maps, Viñoly organized a hub that would take advantage of river views as well as accommodate below-grade connections. Utilizing his artistic talents in watercolor, Viñoly presented the linear quality of the resulting structures in dramatic sketches. In other conceptual images, Viñoly indicated the power of the visual experience made possible by this design.

This summit of architectural talent was particularly important to the formation of THINK. It was here that Schwartz and Viñoly would connect, realizing early on that their ideas concerning the master plan were compatible. Schwartz acknowledges that, among the participants, it was Viñoly and Muschamp who best understood the implications of Schwartz's approach to West Street. By the end of the summer, not only was Schwartz's planning

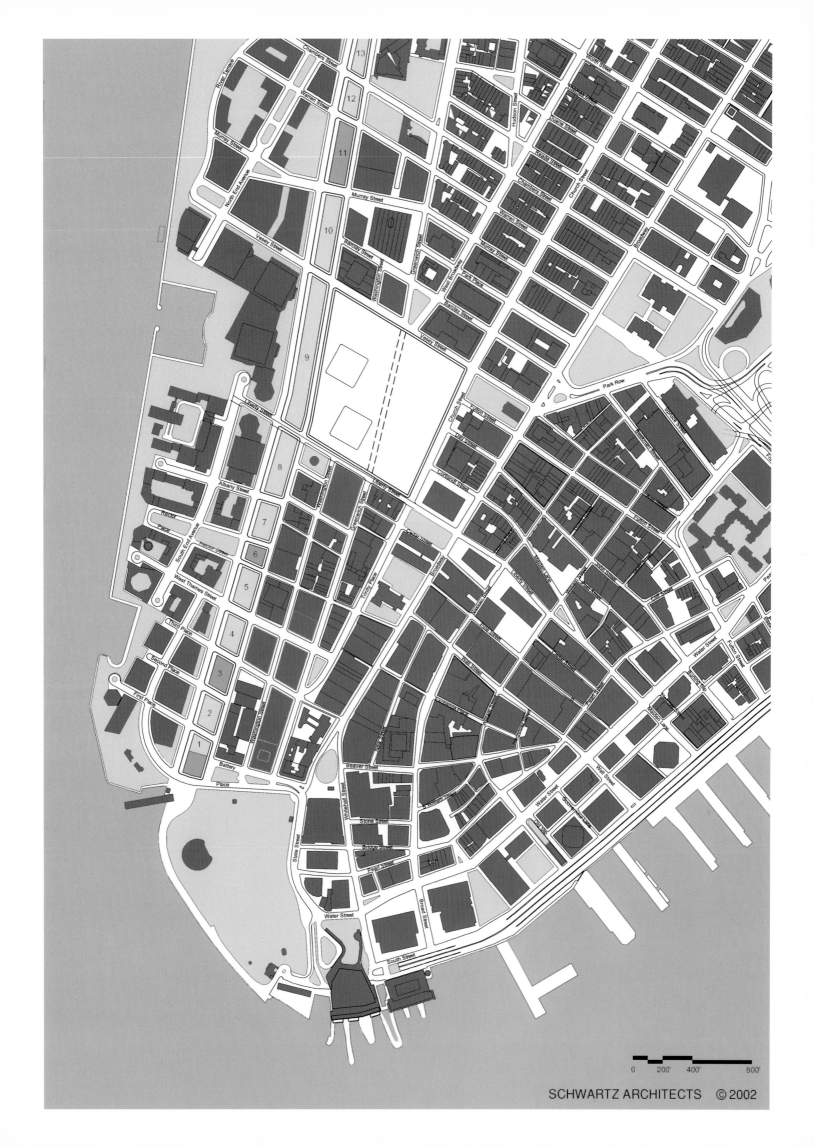

SCHWARTZ ARCHITECTS © 2002

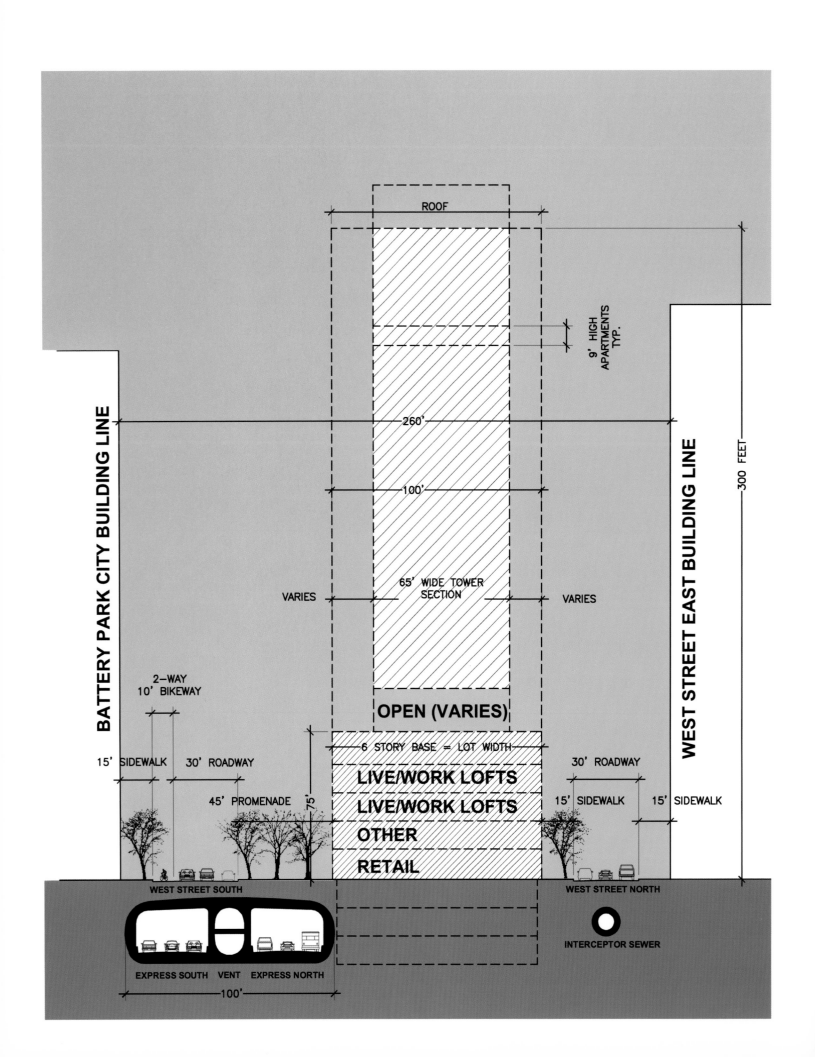

concept at the heart of the ideas presented in the eventual document in the *Times*, it was also common intellectual ground between Schwartz and Viñoly. They would go on to form their own design alliance, soon adding two more principals (Shigeru Ban and Ken Smith) and a number of consultants. THINK was born.

Schwartz and Viñoly's designs would get an audience beyond that of the readers of *The New York Times*. The same month that the magazine was published the Venice Biennale for architecture opened. Schwartz, Viñoly and the other "Masters' Plan" participants exhibited their designs in Venice to an international audience at the biannual showcase of innovative architecture. The cumulative effect of *The New York Times Magazine*, the exhibition and the inevitable press response to both was powerful. By the end of September 2002, there was a sense of excitement about the possibilities of architecture and a potent feeling of entitlement among New Yorkers that the city deserved some of the architectural innovation that was now getting so much play. Perhaps, this influenced the decision-makers at the Lower Manhattan Development Corporation. By October, the LMDC would produce "A Vision for Lower Manhattan: Context and Program for the Innovative Design Study," its request for master planning ideas.

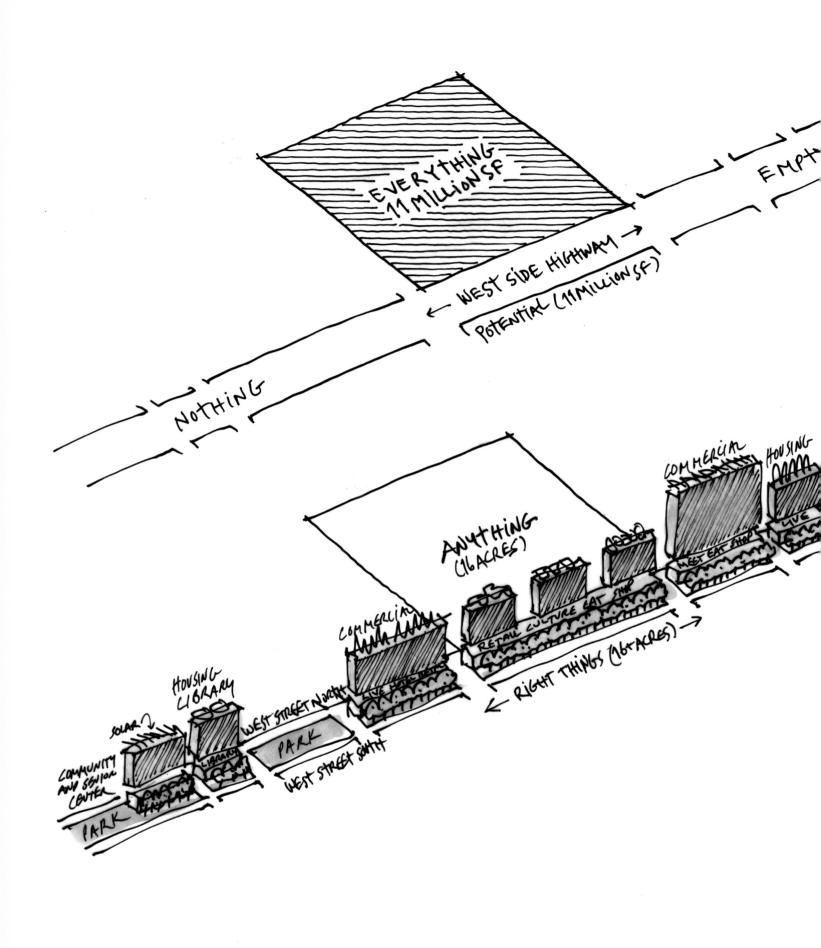

EVERYTHING
11 MILLION SF

NOTHING

WEST SIDE HIGHWAY →
← POTENTIAL (11 MILLION SF)

EMPTY

ANYTHING
(16 ACRES)

COMMERCIAL

HOUSING
LIVE

RETAIL CULTURE EAT SHOP

RIGHT THINGS (16 ACRES) →
←

COMMERCIAL

LIVE PLAY RELAX

WEST STREET NORTH

SOLAR

HOUSING
LIBRARY

COMMUNITY
AND SENIOR
CENTER

LIBRARY

PARK

PARK

WEST STREET SOUTH

07.16.02

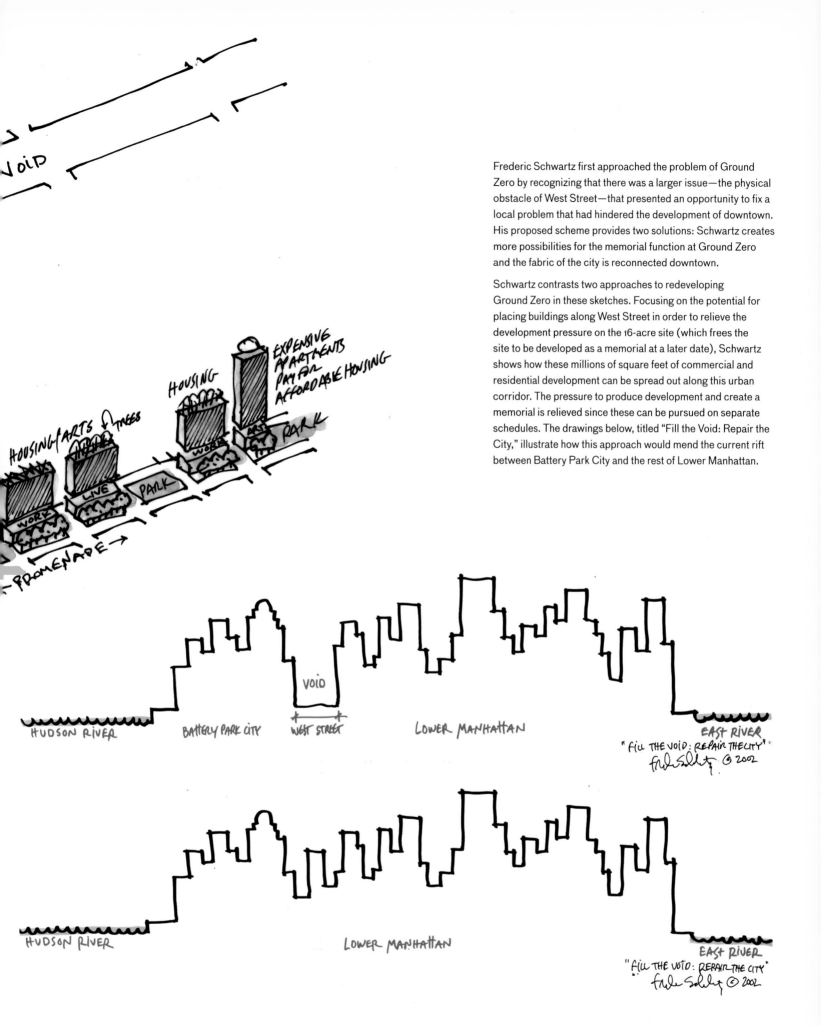

Frederic Schwartz first approached the problem of Ground Zero by recognizing that there was a larger issue—the physical obstacle of West Street—that presented an opportunity to fix a local problem that had hindered the development of downtown. His proposed scheme provides two solutions: Schwartz creates more possibilities for the memorial function at Ground Zero and the fabric of the city is reconnected downtown.

Schwartz contrasts two approaches to redeveloping Ground Zero in these sketches. Focusing on the potential for placing buildings along West Street in order to relieve the development pressure on the 16-acre site (which frees the site to be developed as a memorial at a later date), Schwartz shows how these millions of square feet of commercial and residential development can be spread out along this urban corridor. The pressure to produce development and create a memorial is relieved since these can be pursued on separate schedules. The drawings below, titled "Fill the Void: Repair the City," illustrate how this approach would mend the current rift between Battery Park City and the rest of Lower Manhattan.

This model of Lower Manhattan was produced by Rafael Viñoly Architects and was used by the various designers involved in *The New York Times Magazine* "Thinking Big" project to present their models. The use of low-angled lighting shows shadows across the sizable World Trade Center site. The model clearly conveys the rarity of Ground Zero's 16 contiguous acres available for development in Lower Manhattan. This image is enhanced via Adobe Photoshop in order to highlight in yellow the proposed development corridor on West Street, a crucial element in all of the participants' designs.

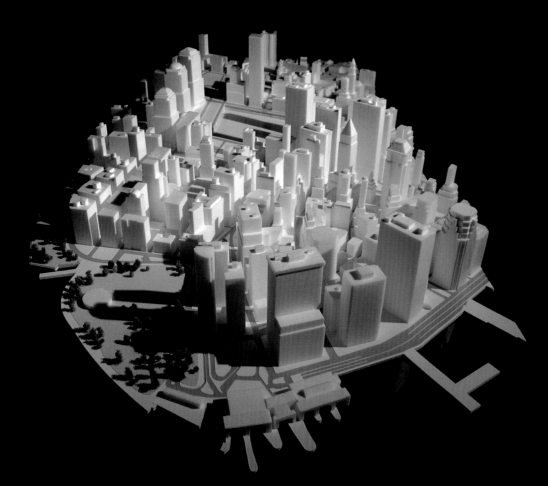

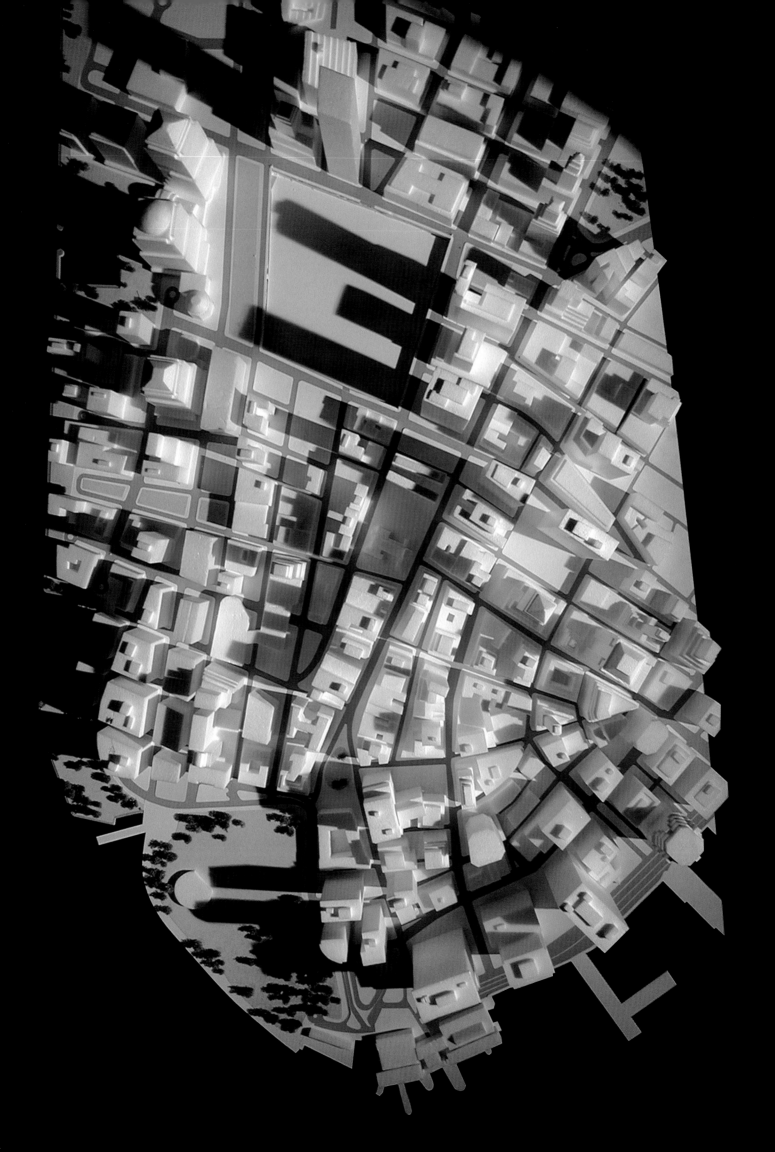

07.22.02

During the summer of 2002, Herbert Muschamp, the architecture critic of *The New York Times*, organized a group of high-profile architects to develop ideas for Ground Zero and areas beyond. This gathering of design talent met regularly in Richard Meier's New York offices. Participants (pictured here) included Steven Holl, Peter Eisenman, Charles Gwathmey, Elizabeth Diller and Richard Scofidio, Tod Williams, Frederic Schwartz, Rafael Viñoly and others.

Over the course of several meetings, a consensus emerged in support of a planning scheme proposed by Frederic Schwartz that moved the majority of new development away from the 16 acres at Ground Zero and on to 14 nominal parcels created by sinking West Street. This solution opened up far greater possibilities for the memorial at the site, which could now have a location and completion schedule distinct from the commercial development. Schwartz's scheme also made it possible to divide the workload into individual assignments that were distributed to the attendees as well as some additional, invited architects and designers. As a result of these summer meetings, a bond of mutual respect emerged between Schwartz and Viñoly and led to their later formation of THINK in fall 2002.

Rafael and Herbert Muschamp understood better than anyone the architectural and cultural implications of my plan for West Street. Following *The New York Times Magazine* design study, we formed a partnership called THINK. Why do I work with Rafael and continue to do so? Because of his intellectual discipline, his fierce determination for a true modern architecture, his competitive edge and take-no-prisoners approach, his understanding of the difference between master planner and architect, his quick thinking and his eloquence and elegance. I am honored to collaborate with Rafael and THINK and look forward to continuing to do so.
Fred Schwartz on Rafael Viñoly

The quintessential New Yorker. An irreplaceable input of enthusiasm, cynicism and emotional charge. The perfect mix of downtown earthiness and craze.
Rafael Viñoly on Fred Schwartz

The conspicuous absence of the Twin Towers inspired designers to suggest new alternatives reminiscent of the originals. This is an example of one of Rafael Viñoly's early concepts for replacing the towers with structures, rather than fully inhabited buildings. In his sketchbook, he shows tall towers that trace the outlines of the original footprints of the World Trade Center. These soaring open structures would be connected by additional suspended constructions that could be used for a variety of non-commercial functions. This initial attempt at creating skyscraper forms foreshadows THINK's **World Cultural Center** and its airy towers linked by a series of public spaces.

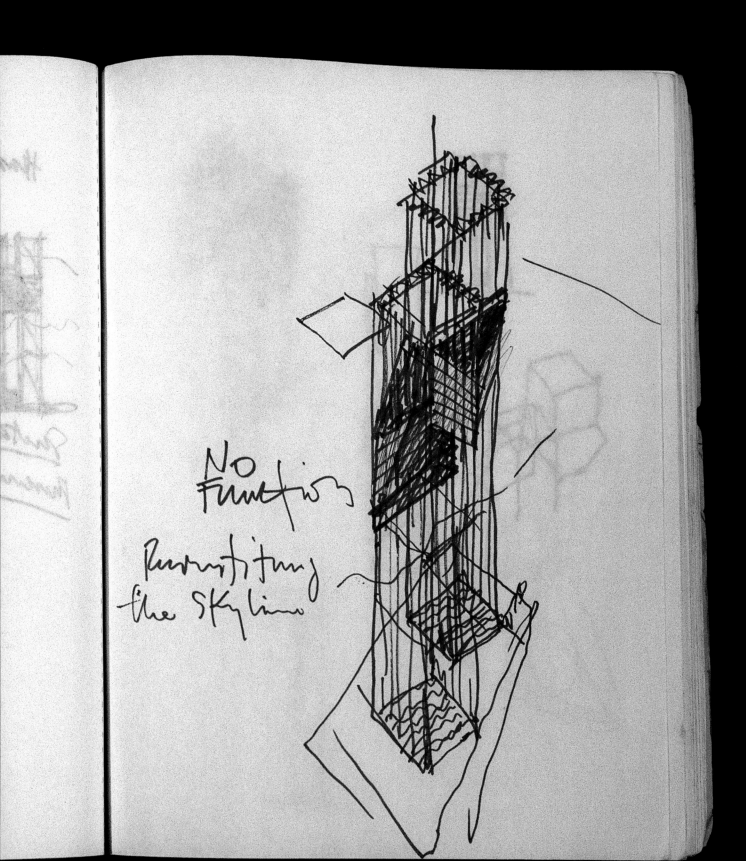

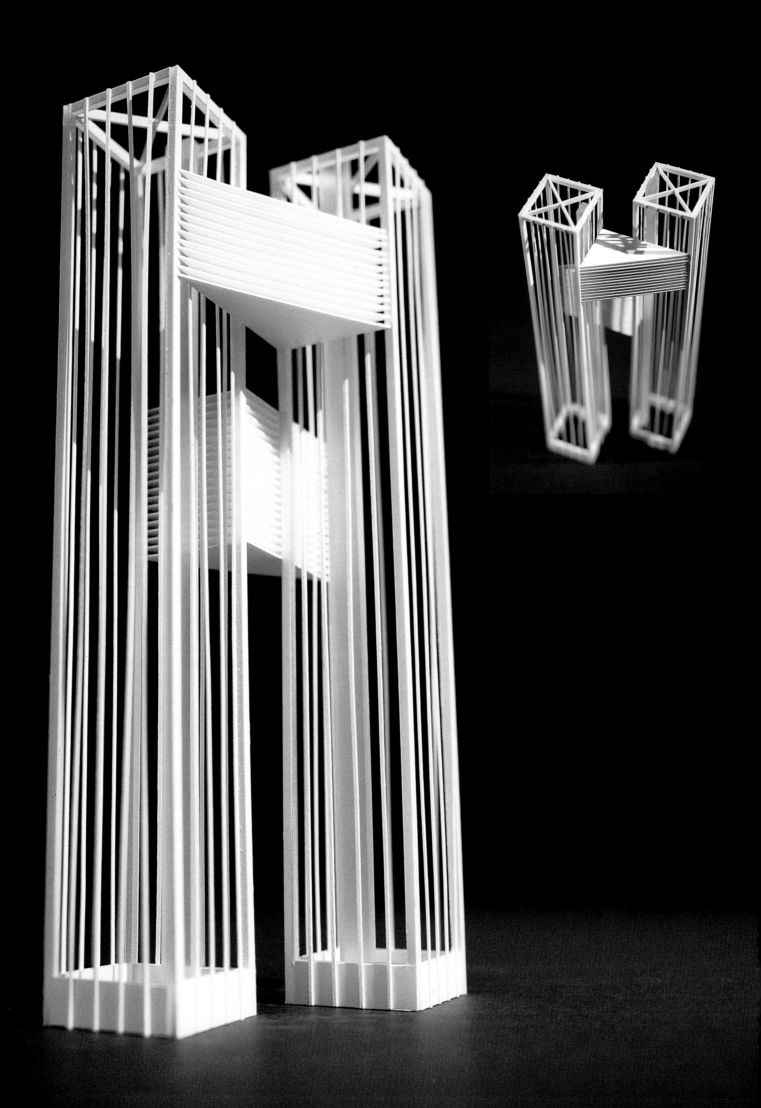

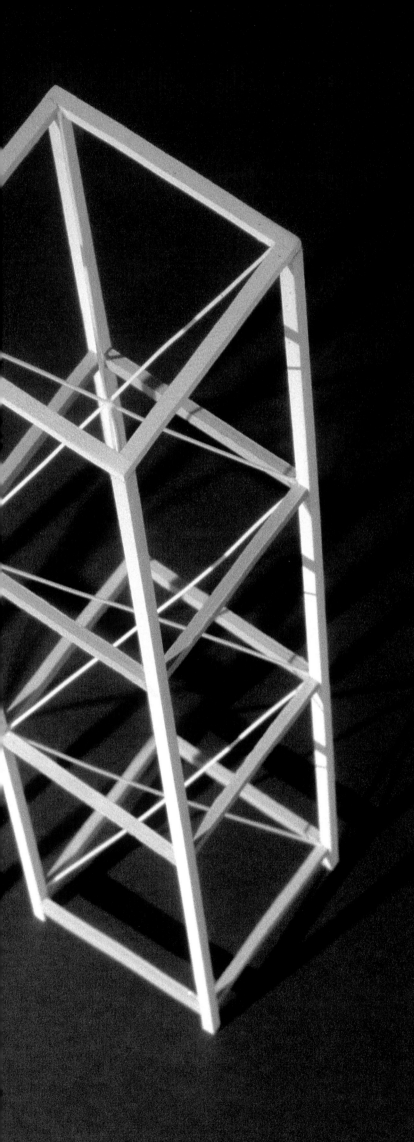
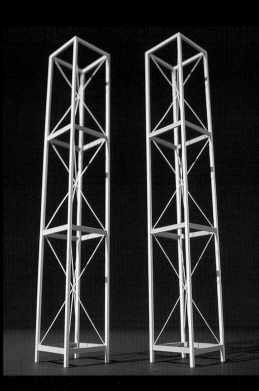

08.10.02

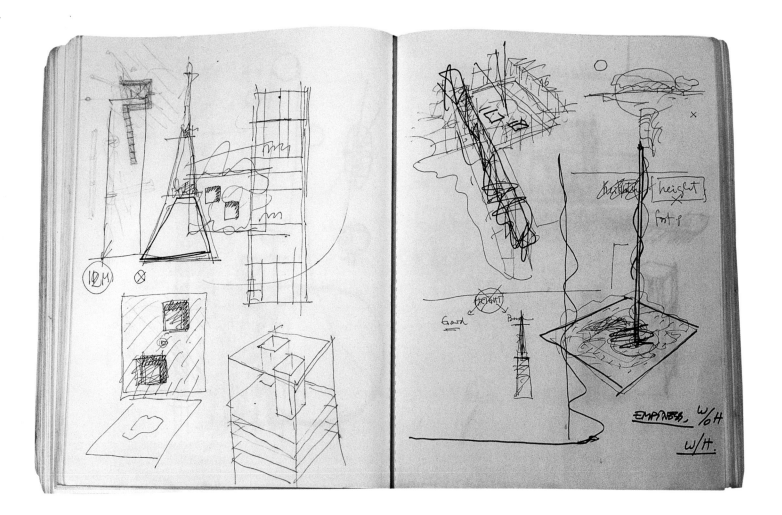

Rafael Viñoly uses his sketchbooks as an important tool, critical to the thinking process. Here we see several pages from summer 2002. On the left-hand page, Viñoly considers the possibility of a tall structure open to the sky. The blue square and black marks at the center represent the sky and birds in this perspective sketch. Beneath it is a sectional representation of the viewpoints when looking up from below-grade (from the footprints—the presumed location of the memorial area). The form of this tower repeats the concept shown on the prior pages. THINK would later employ a similar concept in the **Great Hall**, where massive, cylindrical constructions surround the former World Trade Center footprints.

The sketchbook above shows a number of early ideas. Viñoly is clearly concerned with the site, as seen by the drawings of the footprints, but he is also very focused on the issue of replacing the now-absent height of the Twin Towers with a type of monumental structure. A triangular form on the left echoes his earlier study of the Eiffel Tower. On the right, Viñoly considers a flagpole of massive size, possibly to be accessed by the public through a mechanical ride, similar to elements shown in his previous studies of the London Eye. He also includes a sketch that indicates Frederic Schwartz's West Street concept, which would allow Ground Zero to be left without commercial development. On this page, Viñoly writes the word "emptiness." He also makes a notation on the lower right hand corner of the page, "w/H" and "w/o H," indicating "with height" and "without height," two essential choices for Viñoly.

There are only 2 strategies -

(all or nothing) - / We should offer them both,
(all) means to satisfy the will for height. The
possibility of merging life w/ death - making
the tragedy the source of life - the memory the
present. giving the memory the chance to be [back]
evolve, not denying or foreclose the event
that life or death, not to assume that death
does not exist. - We should not ... the
... component of this site because it
happened there. the footprints are the memorial
the shafts are the memorial / solid over void
(willing) means that ... we do not respond
to a "ground zero" that we respond to a re-
invigoration of the traditional city - that
we say a park a community place ...
... We would not fall for the temptation
of a/fantasy - We put our money on a
gigantic educational project / the
park is a school - We oppose aggression
w/ knowledge with the addition of
civility. -

LMDC and NY New Visions announce
RFQ for members of panel to select
architectural teams.

Viñoly not only uses his sketchbooks for illustrations, but also for jotting down notes and concepts. He begins this text with a basic analysis stating, "There are only two strategies—all or nothing." Recognizing that there are two essential problems at the site—the perceived requirement to rebuild the lost square footage and the crucial need to create a memorial where thousands were murdered, Viñoly examines this tension and potential contradiction. Foreshadowing the challenge of separating development at the site from the creation of a specific place of remembrance, he stresses that "the footprints are the memorial."

Viñoly prepared a series of concepts for a proposed transportation center at Ground Zero at the request of *The New York Times* architecture critic, Herbert Muschamp, for a special issue of the newspaper's magazine focused on the history of the World Trade Center and the rebuilding of Lower Manhattan (and published to coincide with the first anniversary of September 11). He recognized the need to coordinate an intricate system of transportation pathways, all of which would be positioned underground. In this early study, Viñoly indicates the use of landscaping and pathways on the surface, but the real highlight is the complex organization of below-grade connections, which could be seen via transparent surfaces. This model is one of the first that illustrates Viñoly's method of blurring the line between what needs to happen above and below-grade.

This conceptual model represents Viñoly's focus on the complexity of the transportation systems for the proposed transportation hub at Ground Zero and how circulation paths can generate form. Here, he examines the relationship between above-grade and below-grade conditions as well as the ability of the hub to establish a firm connection through the site. The north–south axis is clearly emphasized in the image of the model shown above. The east–west connection became more important as the concept was developed further.

Here, Viñoly wants to raise Greenwich Street so that the transportation hub and the east–west connections can still be at grade. He speculates that the elevation of the street would also afford views of the river. In order to accommodate the transportation hub below-grade, a slight bulge over the site would result. This sketch examines the ground conditions with the inclusion of the "Station." Viñoly also notes the importance of "views to the river." He shows two replacement towers at the World Trade Center site, connected laterally at various levels, just as his sketchbook and models on previous pages indicate. This work presages the much later design of THINK's **World Cultural Center**.

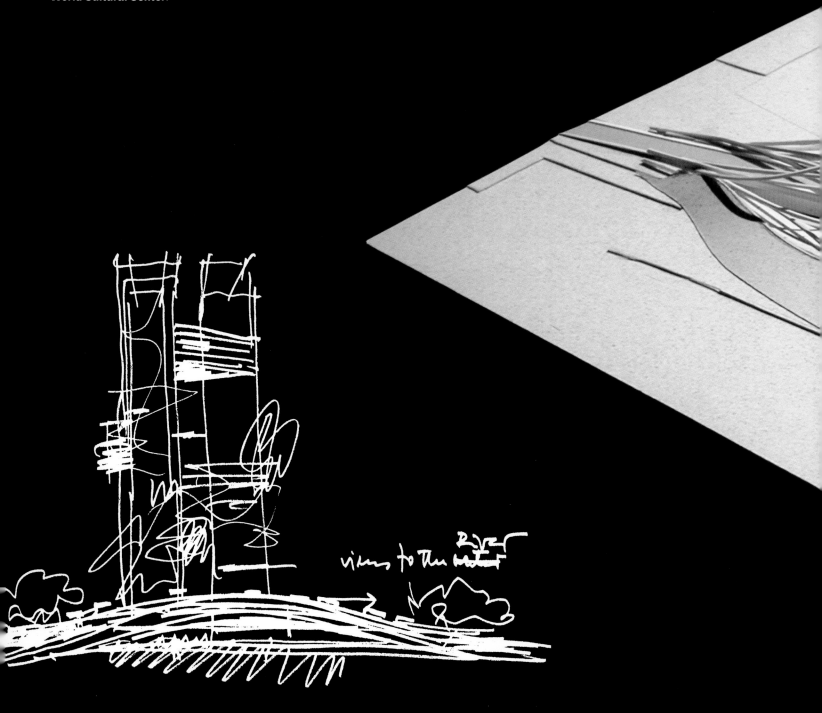

views to the RIVER

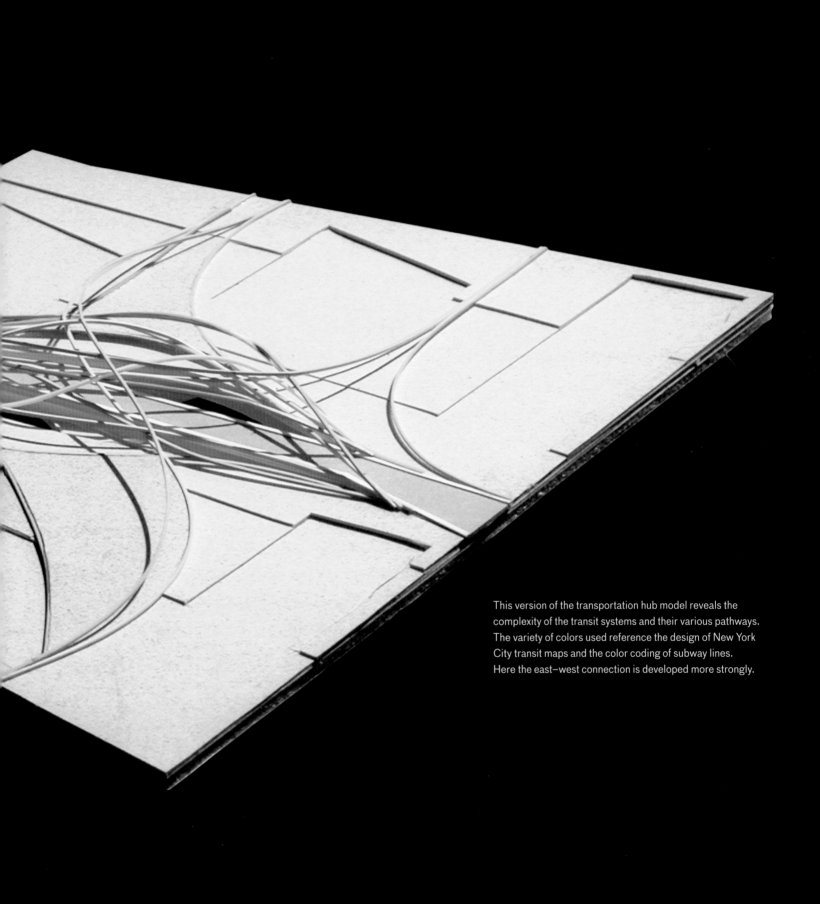

This version of the transportation hub model reveals the
complexity of the transit systems and their various pathways.
The variety of colors used reference the design of New York
City transit maps and the color coding of subway lines.
Here the east–west connection is developed more strongly.

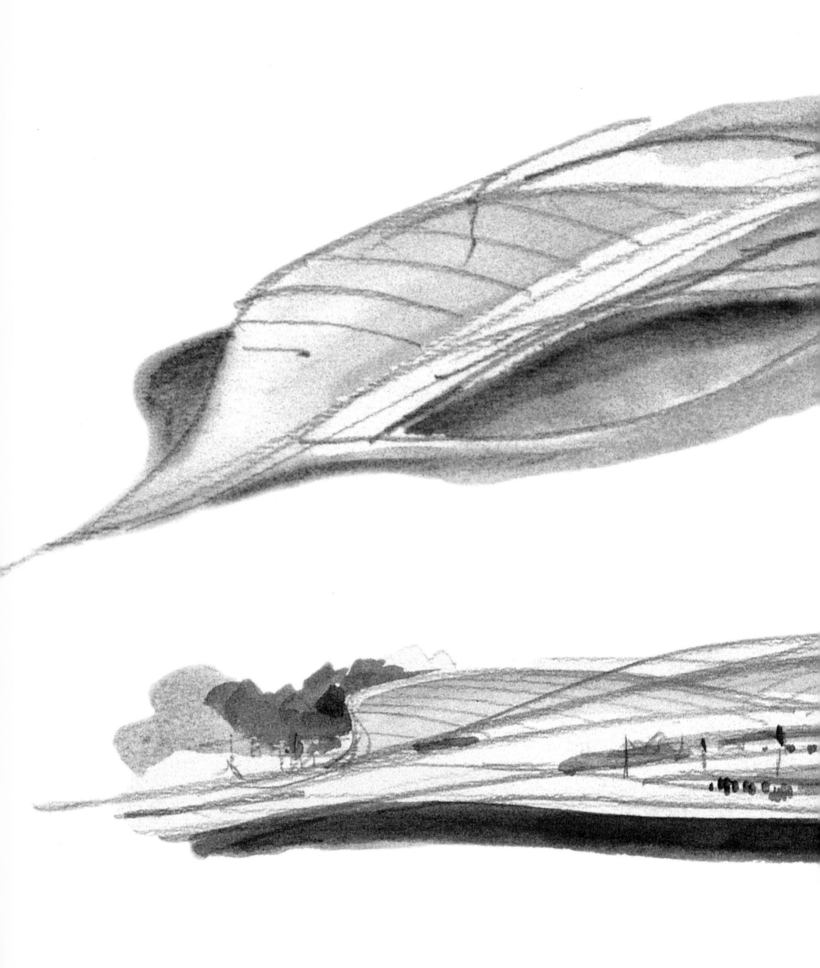

08.18.02

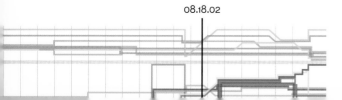

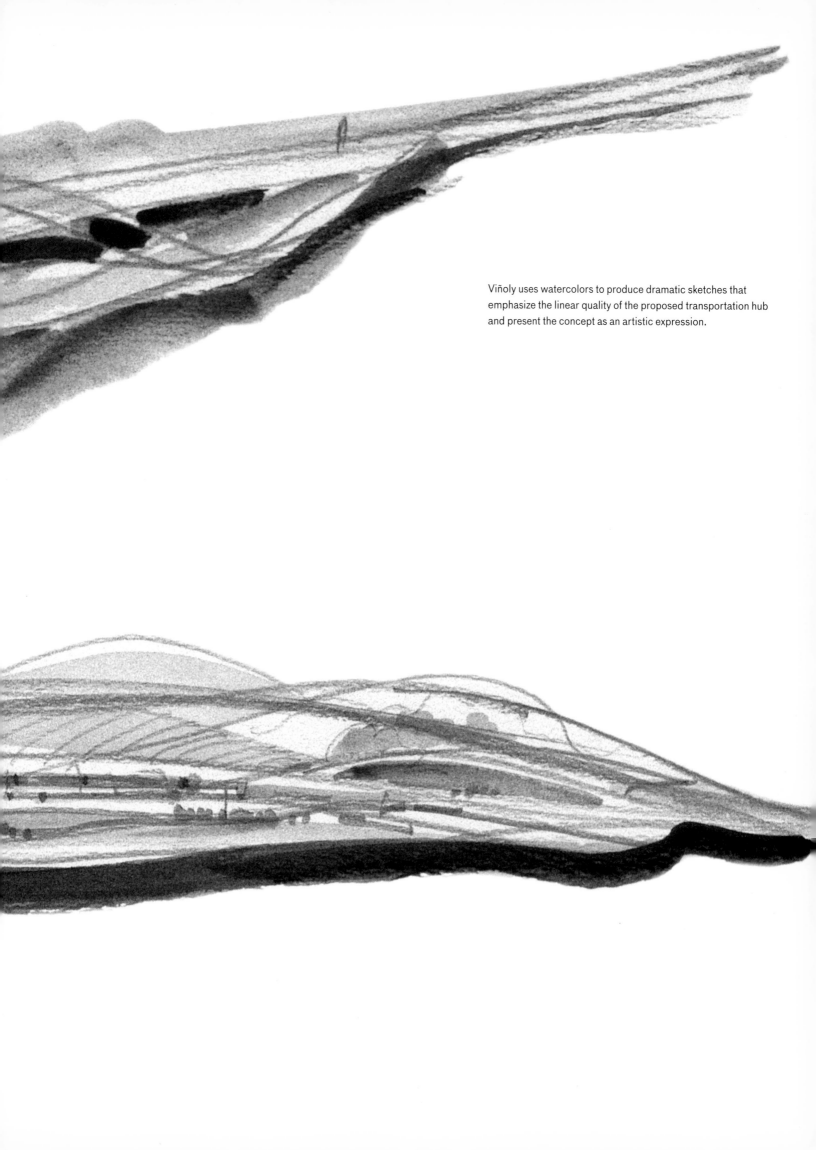

Viñoly uses watercolors to produce dramatic sketches that emphasize the linear quality of the proposed transportation hub and present the concept as an artistic expression.

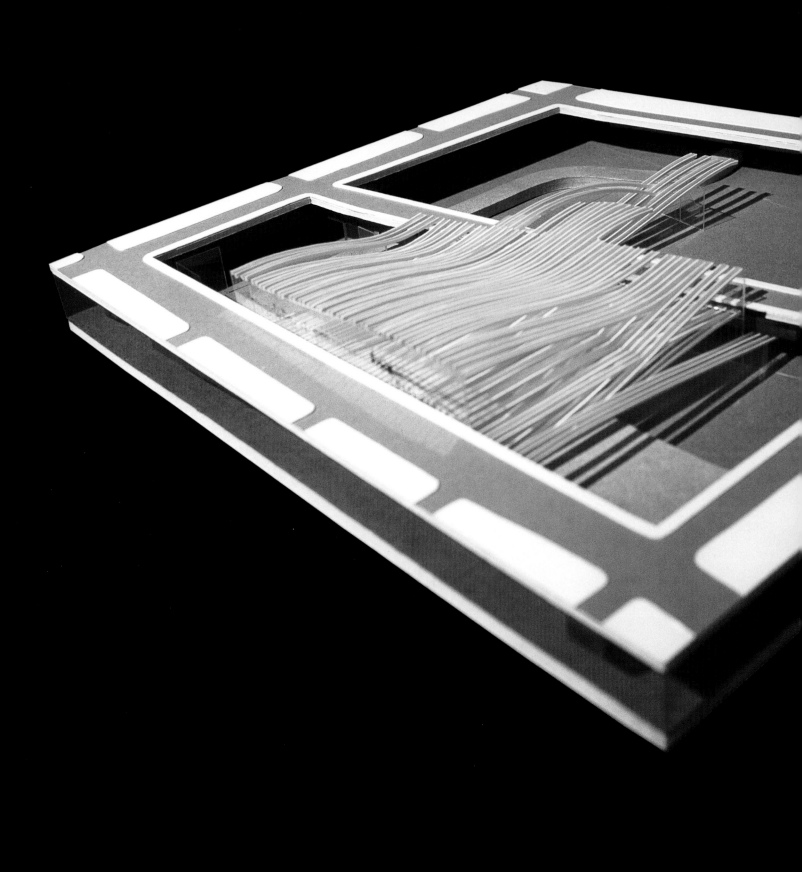

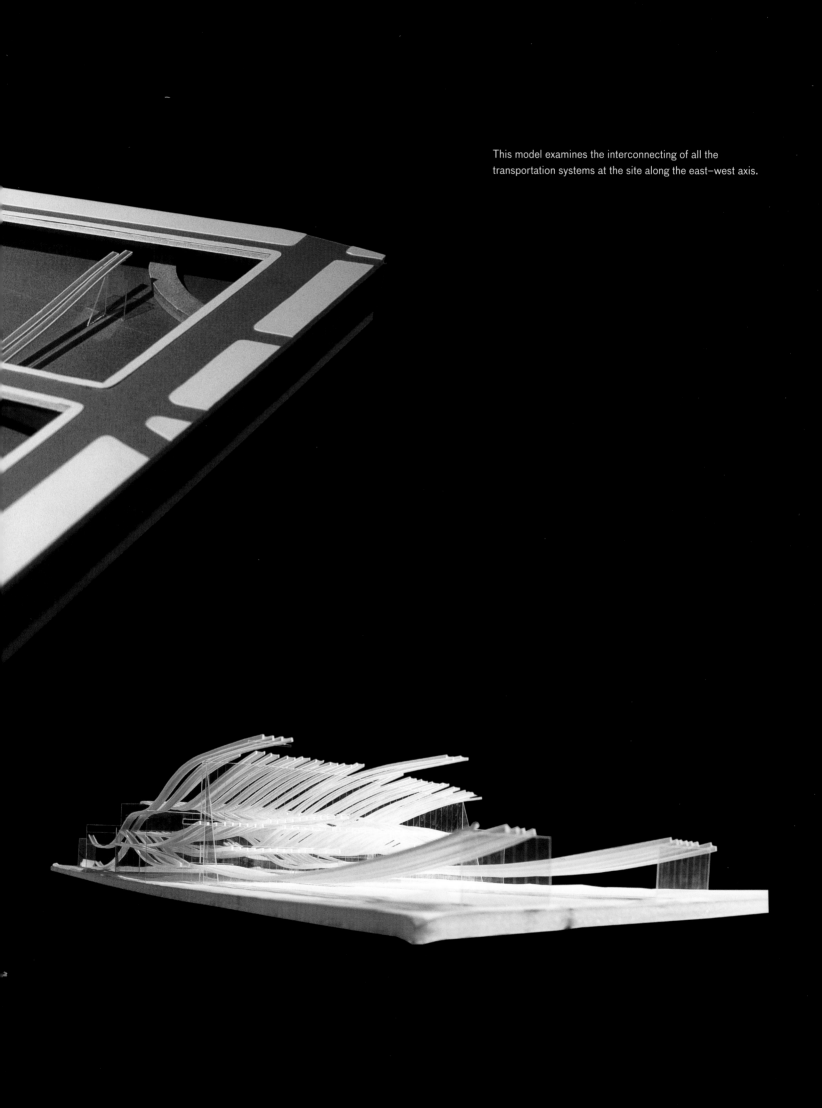

This model examines the interconnecting of all the transportation systems at the site along the east–west axis.

Rafael Viñoly Architects produced a dramatic concept for the Transportation Center at Ground Zero. This image was developed as a potential "iconic" representation of the scheme, which aimed to produce an extraordinary experience for the pedestrian by interlacing the multiple transit lines that already exist at the site. The designers felt that this image was engaging as the representation of an architectural idea, but was potentially confusing due to its realism, because it gives the appearance of a finished design, which it is not. This image was left unfinished.

The New York Times Magazine

SEPTEMBER 8, 2002 / SECTION 6

Towering Ambition

The Rise of the World Trade Center: A History, With Life and Death Implications

By James Glanz and Eric Lipton

The Masters' Plan

Downtown Manhattan Reimagined by a Team of Architects Daring New York to Think Big

Peter Eisenman
Charles Gwathmey
Zaha Hadid
Steven Holl
Rem Koolhaas
Maya Lin
Richard Meier
David Rockwell
Frederic Schwartz
Rafael Viñoly
and others

Curated by Herbert Muschamp

09.08.02

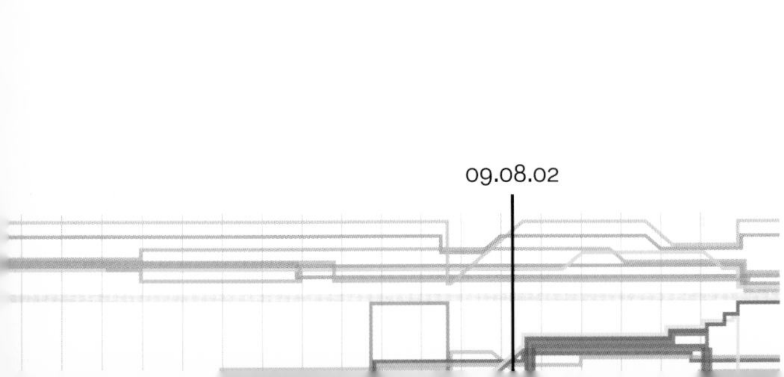

On September 8, 2002, *The New York Times Magazine* published the issue mentioned before, dedicated to the history of the World Trade Center and the efforts to rebuild at Ground Zero. Both Schwartz and Viñoly contributed designs, which were accompanied by the work of many other prominent architects and designers. Peter Eisenman, Charles Gwathmey, Zaha Hadid, Steven Holl, Rem Koolhaas, Maya Lin, Richard Meier, David Rockwell and others participated in the project.

The lead essay by Herbert Muschamp was titled "Don't Rebuild. Reimagine." In this, Muschamp stated, "Now is the time for New York to express its ambition through architecture and reclaim its place as a visionary city." The accompanying image was of Schwartz's West Street development corridor that clearly showed plenty of open green space around the footprints of the former World Trade Center. In fact, Schwartz's plan was the conceptual and physical spine for the other projects, including a housing design by Schwartz (teamed with the young Brooklyn-based firm, FACE), which raised the possibility that the planning agency addressing the Ground Zero challenge would consider this option.

The magazine's cover announced "The Masters' Plan." The full feature, "Thinking Big: A plan for Ground Zero and Beyond" instantly created intense discussions among architects and planners about the need for the LMDC to rethink its approach to rebuilding and may well have been the catalyst for the agency's decision to move forward with its later Innovative Design Study.

The same month that *The New York Times Magazine* published the designs by Schwartz and Viñoly, the two architects traveled to Venice for the biennial for architecture. Viñoly presented his transportation hub and Schwartz showed both his housing scheme and his essential West Street concept at the noted international event. The designs by Schwartz, Viñoly and those of the many others who had participated in the *Times* project were displayed via presentation boards and models, along with the same study model shown earlier—here adorned with smaller models of each participant's project.

At right, Viñoly's presentation board for the exhibition is shown. The plan presents three perspectives in the center, which were intended to be conceptual and not overly realistic. At the top of the board, Viñoly's drawings describe the transit connections across the site.

09.08.02

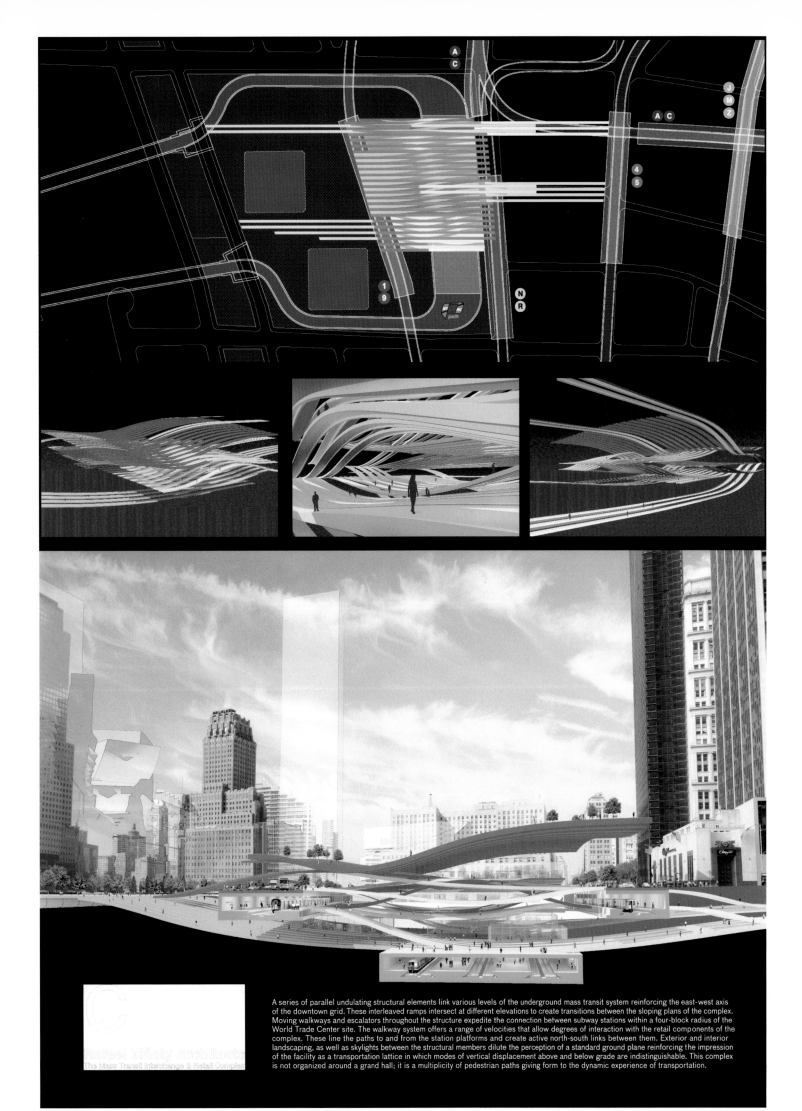

A series of parallel undulating structural elements link various levels of the underground mass transit system reinforcing the east-west axis of the downtown grid. These interleaved ramps intersect at different elevations to create transitions between the sloping plans of the complex. Moving walkways and escalators throughout the structure expedite the connection between subway stations within a four-block radius of the World Trade Center site. The walkway system offers a range of velocities that allow degrees of interaction with the retail components of the complex. These line the paths to and from the station platforms and create active north-south links between them. Exterior and interior landscaping, as well as skylights between the structural members dilute the perception of a standard ground plane reinforcing the impression of the facility as a transportation lattice in which modes of vertical displacement above and below grade are indistinguishable. This complex is not organized around a grand hall; it is a multiplicity of pedestrian paths giving form to the dynamic experience of transportation.

09.10.02

No Subject
Date: 10 Sep 2002 1:12pm
From: Rafael Viñoly
To: Frederic Schwartz

Dear Fred:

It was great seeing you and Tracey.
I am still in Europe but I want to
remind you that since there is little
time left, we need to make a decision
regarding the RFQ. In my view
we should try to stick together as
much as possible and maintain the
integrity of the NY Times group.
Whether that is technically or
politically viable is something we
should look into immediately.

After what we did, and considering
the strength of the idea - your idea
– I think we should try to keep
all of the participants together
(particularly the young ones). Even
if we risk creating difficult working
conditions, I think it would be best
for the process and for our chances
of making a real contribution. In
any case, through time and subtle
leadership, we will surely be able
to introduce some sanity into the
process.

I will be back in NY tomorrow.

We should not give up.

Best,

R

RAFAEL VINOLY ARCHITECTS
50 VANDAM STREET
NEW YORK, NEW YORK 10013
T +212.924.5060
F +212.924.5858
www.rvapc.com

Re: No Subject
Date: 10 Sep 2002 1:12pm
From: Rafael Viñoly *
To: Frederic Schwartz

Dear Rafael:

We had a great time to and hope to
see you both some evening here or
out East.

I would like Tracey to see your
pavilion and hear you play there too.

On the RFP:
I am not sure it is technically and
politically viable.

I am also not sure that I agree with
you on this matter and I will explain
why tomorrow.

We must talk immediately.

Frederic Schwartz

PORT AUTHORITY

LOWER MANHATT

EMBER

DECEMBER

review

11.14.02
4-week LMDC review

d as seventh team

11.18.02
Steering committee meeting; attended by the LMDC, PANYNJ, representatives of the city and state, Silverstein and the architectural teams

11.20.02
Silverstein announces that SOM will design 7 World Trade Center

RVA

12.09.02
Steering committee meeting

12.18.02
Unveiling of g

12.19.02
Winter Ga
intense me
article, "Ar
They Prob

JANUARY 2003   FEBRUARY

01.09.03
Front runners for the competition are
Libeskind, **THINK** and Foster

02.04.03
At press conferer
announces **THIN**
Libeskind designs

sign plans at Winter Garden

01.13–14.03
LMDC holds hearings, open to the public

presentation open to the public;
coverage begins. *The New York Times*
ects' Proposals May Be Bold, but
Won't Be Built" — Charles V. Bagli

01.23.02
SOM-led architectural team eliminated b
LMDC

01.07.03
Ada Louise Huxtable's article in the *Wall
Street Journal*: "Don't Blame the
Architects: Designs are Visionary, but the
Process is Business as Usual."

The Client

When the Lower Manhattan Development Corporation issued its Request for Qualifications (RFQ) on August 19, 2002, it was explicitly searching for appropriate design firms "to generate creative and varied concepts to help plan the future of the site." The architects reading this request must have believed that the LMDC was not looking for firms to design fully all of the elements at Ground Zero, but rather to locate potential consultants to assist the corporation with the arduous task of organizing a master plan for the devastated site. After all, the request noted explicitly, "This is NOT a design competition and will not result in the selection of the final plan." What could be clearer? The LMDC was initially to govern the rethinking process, not yet the redevelopment of the site.

So, what appeared to lie ahead was not a design competition, but rather a high-stakes symposium, where representatives of the design community would educate the LMDC. But what was the LMDC? Was the development organization actually the client, the client representative or something else? Would it have the authority to take the ideas gathered by the upcoming "Innovative Design Study" and put them to real use? According to its own documents, the LMDC not only had the clout, but also the cash. The U.S. Department of Housing and Urban Development had appropriated $2.5 billion for the LMDC's work. There was reason for the design applicants to take the LMDC seriously as arbiter and client.

A wide variety of teams submitted their qualifications for consideration. Often, the team members had competed against each other in previous competitions. THINK's principals came together in part as the result of their familiarity with each other's specific interest in and proposals for Ground Zero. As mentioned earlier, Schwartz and Viñoly had already had the opportunity to observe each other's commitment to rethinking the former World Trade Center site as part of their collaboration with *The New York Times*. There was a mutual respect for their shared work ethic, which would lead them to many late nights and intense work sessions.

Schwartz and Viñoly are both architects with experience in planning. They sought an additional figure with landscape expertise, which led them to Ken Smith. Japanese architect Shigeru Ban also joined the team, adding another level of artistic depth and an international perspective. Ban had garnered considerable attention from the architectural world with his designs for Kobe, Japan in the wake of the 1995 earthquake. These included his Paper Loghouse and Paper Church that won praise for their monumentality, despite their inexpensive and simple construction techniques.

It cannot be stressed enough how rare this type of collaboration is in the world of architecture. While architects may join forces in order to produce different elements of a major project, they do not usually work as a team of equals on specific components. Here, collaboration was the norm rather than the exception. In this, THINK was not alone.

Like so many of the teams that would emerge as competitors, THINK sought additional members to add varied perspectives and talent. Beyond the four principals, THINK included a number of noted consultants in different specialties. David Rockwell, lauded for his work in entertainment, dining and shopping environments brought his expertise to the retail environments that THINK would include in the master plan. For engineering, THINK invited Jörg Schlaich, the German structural engineer who has garnered attention for his combination of artistic and technical approaches. Schlaich's contribution would be essential to the refined design of the cultural towers, which would emerge as one of the main design schemes. Engineers Buro Happold brought novel technological solutions to the group, especially in the area of sustainable systems. Due to the extraordinary complexity of the technical aspects of the proposed plans, THINK brought in yet a third engineering firm, the well established Arup. Finally, a noted academic, William R. Morrish of the University of Virginia added his abilities to the mix by organizing a structured process to assist THINK in considering the effects of each design alternative.

On September 26, ten days after the application deadline, THINK found itself one of six selected teams (eventually a seventh would be added) that would move forward with the LMDC's "Innovative Design Study." From that time they would have slightly less than three months to develop designs, concepts and suggestions for the LMDC, which would present with much fanfare the work of the selected teams to public officials and the press on December 18, and then to the public on December 19, 2002. What awaited THINK and the other participants was one of the most intense periods of design, discussion and reflection that any designer could experience—all for $40,000 in compensation, which would cover only a small fraction of the team's expenses.

On October 11, the LMDC released its publication, *A Vision for Lower Manhattan: Context and Program for the Innovative Design Study*, which set the parameters for the master plan. This document described the authority's desire to remake "the nation's third-largest central business district into a 21st-century downtown." The first paragraph spoke of the important elements to be included in this urban environment, which comprised the obvious combination of uses: retail, residential, cultural and transportation. Surprisingly, commercial activities such as office space were not mentioned here (they would be addressed later in the document); unsurprisingly, the focus was the symbolic aspect of the site. At the outset the LMDC stated, "most importantly, a memorial will sit at the heart of this downtown."

The memorial may have been declared the focus of the redevelopment, but it was also the one element that the LMDC chose to exclude from the work of the selected master planning teams. The Innovative Design Study document made this restriction clear: **"You are not to design the memorial."** The selected consultants could only respond by producing an appropriate setting for the future memorial, and that design would be determined through an international competition.

Of course, the entire redevelopment could be deemed a memorial. The sheer act of rebuilding on the foundation of the former Twin Towers and the remains of so many of their occupants was already endowed with the memorial function. However, the designers accepted that another architect or artist would create the formal memorial. The challenge of making the appropriate environment for this emotionally charged space cannot be overstated.

With the LMDC's requirements in hand, the team assembled, and with a mere two weeks to prepare for the first client review, THINK got to work creating a variety of approaches for the master plan. Indeed, that was the mandate—to create a master plan, or at least the preliminary work that would lead to one, which could accommodate both the early essential uses and future development—but with the caveat that the LMDC might elect to use all, part, a combination of, or none of the suggested designs. The teams were asked to create infrastructure, not specific architecture.

What ensued was a nonstop design studio, or *charrette*, which would not end until the crucial final presentations on December 18. THINK took to heart the LMDC directive to provide ideas rather than complete plans and proceeded to work on several schemes from the start. Beginning with an analysis of the essential qualities of New York's urbanism, including a comparison of the World Trade Center site and the architectural conditions surrounding Central Park, THINK seriously considered not only the importance of verticality in New York's urban form, but also the specific conditions usually found in New York where landscape and buildings meet. In Manhattan, that usually means a wall of buildings along the street line that comes up directly against open space. As the team focused more closely on the World Trade Center site, they explored issues of access. What might the options be for reopening streets once closed due to the former super block of the Twin Towers? In the post-9/11 world, safety had to be a primary consideration, and would also affect the connections between the site and the street grid.

Without firm direction from the LMDC, THINK had to make assumptions about the division of areas devoted to redevelopment and remembrance. Keeping to their commitment to take different tacks in order to show their client the widest range of options, the team members explored some alternatives where commercial development took up a greater percentage of the ground area and others where such uses were restricted so that the memorial function could be spread over additional territory. Understanding that the budget for the project would determine which approach would make the most sense, THINK felt it was best to counsel the client on these various options.

Returning to the principals' initial artistic responses to the destruction of the World Trade Center, the team reconsidered the idea of rebuilding the towers, albeit in a new fashion. Here, the work of Shigeru Ban played a significant role. Basing his concept on floating memorial lanterns from Japan, Ban suggested a compelling form for the new towers. The luminescent cylinders could be both visual symbols and protective containers for functional buildings.

But THINK was not solely fixated on the idea of replacing the towers. In fact the team members accepted that a workable scheme may not include new towers, and entertained the possibility that a horizontal solution could be best, leading them to a series of explorations of garden-based designs. In his own sketchbook, Rafael Viñoly jotted a series of notes, which posed questions such as, "Why should it be a tower?" Never fully convinced that tall commercial structures were the inevitable answer, early on Viñoly weighed the options of rebuilding "all or nothing." Could a vast, open space be the answer at Ground Zero?

According to the rules laid down by the LMDC, "nothing" was not possible. Within its vision of Ground Zero, THINK accommodated the required 6.5–10 million square feet of commercial office space stipulated by the LMDC. Of course, the team accepted the restriction that no building could occupy the original footprints of the World Trade Center towers. The closest thing to a plan for an open landscape on the site would be THINK's later **Sky Park** scheme, which grew partly out of several earlier schemes. It proposed restoring the street grid and covering the entire site with 5 million square feet of mixed-use space (including retail, office, cultural facilities and art galleries) while preserving the footprints as protected areas for the future memorial. This was to be covered with an expansive park that pedestrians could reach directly from the street via ramps and an esplanade, complete with views to the water from an elevated great lawn.

For the first meeting with the LMDC, THINK prepared several schemes—or perhaps one should call these "approaches"—for consideration, each addressing a different way to assemble the required amount of square footage. One scheme that did not make it to the final design stages was known internally as the **Mountain** scheme, which expressed the essential New York characteristic of density by concentrating buildings, including two towers, at the center of the site. Another focused less on structures than on infrastructure. Termed "**Broadway Boogie-Woogie**" for its relation to the well-known painting by Piet Mondrian, this scheme rethought the idea of New York's street grid and how to channel or express its energy.

This scheme asked: if you can take buildings upward, why not take the streets skyward too? This would have required the construction of vertical structures that would act as foundations for future buildings and perhaps most importantly would have extended the sidewalk—and therefore public access—upward, offering views usually exclusive to high-priced private real estate. Fascinating for its conceptual leap, "**Broadway Boogie-Woogie**" would greatly influence some of the thinking behind the later **World Cultural Center**.

The pace of client meetings was relentless. Every two weeks the LMDC would host sessions where each team would present its new work in response to client suggestions. Additionally, regular Steering Committee meetings were part of the mix. In attendance were decision-makers such as John C. Whitehead, Chairman of the LMDC and Deputy Mayor Daniel L. Doctoroff, the city official charged with overseeing the redevelopment of downtown, as well as top officials of the Port Authority. Also in attendance was Roland Betts, an LMDC board member who is also a close friend of President George W. Bush and a veteran of Manhattan development. (Betts is co-creator of the New York waterfront project, Chelsea Piers.) At each meeting, new requests were made to refine ideas and schemes and eventually to present specific engineering and transportation solutions—somewhat surprising considering the original scope of the "Innovative Design Study," which was to elicit ideas as opposed to finalizing concrete plans.

Nonetheless, THINK followed the lead of its client. If the LMDC wanted polished, complete designs, then that was what the agency would get. THINK began to consider and eventually accept that the process could turn out to be a competition after all. THINK would go on to present three very different designs as fully articulated schemes: the aforementioned **Sky Park**, the **Great Hall** and the **World Cultural Center**.

The **Great Hall** offered a gigantic glass-roofed space that was symbolically covered, yet not fully enclosed. At 13 acres, this would have been the largest public space of its kind. Cylinders (reminiscent of Ban's tower designs) would surround and protect the World Trade Center footprints while remaining open to the sky. The considerable amount of commercial space required for the scheme would be built on the Hall's periphery with an additional portion of the required surface area actually contained in a dramatic conical glass tower occupying a site immediately adjacent, but not directly on, the actual Ground Zero site.

While all three schemes had their individual advantages, the **World Cultural Center** eventually captured the most attention for the team. The most expensive and elaborate of THINK's suggestions, this project would have replaced the missing elements of Manhattan's southern skyline by providing not one but four spectacular areas for memorial spaces (at the base and top of each of the two towers) with the elevated areas sited at the exact height of the original World Trade Center towers. These were proposed as an alternative to the typical model of tall towers as commercial space. Instead, cultural uses would populate the framework of these new, reimagined towers.

Adamant that budgets be explicitly addressed, THINK felt that the three schemes clearly illustrated a range of possibilities corresponding to differing amounts of public funding that might ultimately be made available. In one of the presentations to the LMDC, THINK illustrated this with a graphic that broke down hypothetical funding scenarios—ranging from $150 million to $600 million—with different proportions of public to private components. The team reminded the LMDC that where the money came from would greatly affect the type of project that could be produced. The message was clear: if the client wanted a memorial on the footprints, and a dedicated cultural component in this important part of downtown—an essential part of the 24-hour street life ostensibly desired by the LMDC—the price needed to be paid through public funds, because private developers rarely provide such amenities and infrastructure. In other words, if you envision a district with museums, performing arts spaces and public recreational areas, you had better dedicate funds for this purpose from the public sector. For THINK, the cash—the budgets and sources—for the project was an essential component in the design and this was made perfectly clear to the LMDC. Nonetheless, the client maintained that cost was not to be a focus—the agency seemed confident that sufficient funds would be available when the time came to build.

Until December 18, THINK could stay focused on the LMDC's desires and demands. But once the elaborate models, animations and poster boards were mounted in the exhibition area of the Winter Garden in New York's World Financial Center (directly across from Ground Zero), the team would have to broaden its efforts at education from the small, yet powerful audience in the conference room at the LMDC to the public at large. This was contingent on THINK's advancement to the next level of the secretive selection process, which was now clearly more of a competition than any consulting arrangement. The "winners" of the next stage of the LMDC process would have to shift gears and make their case not only to the city's power brokers, but also to average New Yorkers by distilling all of the complexity of master planning into a few compelling images. What awaited the competitors was a political campaign.

A Vision for Lower Manhattan

Context and Program for the Innovative Design Study

October 11, 2002

10.11.02

Innovative Design Study begins.

2 Memorial, Cultural and Parks and Open Spaces

The symbolic memorial and memorial related elements will be the subject of an international competition. You are not to design the memorial. The overall site plan should define the geographic area(s) for the competition and situate memorial elements within the broader framework of the urban planning program. Every effort should be made to allow for the most creative ideas and opportunities for a subsequent memorial competition.

A cultural and civic program is currently being developed with the goal of an area active day and night for visitors, residents and workers. There will be a diversity of facility types and programs—large and small—that contribute to the cultural pre-eminence, vitality and quality of life in New York City. Cultural and civic facilities must also act as an economic driver to the financial revitalization of Lower Manhattan.

As a densely developed and historically rich place, Lower Manhattan has relatively little park and recreational space. The lack of park and open space in Lower Manhattan is a major problem, because such space provides the public realm around which the private realm can grow. Residential squares, new parks and commercial plazas provide a framework for intelligent urbanism. Such spaces need not be large, but they must be varied and accomodate a wide variety of activities.

PROGRAMMATIC REQUIREMENTS

Memorial Area(s)

We have a strong preference for preserving the footprints of the twin towers for memorial or memorial related elements. There should not be any commercial/retail development on the footprints. A preliminary program for the memorial is under development. Some of the elements under consideration include a symbolic memorial structure(s), a private contemplative area or structure, visitor/information center, related museum, and/or open-air plaza or parks. The immediate area surrounding the footprints and the space between should be respectful and enhance the significance of the site. Preserving or acknowledging the footprints does not preclude ideas for the memorial or associated elements to be located on a different area than the footprints or on memorial sites.

Consideration should be made for creating inspirational view corridors and respectful approaches to the memorial area(s). Adjacent transportation, street grid, cultural facilities, parks or plaza, and commercial/retail development must be thought of in relation to the creation of the memorial area(s).

Do not design the memorial. Although there is no way of knowing what the memorial will be, do indicate appropriate location(s) and setting(s) that will be included in the competition.

Cultural and Civic Amenities

Cultural and civic elements may be permitted in or around the memorial area(s) or elsewhere. Consideration should be made for how cultural institutions could play a

10.11.02

Roland Betts

Daniel Libeskind

Steven Holl and Richard Meier

Frederic Schwartz

Rafael Viñoly

Lord Foster

General Programmatic Requirements

Sense of place:
Develop a distinctive identity for the site. Create interior and exterior spaces of special character, at appropriate scales, that relate to the urban fabric of Lower Manhattan, including its skyline, and create a unified street architecture and landscape.

Phasing:
Redevelopment of the WTC site is likely to take place over a multi-year period. Site proposals must identify the likely phases of development, and describe the critical components that will assure that each phase will result in a "complete project" at each stage of development. Proposals without clear staging plans, and proposals that must be built all at once, may have a strong negative impact on the existing community and will be difficult to implement.

Environmental Planning:
Site planning proposals must be sensitive to the natural environmental conditions at the site, and ensure that the placement and orientation of buildings and open spaces takes advantage of opportunities to incorporate sustainable design and technologies.

Distinctive Skyline:
New York City lost a critical part of its identity when the World Trade Center towers were destroyed. A tall symbol(s) or structure(s) that would be recognized around the world is crucial to restoring the spirit of the city.

Excerpt from *A Vision for Lower Manhattan*

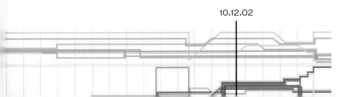

10.12.02

First **THINK** meeting at
Rafael Viñoly Architects.

9/11/01

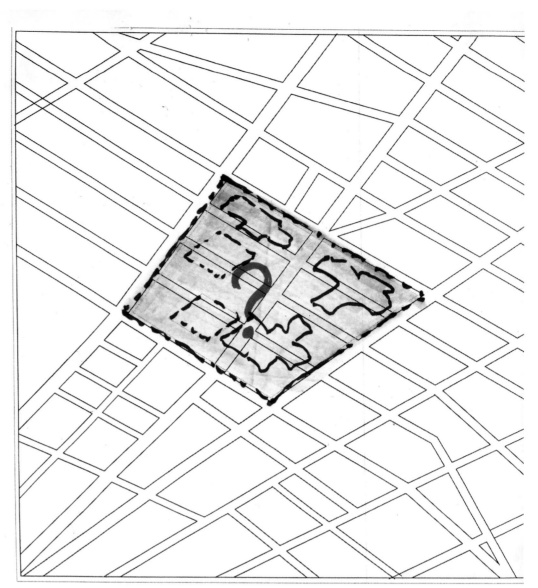

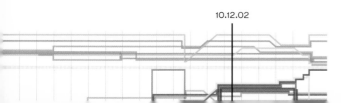

10.12.02

CENTRAL
PARK

& POOM
W/
BLDG WALLS

INTERNAL WORLD
NATURE
PUBLIC
SPACE

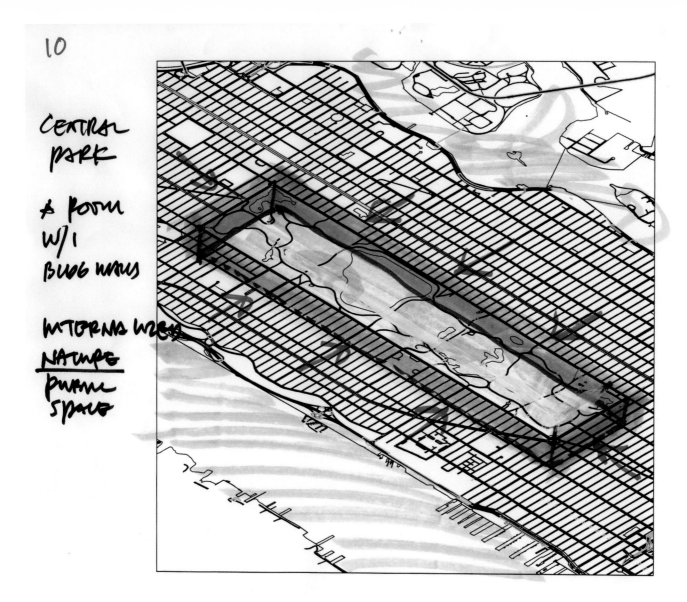

Immediately following September 11, the question for designers was how to reconsider the World Trade Center site. Addressing this as a specifically New York condition, THINK analyzed other districts in Manhattan in order to assess local urban conditions and determine whether they were applicable to Ground Zero.

New York has both small green spaces and massive ones, ranging from intimate greens ringed by mid-rise buildings (Gramercy Park comes to mind) to parks along the water flanked by roadways and buildings, such as Riverside Park on the West side. Ground Zero would probably contain both public space and skyscrapers, so THINK looked toward the few examples where green space is juxtaposed with extremely tall structures.

One example is Bryant Park, located to the west of the main branch of the New York Public Library at 42nd Street, between Fifth Avenue and Avenue of the Americas (Sixth Avenue). This well used public space combines an open lawn with landscaped paths and sits in the shadow of extremely tall buildings to the south. Of course, Bryant Park is far smaller than Ground Zero's 16 acres.

Another example of green space surrounded by a tight urban fabric of buildings and streets is Central Park, distinctive for the manner in which tall structures, especially at the park's southern end, come right up to the edge of the green space. In the drawing on the right-hand page, Rafael Viñoly points out the verticality of the buildings that line the park's boundaries, essentially making a wall enclosing Central Park. Viñoly was especially interested in this quality and remarked on it in detail in his published essay "My Kind of Town," which appears later in this section.

October 15, 2002

Following the October 11 meeting with the LMDC, THINK's principals assembled and began a renewed analysis of the site. THINK understood that the site either could be considered as a single entity (as seen in the sketch near right), or as three separate sites, since it could be argued to include the Deutsche Bank building and St. Nicholas Church (as shown in the drawing far right). Also, the team discussed ways in which parkland and green space could be used to create connections across the site. The video stills show the beginning of THINK's development of a structured process for analyzing the feasibility of various site plans.

The LMDC made its attitude toward the site clear. The teams were to address the site—within an expanded context called the "Vision for Lower Manhattan," which included the West Street promenade, the Fulton Street corridor and other downtown initiatives within a loose urbanistic framework. THINK felt that the scope should have been even larger— an approach to Lower Manhattan overall.

10.15.02

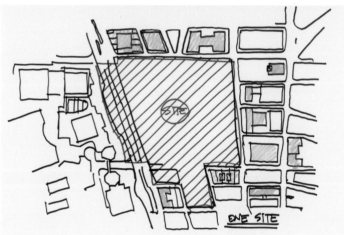

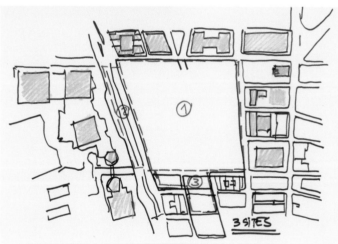

Ken Smith suggested a number of approaches for introducing landscape to the site. Above, he shows landscaping along the east–west axis that addresses the overall image of a possible green space, as opposed to a solution of specific elements. In a sense, Smith is showing the forest rather than the trees.

The drawings on the facing page illustrate the drop in elevation from east to west (from Church to West Street) across the site. The suggested park is one of the tools that could be used to negotiate this change in elevation. These drawings show the option of building a platform that would adjust the slope rather than working along the normal topography of the site. They also relate to THINK's attitude toward the redevelopment of West Street, which would be bridged by extensions from the platform.

10.15.02

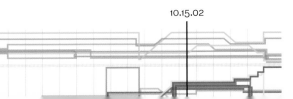

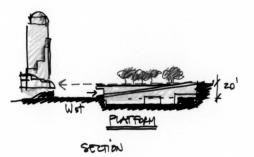

W st.

PLATFORM

SECTION

20'

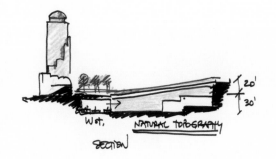

W st. NATURAL TOPOGRAPHY

SECTION

20'
30'

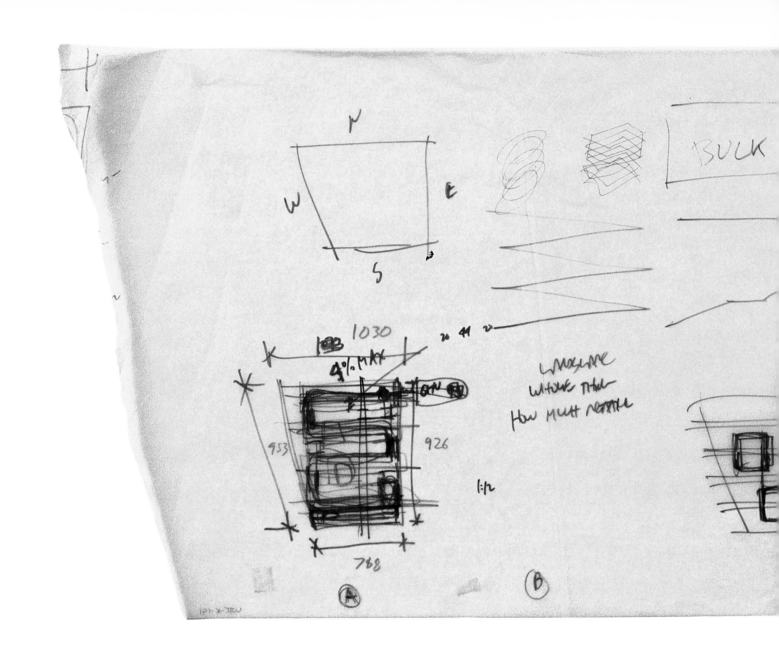

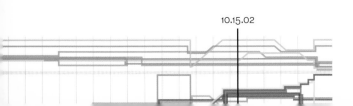

10.15.02

A series of sketched studies for the site using a collaborative process to develop different aspects of the plan. It is one example of the many pieces of yellow trace paper that were used to exchange ideas among the principals of THINK. These drawings include the proposed ramp through the site and also the layout suggested by the team of architects involved with *The New York Times Magazine* project.

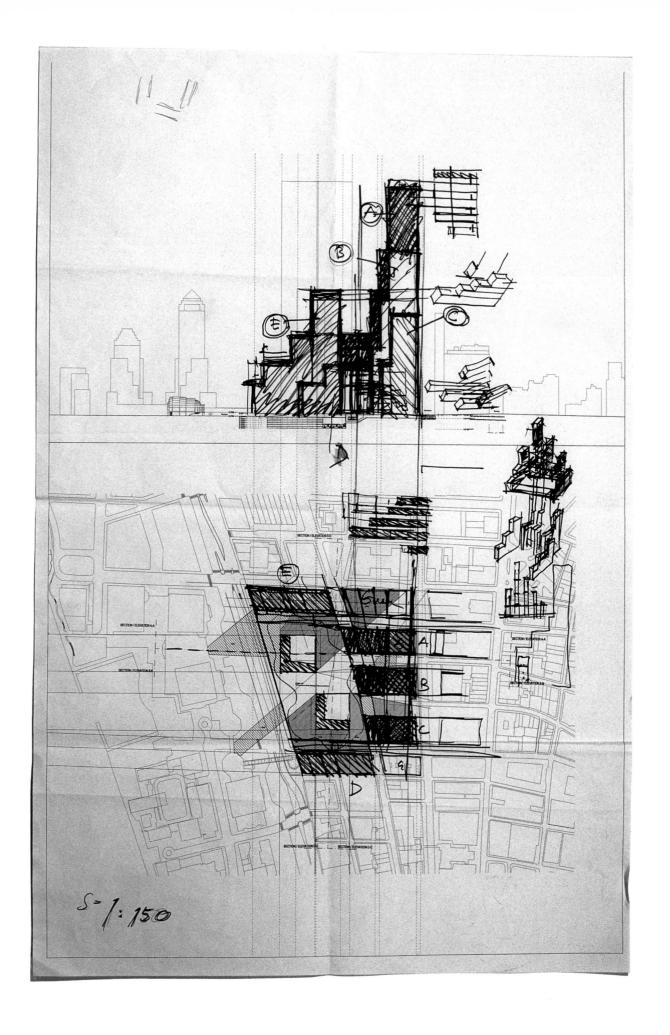

S = 1 : 150

Second **THINK** meeting at RVA

PUBLIC ACCESS FORCES

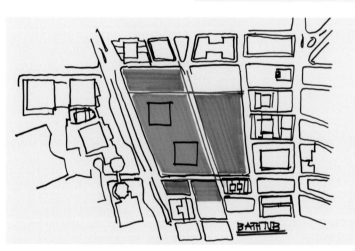

BATH TUB

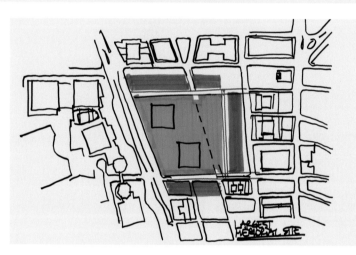

LARGEST MEMORIAL SITE

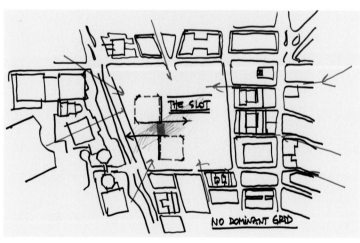

THE SLOT

NO DOMINANT GRID

The drawings opposite illustrate a plan and an elevation of a massing study that moves the bulk of the required square footage away from the sacred precinct at the footprints of the original towers. The idea of building at the periphery of the footprints and the constraints of space at the site are explored.

The upper image on the right shows the placement of the rebuilt St. Nicholas Church directly behind St. Paul's Chapel—appropriately situated along Church Street. The image below indicates the location of the tunnel for Greenwich Street, which is designed to extend the memorial precinct. Both images in the middle of the page use color to show the division between memorial (green) and redevelopment (blue) on the site. The image on the right acknowledges the need to bury Greenwich Street in order to extend the memorial precinct by concentrating the massing (as detailed in the sketches on the left of the spread).

As illustrated in the lower image—the "slot" is considered by THINK to be an important organizing principle for the site, emerging as it does, from one of the most powerful elements of the original World Trade Center composition. By orienting the towers in different ways, this space can be transformed.

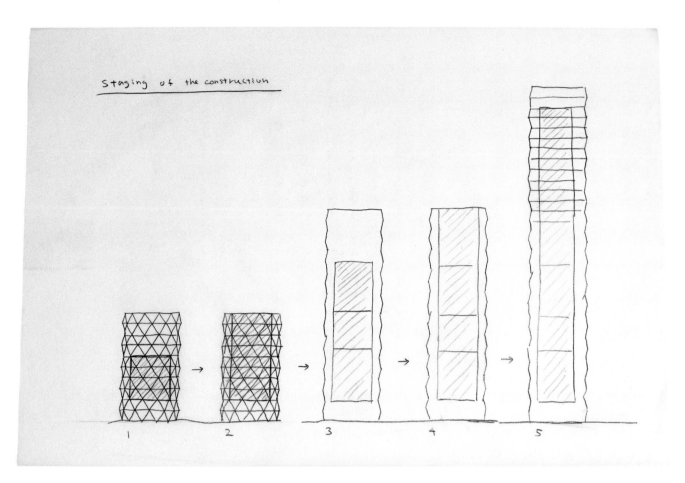

Staging of the construction

1 → 2 → 3 → 4 → 5

Shigeru Ban's design for replacing the towers adapted the Japanese tradition of floating memorial lanterns. Using illumination, great size and height, Ban created designs that could function both as inhabited buildings and symbols. His drawing at the top of the page examines the phasing of construction, while the drawing below explores different structural designs.

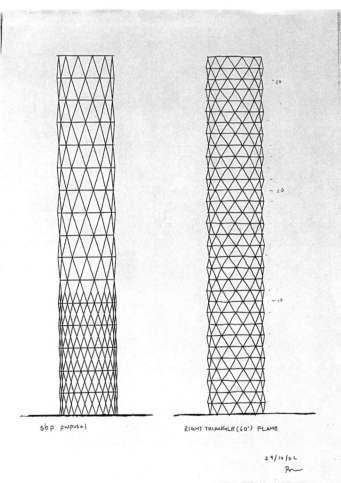

sbp proposal

RIGHT TRIANGLE (60°) FLAME

29/10/02

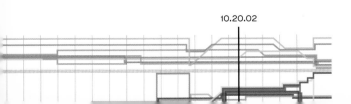

While the master planning of the site was of paramount importance, THINK carefully considered the restoration of the skyline. Part of its analysis was an examination of not only existing conditions in New York, but also the formal qualities of other great urban cityscapes. Clearly, iconic skyscrapers and other major structures leave their imprimatur on a city. Imagine Chicago without the Sears Tower or Sydney without the Opera House; the image of the city is defined by its landmarks. From New York's former World Trade Center to Paris's Eiffel Tower, tall buildings and monuments are essential to our recognition of each place.

On the left is a study of New York, Chicago, San Francisco, Kuala Lumpur, Seattle, Paris, Hong Kong, Berlin, Frankfurt and Sydney. On the right is an examination of various massing solutions for Lower Manhattan from different vantage points.

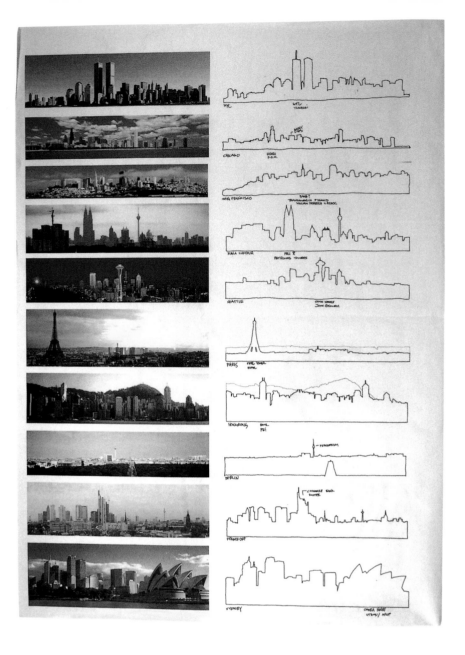

10.20.02

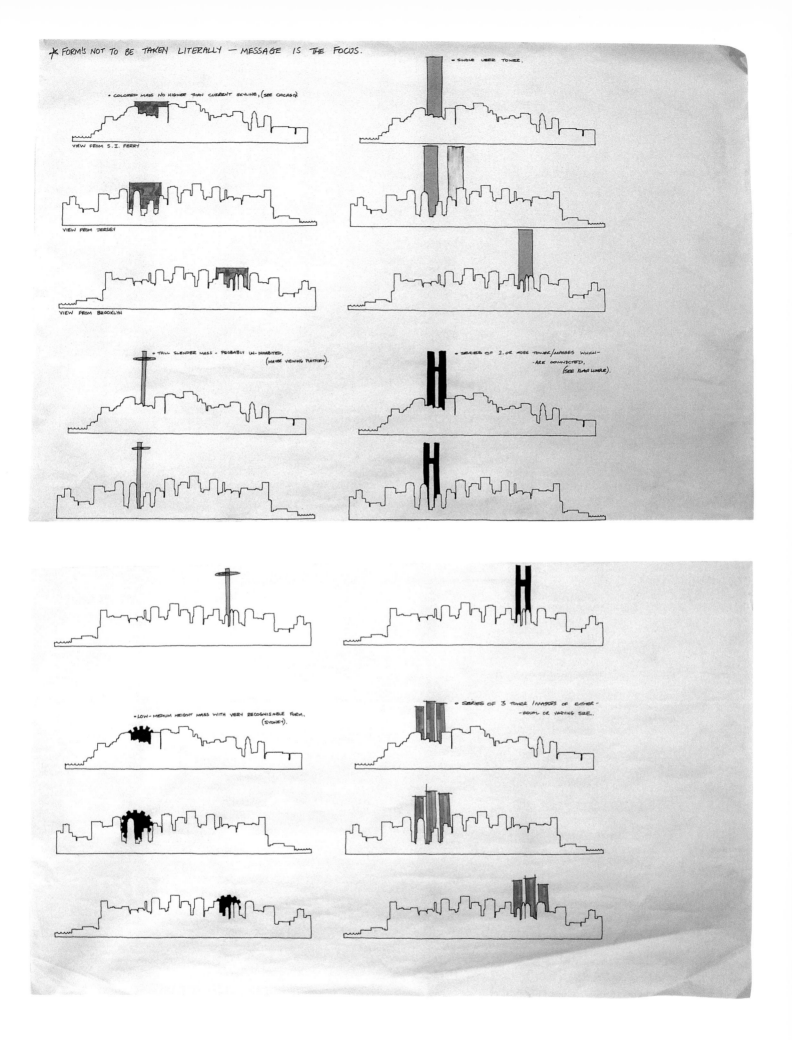

★ FORM'S NOT TO BE TAKEN LITERALLY — MESSAGE IS THE FOCUS.

• COLORED MASS NO HIGHER THAN CURRENT SKYLINE, (SEE CHICAGO)

VIEW FROM S.I. FERRY

VIEW FROM JERSEY

VIEW FROM BROOKLYN

• SINGLE UBER TOWER.

• TALL SLENDER MASS - PROBABLY UN-INHABITED, (MAYBE VIEWING PLATFORM).

• SERIES OF 2. OR MORE TOWER/MASSES WHICH- -ARE CONNECTED, (SEE KUALA LUMPUR).

• LOW - MEDIUM HEIGHT MASS WITH VERY RECOGNISABLE FORM. (SYDNEY).

• SERIES OF 3 TOWER/MASSES OF EITHER- -EQUAL OR VARYING SIZE.

Following these early LMDC meetings and the first meeting of the entire THINK team, Rafael Viñoly took some time to jot down a list of concepts and larger issues relating to developing the master plan. Well aware of the politics and possibilities of the site, Viñoly assessed a wide range of qualities and ideas, some of which are in conflict with one another. For example, there is a desire for re-creating tallness on the site, "the will of height," yet he also acknowledges the desire to allow for a memorial space that is not complicated by building. As Viñoly develops a greater understanding of the site's potential, he asks, "Why should it be a tower?" He also speaks of a "non-skyscraper" and "the ethics of doing nothing," which questions the task of rebuilding.

10.20.02

"It does not put in conflict
(past|present) memorial w|work
Could you call
How could you be there w|o knowing
why you were able to be there
it changes the relationship between
towers + lateral stability
Height + the City
fear + knowledge + perspective +
totalizing experience
not being alone
nothing or everything
Nothing is cool because it is <u>non-confrontational</u>
do not respond w| the same action
the ethics of doing nothing
<u>The will of height</u>
Why should it <u>be a tower</u>
Not a point

A place generated by the ghost
A non-skyscraper a space _____?
(only possible for the availability of the
super-block)
Eliminate the super-block|traditional
pattern of circulation
predetermined (?) of trans-physical displacement
a non-building
non gravity
a non-monument
"an embrace" "a hug"
generated by the logic of history
is historically contextual
solid-void
it does not perpetuate the tragedy it
"builds on it" it changes agression (sic)
for desire
relationships w|and between work +|
dwelling

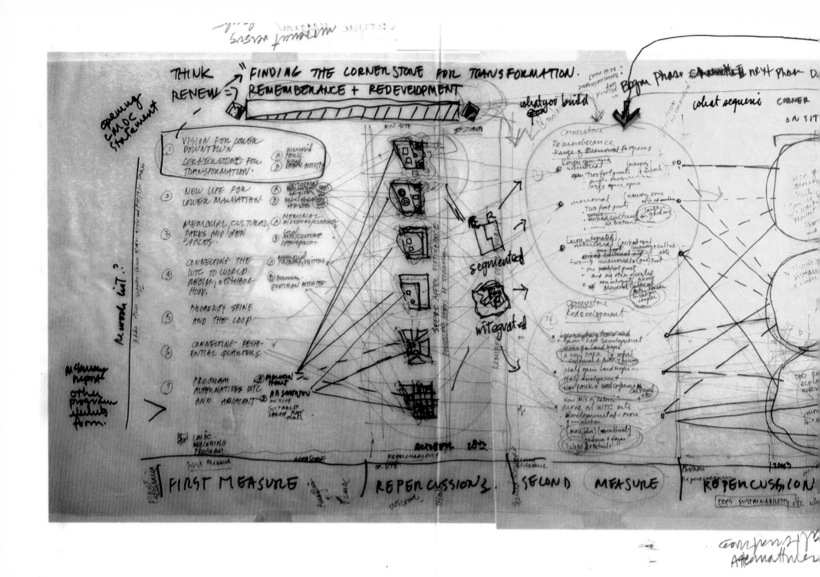

True to its name, THINK examined multiple scenarios and their ramifications using a variety of methods including this system for analyzing the decision trees that emerge through the systematic consideration of architectural, planning and transportation issues. This navigable tool for analyzing the World Trade Center site was an outgrowth of THINK's understanding of the LMDC's intent to select a design consultant as opposed to a specific design.

On the tracing paper above, the team started by identifying six typologies, or "seed" scenarios, that generate a visual decision tree of design options. THINK strongly felt that all six of these scenarios were essential for not only the LMDC to consider, but also for New Yorkers to utilize as part of the process of public participation.

These "seeds" included a series of six plans, reduced to their essential elements, which could evolve into all possible plans based on requirements of the site. The system used an iterative process where different goals and elements were applied to the seeds in order to produce more developed plans. The idea was to create a logical design system that could record the thinking behind the team's master planning process.

The system could accommodate those elements predetermined by the LMDC, such as the location of the memorial, the establishment of a West Street promenade and added greenery, the reclaimed skyline and various aspects of a renewed vision of Lower Manhattan.

THINK was enthusiastically obtaining public input as well as educating the public—an important constituency—and believed that a website would be a ideal mechanism for this purpose. The idea was to build public support through education, transparency, patience, and enfranchisement. Working with information architects R/GA, THINK developed an interactive archive and polling system based on the architectural analysis described above and went so far as to develop a sophisticated mock-up of the web-based system that could be implemented in short order. The images on the right are screenshots from the mock-up. The whole process was developed, presented and rejected by the LMDC within the space of five weeks.

10.26.02

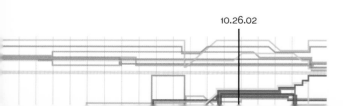

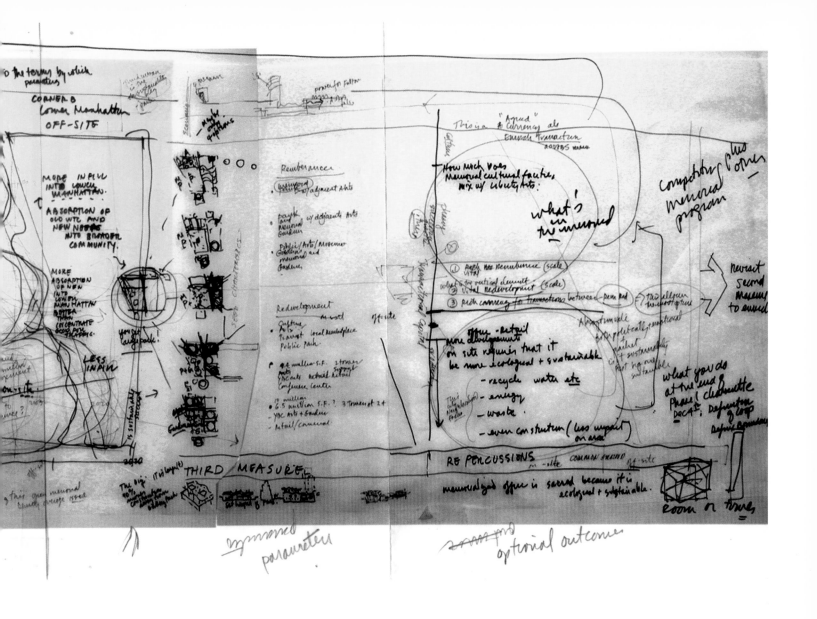

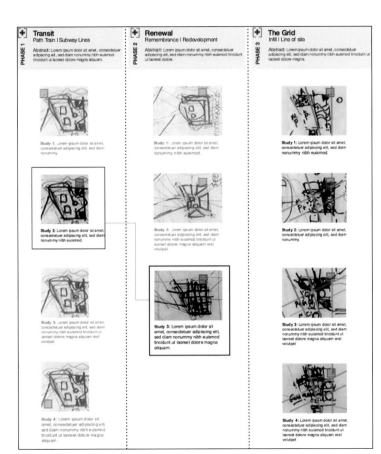

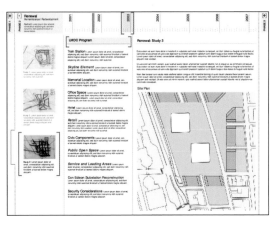

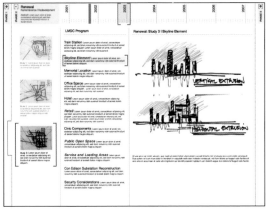

Rafael Viñoly's essay for *Architecture Today*, "My Kind of Town," detailed his appreciation of the distinct urban qualities of Manhattan. In particular, Viñoly stresses the importance of verticality in New York, something which will greatly influence his work with THINK and the team's approach to vertical infrastructure.

10.26.02

MY KIND OF TOWN

Rafael Viñoly

Principal in Rafael Viñoly Architects, whose recent projects include the Kimmel Centre in Philadelphia

I left Buenos Aires in 1979 because I wanted out of what had become an economically and politically unfeasible environment for my family and me. I could have easily chosen Europe over the United States, since I barely spoke English at the time. But I chose the US because it was in New York that I wanted to settle and practice.

Since its earliest days the city has been driven by an ever-increasing density of people, talent and resources that are drawn to each other and to the city's spectacular form. Even in the late 70s, when the city was just beginning to emerge from a serious financial crisis, and even viewed from as far away as Argentina, it seemed full of opportunity. Like most immigrants to the city, I was drawn to its intensity because even though it always threatened to come apart at the seams the demise never seemed to materialise. Today the city continues to grow into Long Island to the east, Westchester County to the north and New Jersey to the west, but it is its growth in Manhattan that really makes it such a compelling and unique place.

Manhattan is especially 3D. The borough's primarily vertical response to the pressures of its growth has not been dictated by the geographical constraints that have shaped a city like Hong Kong. And unlike the urban centres in places like Tokyo or Frankfurt, Manhattan is exceptionally integrated programmatically. Amazingly, this most exuberant sort of growth, this upwards expansion, is occurring in a place where the physical barriers were overcome by bridges or tunnels long ago. Manhattan, as an iconic image of New York City, is a land of psychological frontiers, bounded by identity, not geography. The city is perceived as an object about which most people, especially New Yorkers, feel a deep sense of proprietorship. One experiences a common identity that is predicated on the insular condition of being a New Yorker, a condition that is as apparent from within as without. Like the number of people who claim to have attended the Woodstock Festival in 1969, I suspect that more people in the world identify themselves as New Yorkers than have actually lived here.

But that's all right with me; there should be billions of New Yorkers in the world. I think what makes New York City attractive is the plurality and democracy that exists on the streets and the fact that individualism can so easily coexist with a sense that somehow we all participate in the New York project. I believe this effect can be attributed to an urban morphology that produces effective transitions of scale. In the canyon streets between its tall buildings, as in its subway and most of its dense cityscape, New York is a close-up of architectural and human detail. It may have real social boundaries and frontiers but the streets unify experience by denying everyone insulation from the messy process of social, economic, cultural and political integration.

Manhattan is socially and economically stratified but this is a primarily vertical phenomenon that occurs above a highly democratic street. Since rooftop helicopter landings were deemed too dangerous and outlawed, not even the wealthiest or most influential people have been spared having to go down to the street and mix it up with everyone else, participating in globalisation on a face-to-face scale. On the street you are immersed in pragmatic plurality. It's not ideal and could certainly improve, but at least it's there.

There are also places, always nearby, where the scale shifts and you come face to face with the city as a whole. Verticality allows the perception of scale to shift towards the very large and it is easy to perceive the city as a complex, highly integrated system that somehow manages to remain functional even when large sections of it are violently and traumatically amputated. There may have been many ways to criticise the World Trade Center but its ubiquity in the daily experience of the city made it possible to perceive one's self within the larger object. The Twin Towers were a point of reference which, with the Empire State Building, made it easier to triangulate one's position and understand the common project that is New York.

Central Park manages this trick as well. It is the collective backyard from which we can see the city and know that we share it too. I think that common identity is what allows us to share the park so well – that and the fact that it's an extremely well crafted resource which in its diversity manages to please most of the people most of the time.

The democracy of New York depends on being able to see the forest for the trees, so to speak. You have to apprehend the wonderfully functional object past the mess of everything that constitutes it and the people who inhabit it and understand that we are bound in a common identity which we have chosen rather than inherited.

I think there is a minimum requirement for being a New Yorker that has nothing to do with geography. Anyone who has an idea of what it might be like to walk in the streets of a city which, despite its many problems and iniquities, manages to maintain a sense of village even in a very large and diverse metropolis, could rightly call themselves a New Yorker.

Frederic Schwartz

Since the morning of September 11, 2001, in honor of the 2,749 innocent people who were savagely murdered, I have dedicated myself—as an architect and planner, a native New Yorker and a 25-year resident of Lower Manhattan—to finding the best way to remember and rebuild on the hallowed ground of the World Trade Center.

I live in the shadows of Ground Zero and from my office I stare at the empty sky where the missing Twin Towers once stood. I was at home at the corner of Canal and Greene Streets when the first plane went over my head (a sound I shall never forget), and struck Tower One. I walked outside my front door to watch in horror as the second plane struck Tower Two. From the beginning, I have seen the planning process as an opportunity to redefine ourselves (individually and collectively), and to reassert more than ever the values, taught to me by my mother and my late father (a World War II veteran), of democracy, truth and honesty, of community and humility, and of giving instead of taking—values that the terrorists assailed.

In an attempt to help my city and country heal, I immediately began drawing and imagining ways to relieve the pressure on the site in the rush to rebuild on sacred ground. My early independent work first proposed DNA-like memorials (with the help of the brilliant Dr. Mark Phillips of New York University) and a plan to suppress West Street for 13 city blocks (from Battery Park to one block north of Chambers Street) in order to transfer the entire program and build 12 million square feet of offices, mixed income housing, retail, cultural and community facilities and parks in the area adjacent to and north and south of the 16-acre World Trade Center site. I was confident in the value of my plans and in early February 2002, I presented them to Amanda Burden and the New York City Planning Commission, Alex Garvin and the Lower Manhattan Development Corporation, the Battery Park City Authority, and at its request, Community Board One.

On April 24, 2002, The Port Authority of New York and New Jersey and the Lower Manhattan Development Corporation issued a request for proposals for a design for the site. I submitted my qualifications, teaming with Kohn, Pederson Fox (KPF) and Arup. In May, Beyer Blinder Belle (BBB) was selected under a veil of controversy, our team was not. That firm would then spend the next few months leading the effort (along with the LMDC's in-house planning consultant Peterson Littenberg, and off-the-record planning by SOM) to prepare six "different" master plans. On July 20, 2002, at the "Listening to the City" session at Javits Center, those plans were categorically rejected by 5,000 participants for their lack of vision.

Meanwhile, on July 6, 2002, I received call from Richard Meier inviting me to share my plans and vision for Lower Manhattan and participate in a planning and design study that would later be published in *The New York Times Magazine*. A group of architects (Meier, Gwathmey, Holl, Eisenman and others) had started meeting at Richard's office to come up with design alternatives for the World Trade Center site that would later be known as: "Thinking Big: A Plan for Ground Zero and Beyond." During these meetings, Rafael Viñoly and I realized a certain commonality, and though we both felt we were not ready for architectural design (still working on planning), we shared our sketches (literally under the table), of what turned out to be similar DNA-inspired designs. This group (most who had never worked together and many at career-long philosophical odds) agreed to bring ideas and drawings to the table. This was not a time to agree on "The Design" but rather a series of strategies for Ground Zero and all of Lower Manhattan.

On July 25, 2002, Herbert Muschamp took my ideas public in *The New York Times*. He wrote: "The plan offers a conceptual beauty unmatched by the six official proposals. Besides taking the economic and urbanistic factors into account, it has set the stage for focused discussion on historical meaning and cultural values." Adding that, "[p]erhaps it is best seen as an intellectual tactic for clearing the mind, so that thinking about ground zero can proceed on a higher level of historical imagination." The very next day, the *Times* ran an editorial where Governor Pataki finally agreed also to look off-site.

As a result of the work of NYNV, *The New York Times Magazine* and "Listening to the City," the LMDC was put on notice—its efforts to date were resoundingly lacking public support and that of the design community. On August 19, 2002, under increased public pressure to start all over, the Lower Manhattan Development Corporation and the Port Authority of New York and New Jersey took a brave and bold step and issued a worldwide Request for Qualifications for an "Innovative Master Planning Study with Special Emphasis on Transportation." There was jockeying for formation of collaborative teams. I was contacted by a number of prominent architects from around the world. But in the end, partnering with Rafael was born of a similar work ethic (non-stop, day and night for 18 weeks during the competition) and a profound understanding of the difference between presenting a master plan and designing buildings, including his public acknowledgement of my West Street thinking. The addition of Ken Smith to the team confirmed that landscape would be key to the Master Plan. Shigeru Ban brought his brilliance to the team and his extensive experience in designing innovative housing, especially in the wake of disaster. On September 30, 2002, six teams were chosen from among 407 submissions, representing 34 nations, and more than 1,000 architects, planners, engineers and landscape architects. THINK was one of those teams.

Epilogue:

As a founding partner of the international collaborative THINK team (including Rafael Viñoly, Shigeru Ban, Ken Smith, Jörg Schlaich, Arup, Buro Happold, Richard Tomesetti, Janet Marie Smith, David Rockwell and William Morrish), and as one of the two finalists in an extraordinary competition, I still believe that this could be architecture's finest hour.

It is critical that there is an open public dialogue about the rebuilding at Ground Zero instead of the closed-door politics of Governor Pataki that single-handedly reversed the decision the morning after the THINK team's design for the **World Cultural Center** was selected unanimously by a vote of eight to zero by the LMDC steering committee (that was appointed by Governor Pataki and Mayor Bloomberg). Three years after the controversial reversal, the current Master Plan (February 2005) has morphed into the THINK Master Plan (sans the World Cultural Towers): rational city street grid and blocks for new development surrounding an easy to transverse, on grade, eight-acre tree shaded park with two voids for the September 11 Memorial.

It has been both my privilege and my responsibility to be part of this continuing process. I continue to work hard every day and I am honored to have won two September 11 Memorial competitions (New Jersey State and Westchester County) both to remember and honor the magnificent lives lost. I shall never forget.

Fred R. Conrad/The New York Times

CITIZEN

ARCHITECT

Frederic
Schwartz with
sketches for
rebuilding Lowe
Manhattan.
Right, his loft in
SoHo.

Meg Henson for The New York Times

The Man Who Dared the City To Think Again

By ALASTAIR GORDON

FREDERIC SCHWARTZ flinched at a flash of light outside the window of his architecture studio in SoHo. "Did you see that? It's an airplane," he said, pointing at the fuselage of a commercial jet banking harmlessly over the Hudson River.

Mr. Schwartz is unusually sensitive to subtle shifts in light and sound, and with good reason. "I was getting ready to go to work when the first plane flew over my loft," he said. "I called 911 before it even hit, or at least that's how I remember it. It just sounded wrong — out of place, like a missile." He ran to the corner of Church and Canal Streets in time to watch the towers collapse.

Mr. Schwartz then did what came naturally: he began to draw, sketching quickly with colored pens on scraps of paper, restaurant tabs and napkins. On the back of a cardboard coaster he sketched the towers engulfed by black clouds. "I kept drawing horrible things," he said. "I drew what I saw."

Within weeks, the nightmarish imagery had subsided, replaced by Mr. Schwartz's first glimmerings of how Lower Manhattan might be reorganized and restored. "I started to redraw the skyline. I started to draw what should happen," he said.

Those impromptu drawings were the conceptual seeds of a master plan for downtown redevelopment — a plan that was published earlier this month in The New York Times Magazine and is now displayed in Venice at the Eighth International Architecture Exhibition at the Biennale. It was drafted as an alternative to the official versions unveiled in July by the Lower Manhattan Development Corporation, which met with tepid public response.

Under Mr. Schwartz's proposed design, the 16-acre void at ground zero would be left alone, permitting a respectful period of reflection before a permanent memorial can be agreed upon. He would instead bury part of West Street, the forbidding multi-lane state highway, in a tunnel running north from Battery Park to Chambers Street, and build on the reclaimed land on top. He envisions a series of parks and buildings linked by a tree-lined promenade that would

Continued on Page 4

AT HOME WITH

FREDERIC SCHWARTZ

A Man Who Dared The City to Think Again

Continued From Page 1, This Section

reconnect Battery Park City with the old city grid. "People were thinking of West Street physically but not metaphysically. Is that the right word?" Mr. Schwartz said. "They weren't thinking that you could do two things at once."

While Mr. Schwartz's plan has no official standing, it has stirred debate by injecting imagination into the proceedings and showing how aspirational design could help repair the city.

"His presentation stood out from so many others," said Jordan Gruzen, a member of New York New Visions, an advocacy group of architects and planners formed after Sept. 11. "Now everyone else has taken this point of view, and every scheme that comes forward deals with West Street."

After living in SoHo for 22 years, Mr. Schwartz, 50, has an intimate feel for Lower Manhattan. "I walk and look and Rollerblade on all those streets," he said. "I know the buildings and I know what's going on inside them."

He owns a ground-floor loft in a 19th-century cast-iron building in SoHo, where he lives with his girlfriend, Tracey Hummer, an editor at Art in America magazine.

The loft formerly belonged to his friend, the architect Alan Buchsbaum, who helped popularize the loft look of the early 80's and designed loft conversions for Bette Midler, Diane Keaton and Billy Joel. Mr. Buchsbaum died of AIDS in 1987; Mr. Schwartz moved in a year later. Aside from a new shower mosaic depicting an underwater scene, Mr. Schwartz has changed almost nothing; he wanted to preserve the high-tech style that was Mr. Buchsbaum's signature. "Living here makes me remember Alan all the time and how talented he was," Mr. Schwartz said.

The loft is furnished with an eclectic mix of furniture by Mr. Buchsbaum, Frank Gehry, Robert Venturi and Mr. Schwartz's own designs, including a chair from 1985 in the shape of a house. (Mr. Schwartz has edited a book about his friend's work, "Alan Buchsbaum, Architect and Designer: The Mechanics of Taste," Monacelli Press, 1996.)

"He was the master of loft design," Mr. Schwartz said. "He was like the older brother I never had."

The loft's ceilings are stamped tin from the late 19th century, and old beams and columns have been stripped to expose origi-

nal timber. Industrial light fixtures, a mainstay of Mr. Buchsbaum's high-tech style, hang in the kitchen and living area. "I feel it's timeless," Mr. Schwartz said. "That's why I can't change it, because it's not getting old." One of Mr. Buchsbaum's few eccentric touches is an amorphously shaped hot tub.

"I love my loft, but I don't live at home," Mr. Schwartz said. "I live at my office nowadays." Mr. Schwartz starts his mornings at about 8 at the Westside Coffee Shop on Church Street where he greets the proprietor, Johnny Morillo, with a high five. "I drink a triple shot of café con leche — rocket fuel — to get me going," he said. Then he walks to his studio, eight blocks north on Varick Street. "I have a wonderful walk through SoHo every morning, and I'm always aware of the empty sky," he said.

Mr. Schwartz's studio, on the 15th floor of a former printing plant, has expansive views of SoHo and, to the south, ground zero. "When you have this incredible panorama of the city you are more aware of what's missing," Mr. Schwartz said. "When you also happen to be an architect, you're hypersensitive to what's not there."

Mr. Schwartz has worked on New York City projects since 1978, including eight years with the firm of Venturi, Rauch & Scott Brown on Westway, the contentious plan to build a 100-acre park on the West Side. The project was never built, but Mr. Schwartz received an invaluable lesson. "Westway taught me the importance of working with the community," he said. "We

had to listen to the needs of different neighborhoods, including TriBeCa, Chelsea and the West Village."

Since opening his own firm in 1996, Mr. Schwartz has designed dozens of New York projects, including the Whitehall Ferry Terminal now under construction. "I grew up going on that ferry to Staten Island to visit the grave of my great-grandfather," he said. His commercial projects include the offices of Rolling Stone magazine, Joe's Restaurant in Greenwich Village and the

IN PLACE Frederic Schwartz, above left, outside his SoHo loft, which has a table, above, by Alan Buchsbaum, a house-shaped chair by Mr. Schwartz and a sun-shaped chair by Robert Venturi. Left, a "think pod" designed this year by Mr. Schwartz for the Deutsch advertising agency's offices in Los Angeles.

Meg Henson for The New York Times; left, Fred R. Conrad/The New York Times; below, Benny Chan/Fotoworks

offices of Deutsch, an advertising firm based in Chelsea.

Mr. Schwartz has no official planning role, but he has managed to insinuate himself into the redevelopment process by becoming a regular presence at public hearings. Many days he would attend a development corporation meeting at 8 a.m. and then, in the evening, go to a community board meeting. "It started to get insane," he said. "I'd go to meeting after meeting." He would listen patiently before taking the floor to remind the assembled that the objective was to create a plan that would include all of Lower Manhattan, not just ground zero. "Sometimes, I would go ballistic," he said. "I would say: 'Don't you get it? If you keep thinking about the site, you're stuck.'"

While Mr. Schwartz does not have an official title, his persistence has paid off. In April he presented his ideas to Amanda Burden, chairwoman of the City Planning Commission. He also showed his plan to the Battery Park City Authority and to Alexander Garvin, head of planning and design at the development corporation. "He's tenacious," said Nancy Owens, a chairman of the land use committee of Community Board 1.

In July, Mr. Schwartz began meeting with

a group of other architects dissatisfied with the development corporation's six designs. "He unrolled these drawings, and we all realized that he had done a tremendous amount of research," said Charles Gwathmey, one of the participating architects. "It was the one thing that we all universally agreed on. The West Street move clarified the opportunities and de-obligated one from having to deal with the 16 acres of the World Trade Center."

Rafael Viñoly, another collaborating architect, said: "Fred's plan removed the limitations on the thinking process."

Two weeks before his plan was published, Mr. Schwartz entered the Ear Inn on Spring Street, a favorite neighborhood spot.

A waitress nodded in recognition as he took a seat at a back table. "I live here in the city, and I made it my mission to understand," he said, drawing a quick sketch on a paper napkin. "Urban planning has to find a way to make it all work together."

Mr. Schwartz continues to refine his ideas and has begun to focus his attention on what might be done with ground zero itself. "This is different than other memorials," he said. "You have to have bigger ideas. You're dealing with heaven and hell."

October 26, 2002

THINK met as a group for the second time on October 26, 2002. David Rockwell joined the team at this session and contributed his expertise on the retail component for the site plan. The two drawings (upper right) represent early iterations of the "mountain" or "slot" scheme, which combined a concentration of massing at the center of the site with a reinterpretation of the street grid.

10.26.02

In these sketches, Viñoly focuses on the layout of the site, while Schwartz considers the challenges of the towers. The sketch immediately below shows the topography of the site from Church Street down to the river (toward the West). An essential part of the master planning process was always to address the connection to the waterfront. The sectional view highlights (and exaggerates) the drop in elevation from Church Street (toward the east) to West Street and the waterfront to the west. Also illustrated here (in conjunction with the plans below) is THINK's concern for the physical and visual connection to the waterfront using low-slung massing at the western boundary of the site and the elevated viewing platforms to the east, which could afford views to the Hudson.

Just below are several sketches illustrating various characteristics of the site's configuration. They show variations in which Greenwich Street does and does not cross the site and consider the orientation of the peripheral structures in the site plan—whether they face or turn their backs on the sacred precinct at the center.

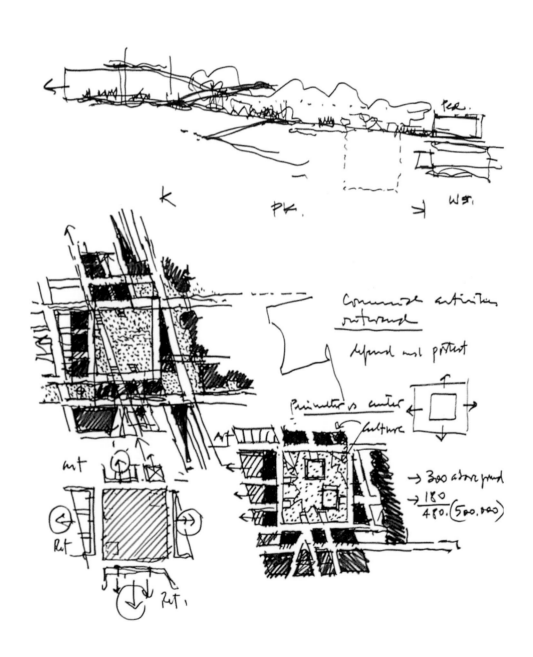

10.26.02

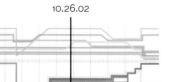

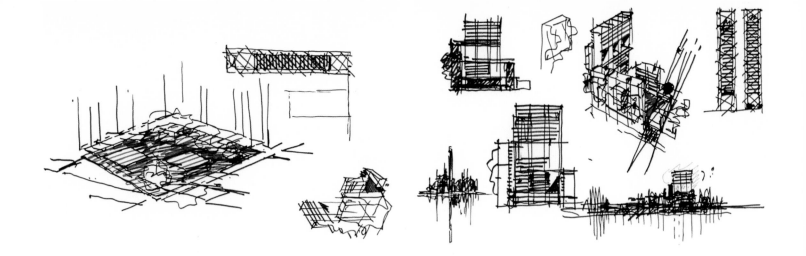

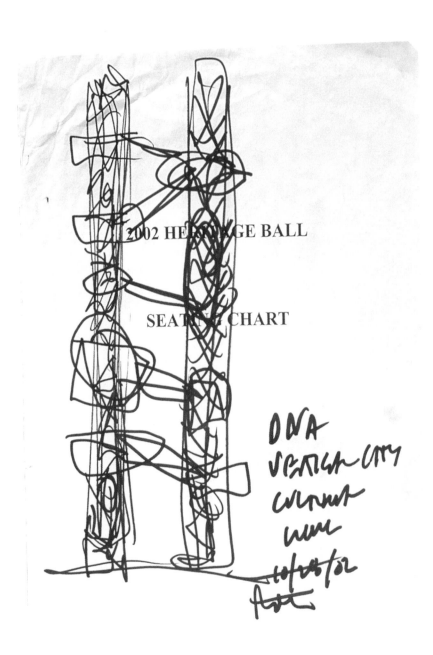

2002 HERITAGE BALL

SEATING CHART

DNA
VERTICAL CITY
CULTURE
WELL
10/18/02

In this series of sketches to the upper right, THINK explores the idea of vertical infrastructure—an idea that would morph into a scheme known as "**Broadway Boogie-Woogie**," later discussed in greater detail. Here the architecture is not to be defined, in fact, THINK proposed it as an infrastructure solution that could accommodate buildings by other architects at a later date. Also in this series we see an early idea of the towers lifted above the site, freeing it for the memorial use. The image to the left shows a quick conceptual drawing by Schwartz done at the 2002 Heritage Ball, an annual New York AIA event. Schwartz notes DNA as an influence and refers to the concept as a "vertical city." Already, he is depicting potential cultural buildings that could be developed at higher altitudes from this new infrastructure.

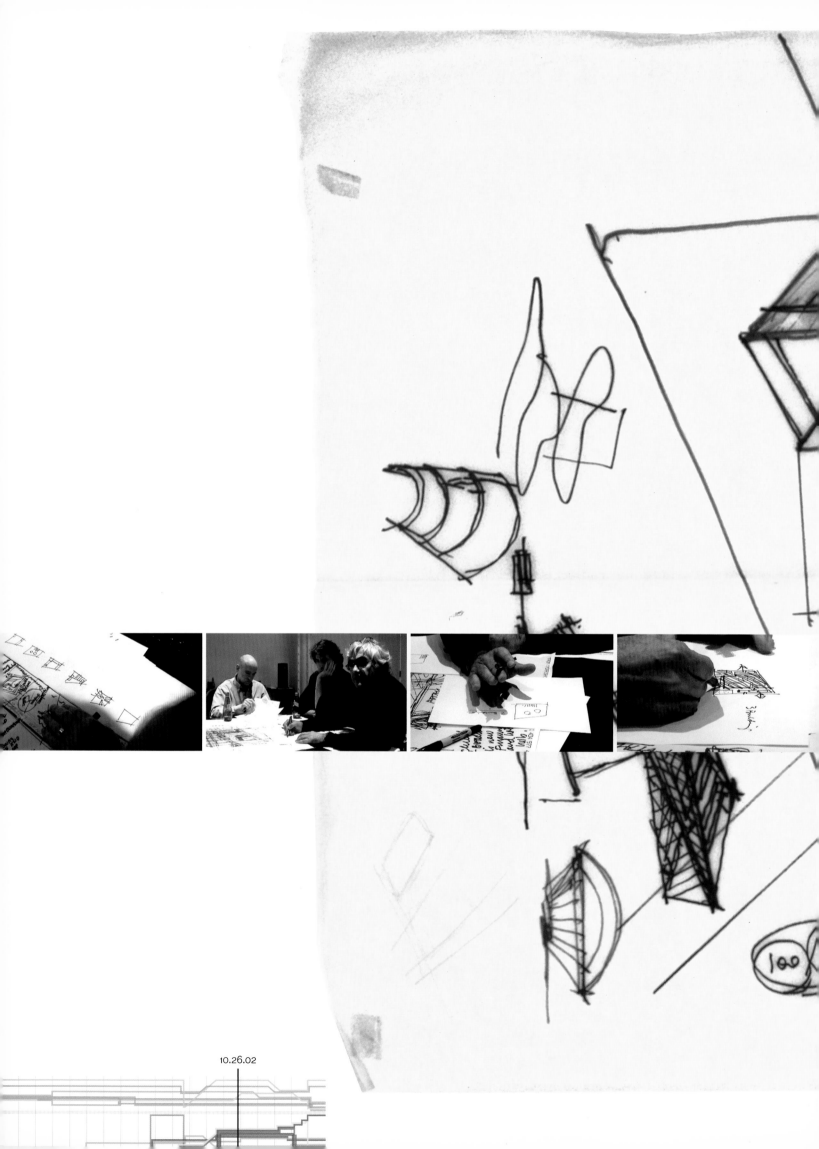

10.26.02

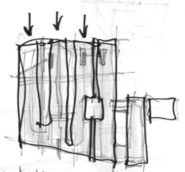

Peter Somerthing

TIMBERLAKE HARRIS

BUDGETARY
TRULY FUNDED
CORE BUILDING
TO EVERY BUILDING TO EVERY COLLEGE

ACCESS...
PLUNKED DOWN IN PARKING LOT
FOCAL POINT | FLANKED BY
  ACCESS IN DESIGN | UGLY BUILDING
  PSYCHOLOGY NEEDS | URBAN ISSUES
INVITE + DISPERSE | CAMPUS PLANNING
  "HUB"

10.26.02

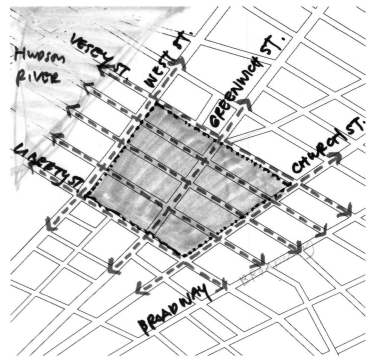

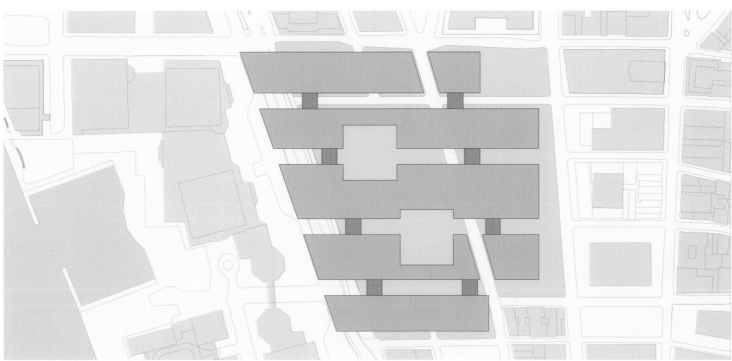

One of the principles underlying this scheme, which became known internally as the **Table** scheme, was the restoration of the traditional street grid at the site before the first World Trade Center was built. In order to reestablish the grid and allow streets such as Vesey, Liberty, Church, Greenwich and West to cut through the site, the master plan would have to conform to older, non-super block conditions.

However, this was challenging given the mandate of rebuilding 10 million square feet of commercial space. THINK developed a scheme based on this need for access and substantial development. Lifting the development off the street via the use of pilotis (column-like elements that raise the building) both demands could be met.

This scheme reserved its roof for green space; the problem, of course, was how to incorporate sufficient light into the development and streets below. However, this scheme would not be able to accommodate the phasing of development as well as some other solutions from THINK. Note that the image, bottom right, presents a variant that does not restore all of the former streets.

The film strips show Rafael Viñoly and Frederic Schwartz collaborating on the same sheet of paper.

Early on, THINK recognized the inherent problems of the scheme (getting light down to the street was paramount among these), but also saw advantages, which would lead to some of THINK's ideas in the **Sky Park** plan. The low-slung distribution of mass and volume separated it from THINK's other concurrent ideas that focused on height.

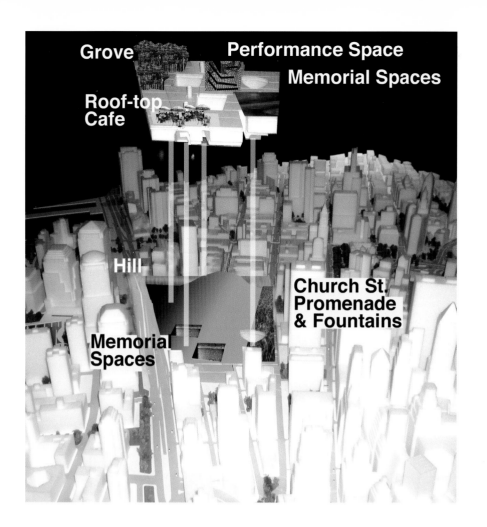

10.26.02

690,000

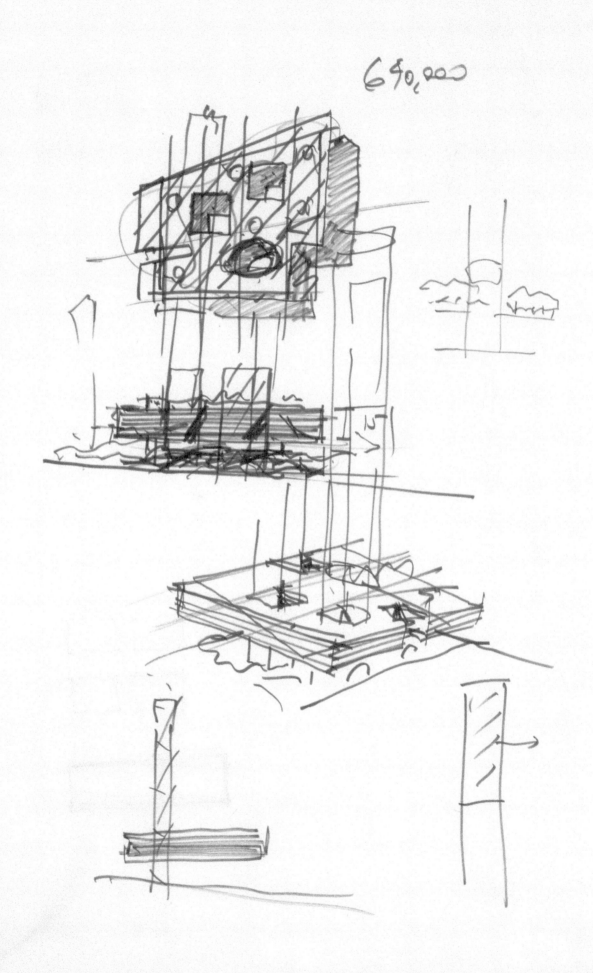

the work
of
Rockefeller
Center

10.27.02

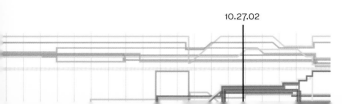

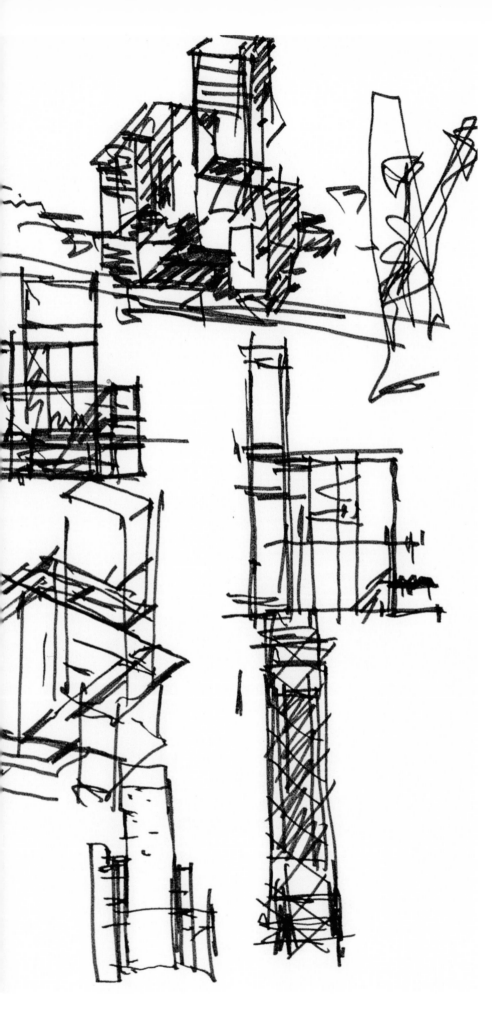

These sketches by Rafael Viñoly continue to examine aspects of vertical infrastructure and the possibility of suspending the Trade Center replacement buildings within towers. They show similarities with Viñoly's towers scheme and the influence of Shigeru Ban's idea of protective shells for the towers.

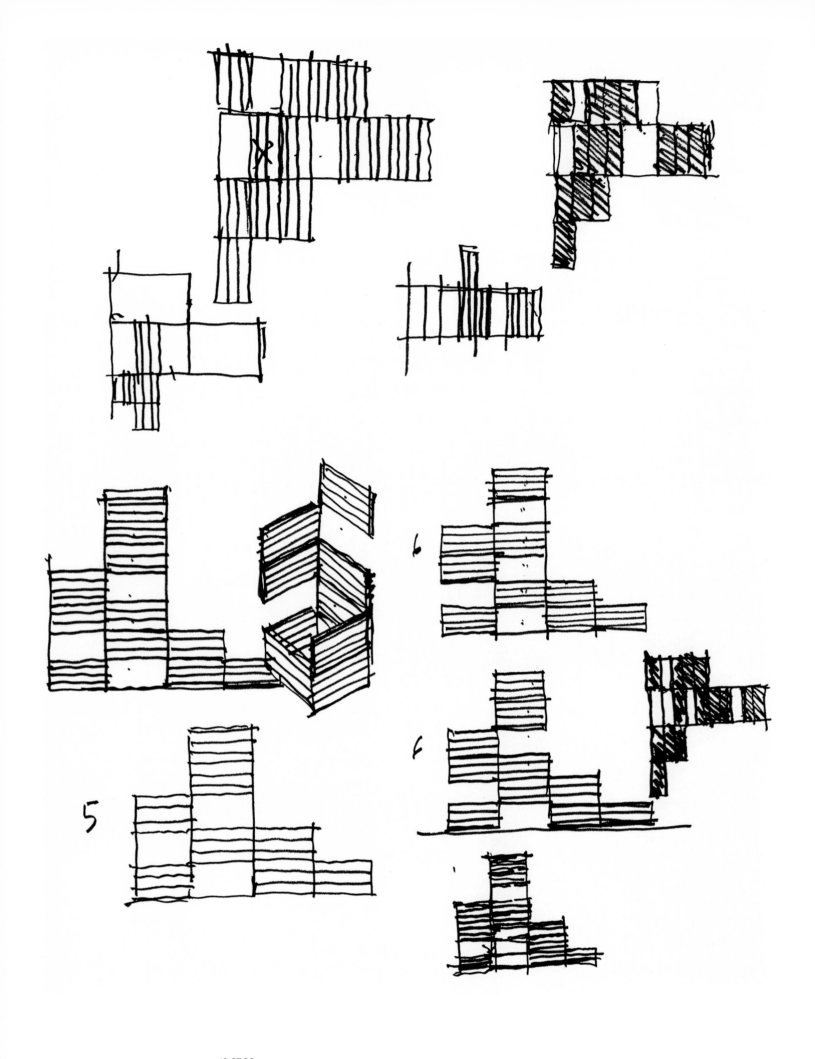

5

6

6

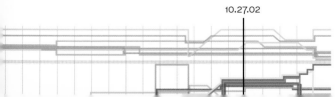

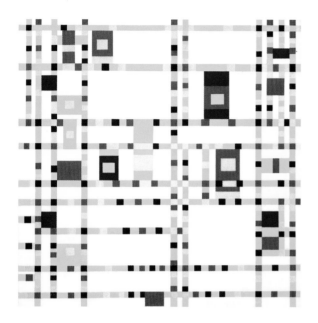

Carefully considering the qualities that make Manhattan so recognizable, THINK explored a concept based on New York's essential planning principle — the street grid. In this 21st-century twist however, the grid is not only expressed on the ground plane. Starting with the idea of vertical extrusion from that basic horizontal grid, THINK examined the possibilities of horizontal extrusion from a vertical grid. Taking both a cue and a name from Piet Mondrian's ode to New York, THINK produced **Broadway Boogie Woogie.** Like the painting, the scheme assumes an active street life within the infrastructure of the grid. These structures would have acted as vertical streets from which other buildings could be supported and visited. Key elements of this concept would emerge in the team's later presentations to the Lower Manhattan Development Corporation, especially the idea of extending the grid skyward, which was acknowledged in the towers of the **World Cultural Center.**

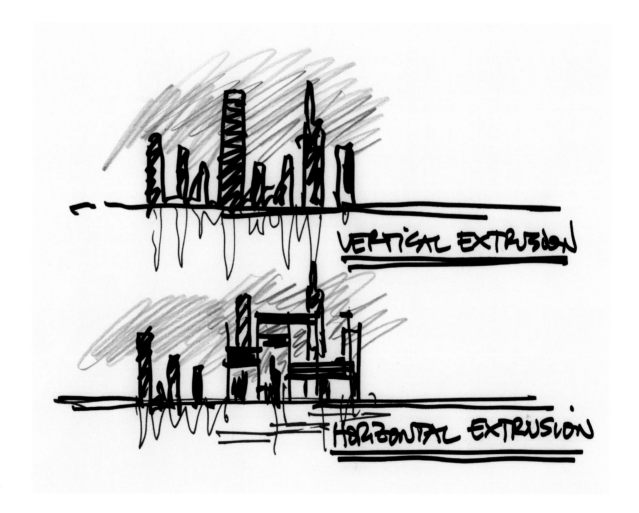

VERTICAL EXTRUSION

HORIZONTAL EXTRUSION

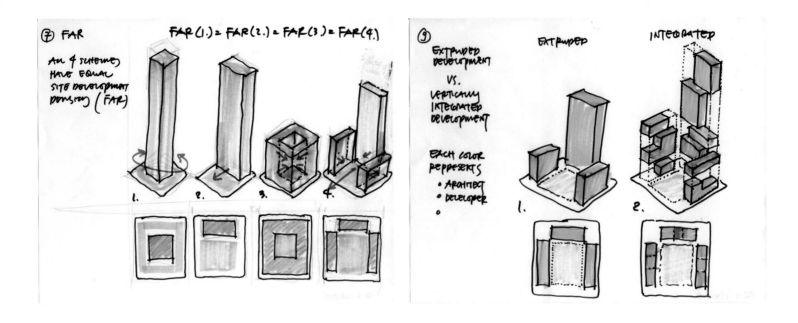

During this LMDC Land Use Committee presentation on October 27, 2002, THINK displayed its analysis of the variety of ways massing could be distributed on the site using a reductive approach to the site plan—top left image. Next to this image is an example of how one of these "seeds" could be articulated as part of the analysis. In this case, the result raises zoning issues.

In the drawings, different colors indicate various zoning uses. These images showcase THINK's belief in the possibility of employing vertical infrastructure as a method of extending a mix of zoning uses skyward. This indicates a key zoning consideration—the provision of enough free space in the vertical grid to allow sunlight to penetrate into the sacred precinct at the center of the site.

10.28.02

2-week **LMDC** meeting

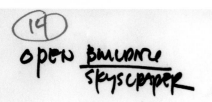

open building
skyscraper

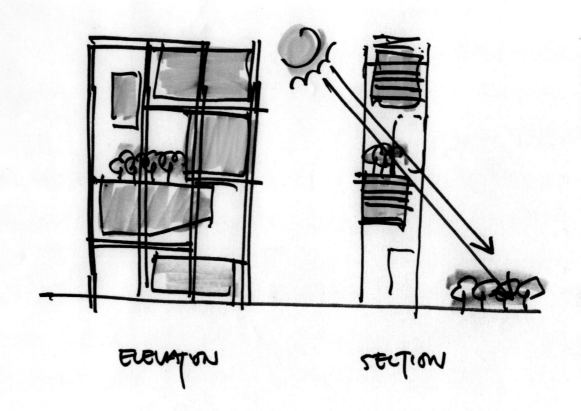

ELEVATION   SECTION

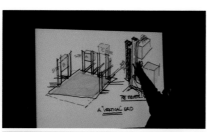

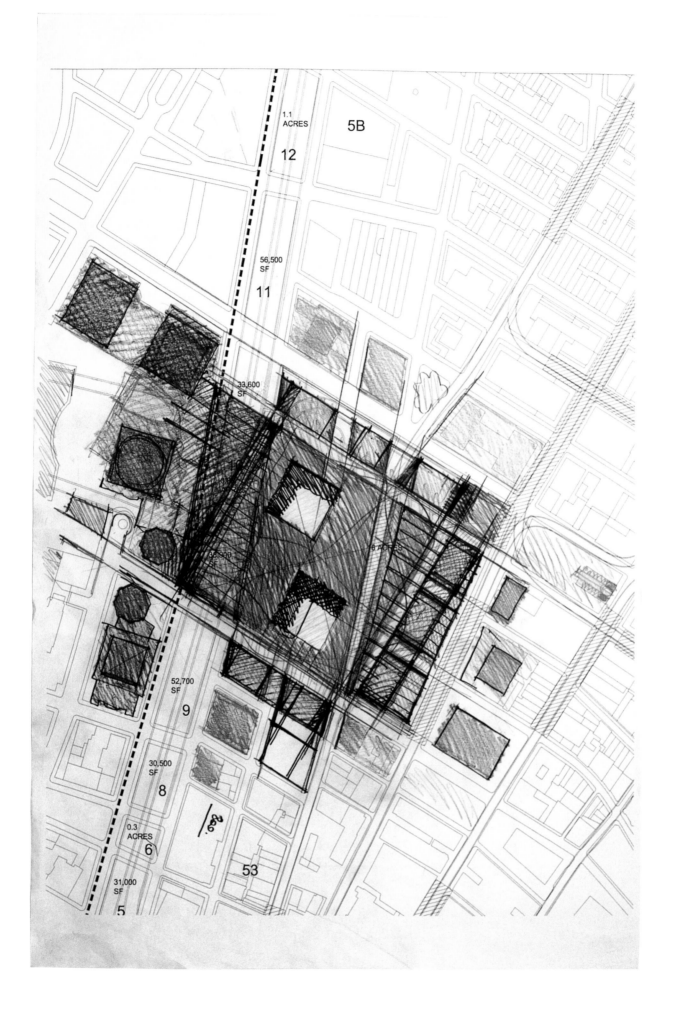

5B

1.1
ACRES

12

56,500
SF

11

33,600
SF

52,700
SF

9

30,500
SF

8

0.3
ACRES

6

31,000
SF

5

53

10.28.02

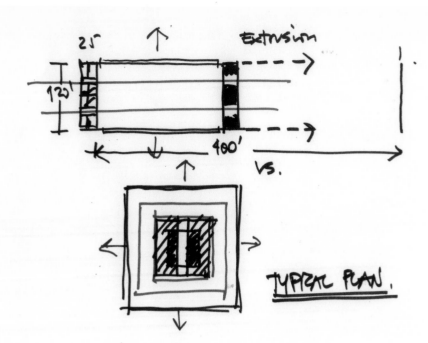

25'

Extrusion

125'

400'

vs.

TYPICAL PLAN.

Opposite is a site plan corresponding to the **Broadway Boogie-Woogie** idea. On this page are illustrations of the publicly accessible vertical infrastructure that would serve the different airborne development sites and an analysis of the efficiencies that this approach would afford.

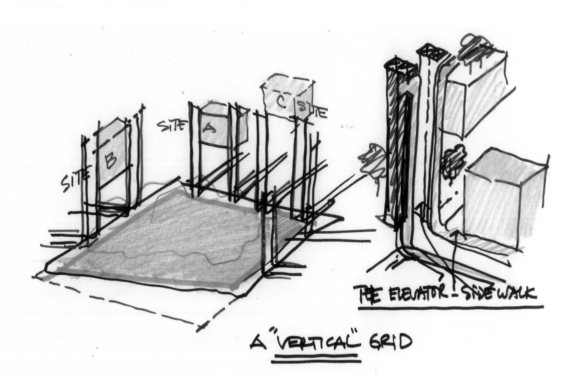

SITE B

SITE A

C SITE

THE ELEVATOR - SIDEWALK

A "VERTICAL" GRID

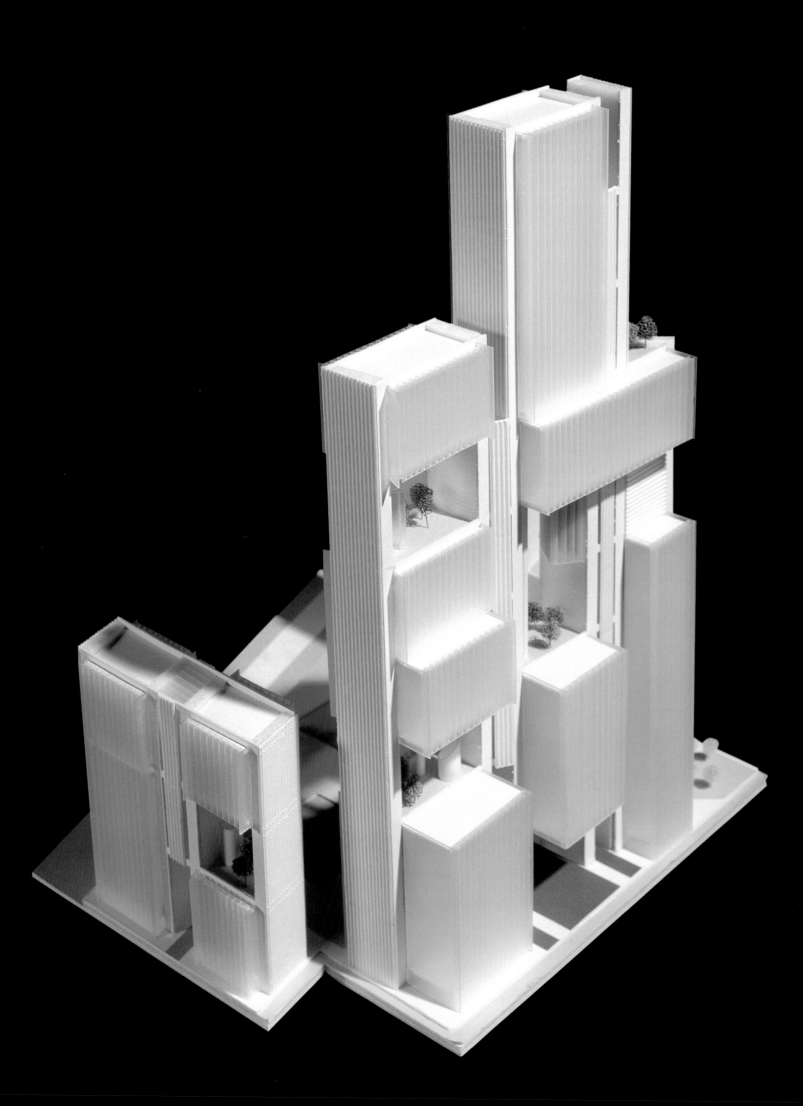

Positive volume

Negative volume

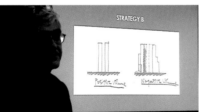

10.28.02

Giving presence to the absence of the towers, THINK offered a solution of buildings that would capture the former volumes of the Twin Towers as negative space. Instead of rebuilding the towers on their former site, new buildings would wrap around the space once occupied by the towers. This proposal would produce interesting options for the procession through the space as well as dynamic massing for the new structures, all affected by the placement of the transportation hub. The drawing to the left shows the traffic patterns for the proposed plan and the tight space at the nexus of the complex (the "slot"), which orients the entire plan.

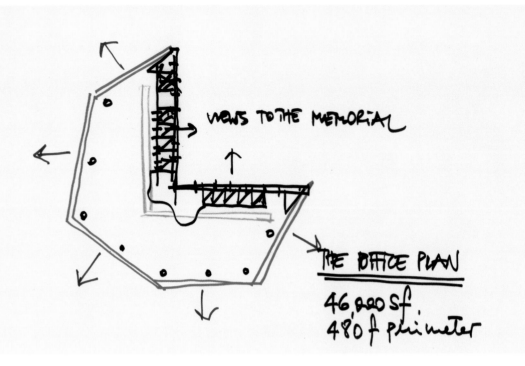

VIEWS TO THE MEMORIAL

THE OFFICE PLAN
46,000 sf.
480 f perimeter

As the **Negative Space** plan continued to develop, details such as the circulation layout were described. In the drawing at top left, it is clear that the traffic flow will be focused on the interior of the site, where the former towers stood. In the model, the treatment of the interior façades suggest the old exteriors of the Twin Towers, while the exterior façades have a different articulation. The massing suggests a hill or mountain, with lower buildings on the periphery and the tallest toward the center. The small detail (upper right) shows the dynamic juxtaposition of the two voids as well as the main passageway through the site, or "slot" where the massing culminates.

10.28.02

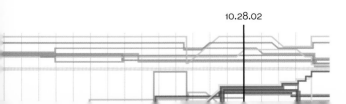

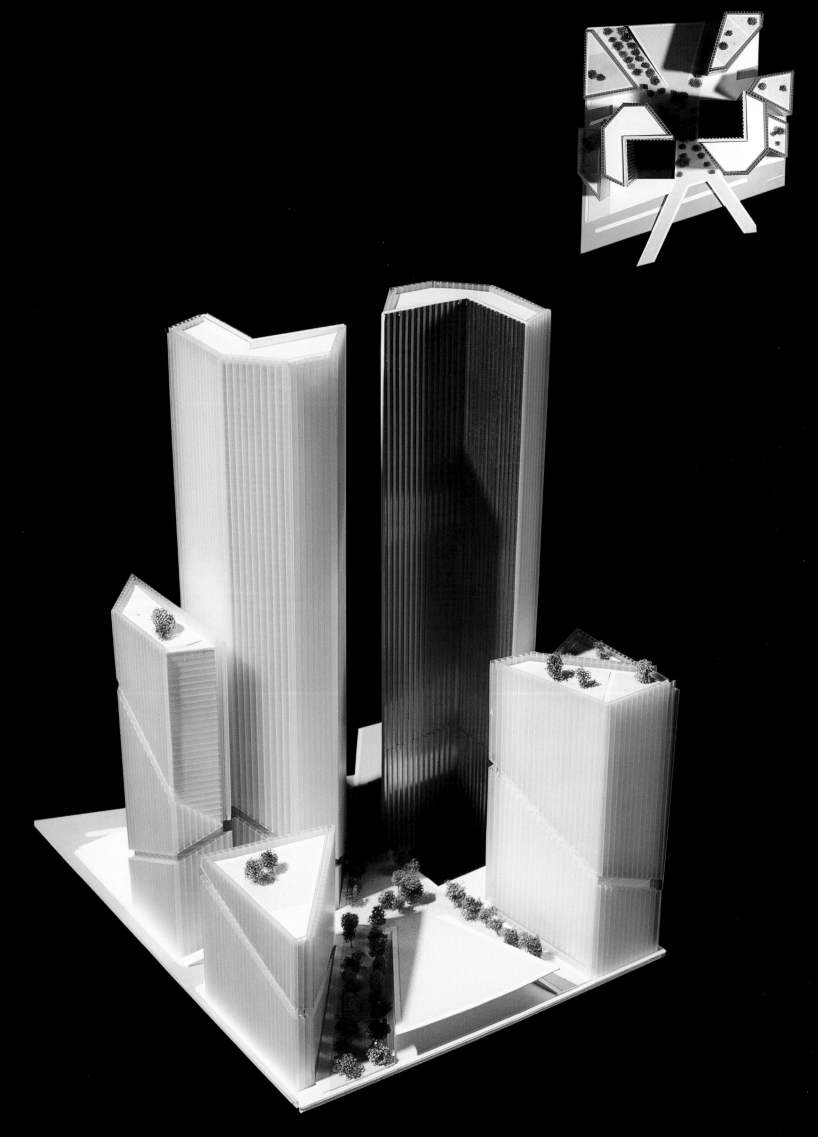

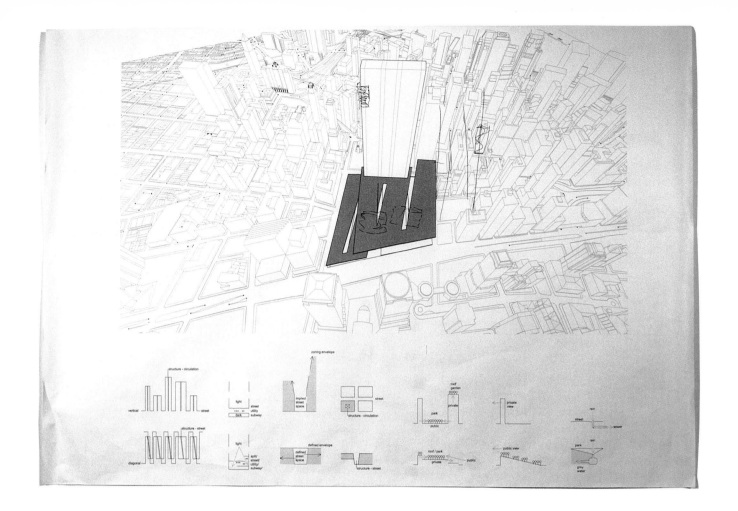

Using a ramp to take pedestrians from grade to a roof garden, THINK's **Sky Park** restores the street grid and provides an extraordinary green space for the public. Without the problems of access to light that hindered the **Table** scheme, **Sky Park** would remain under consideration by the LMDC until THINK was named a finalist. The image at upper left presents the basic concept of the ramps and the image to the far right shows the layout in greater detail with area calculations and grading considerations. The hatched areas represent flat areas (or meadows) as opposed to the inclined passages.

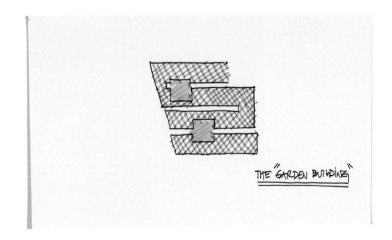

THE "GARDEN BUILDING"

10.28.02

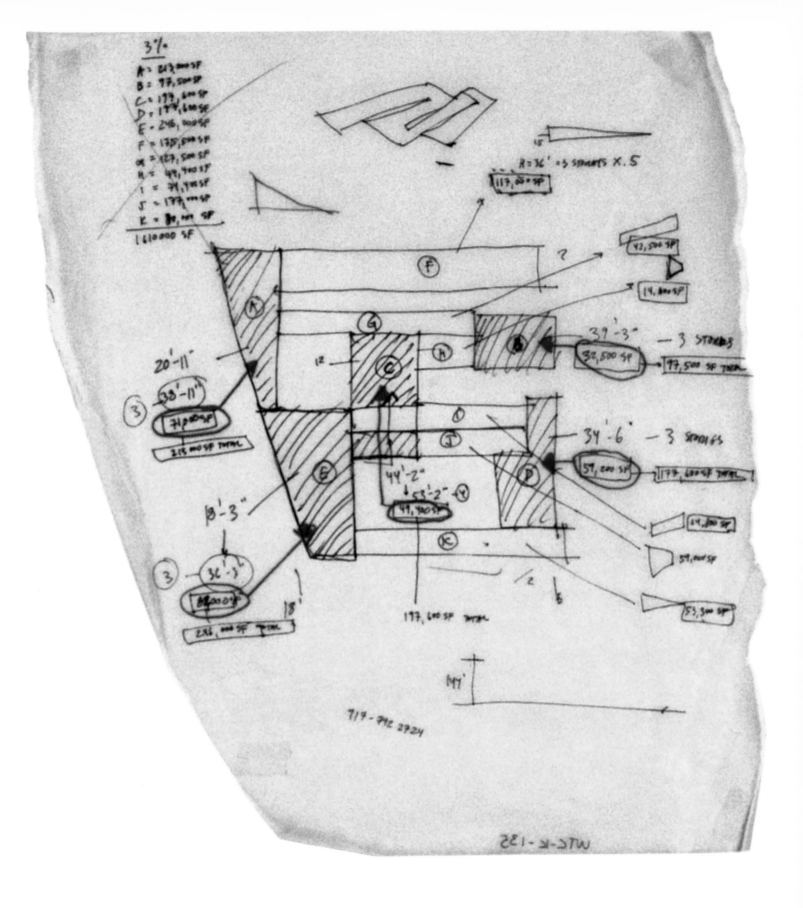

The Coalition of September 11th Families contacted Frederic Schwartz concerning THINK's work on the master plan. THINK was pleased to work directly with the families of victims who had, and continue to have, such a great emotional stake in the memorial and rebuilding process. Unfortunately, the LMDC imposed a requirement that the design teams not consult with such groups, perhaps in part because the LMDC had determined that the memorial would be separate from the master plan. Therefore, the master plan had to accommodate a future memorial, yet not create one, a difficult and, in many ways, contradictory requirement.

The images to the right show a solution from THINK to replace the towers with structures that could both be inhabited and support memorial functions as required by the LMDC. This concept was the opposite of the **Negative Space** proposal (both schemes were explored at the same time). At the top of the page, the drawing shows the only two conceivable ways of preserving the footprints while also rebuilding the towers. Either they can be moved in plan or in section (lifted over the footprints). In both cases, the footprints are treated as sacred ground.

The image, middle right, shows a "protective shield" or sheath that could go around the footprints. No actual structure would be placed on the former footprints, again preserving them for the memorial.

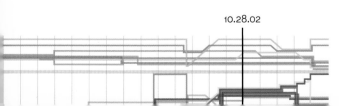

10.28.02

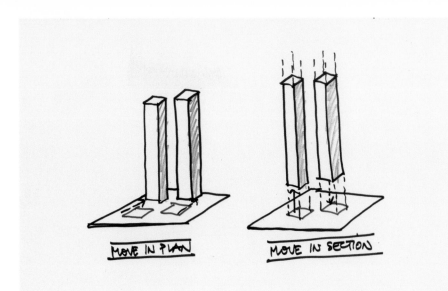

MOVE IN PLAN   MOVE IN SECTION

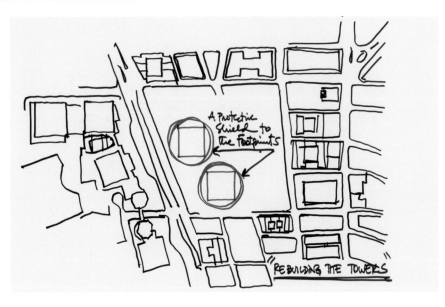

A Protective Shield to the Footprints

"REBUILDING THE TOWERS"

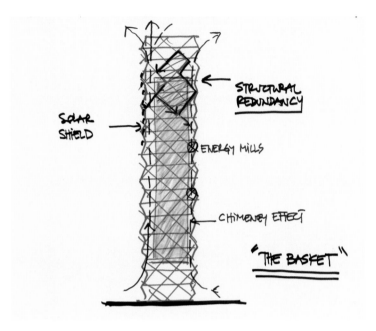

SOLAR SHIELD

STRUCTURAL REDUNDANCY

ENERGY MILLS

CHIMNEY EFFECT

"THE BASKET"

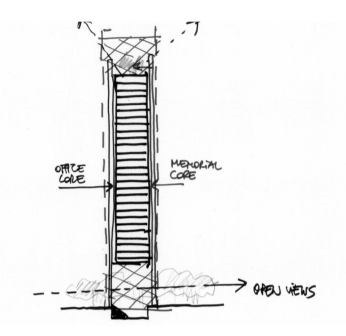

OFFICE CORE

MEMORIAL CORE

OPEN VIEWS

The LMDC received the suggestions on the prior pages with enthusiasm and encouraged THINK to pursue the development of this idea at greater depth. The images seen here show various aspects of structural redundancy of the proposed towers. Here, a basket surrounds the volume of each tower. The structure multitasks: it contains an office tower capped by a "sky memorial," all placed above a "ground memorial." Innovations such as a "solar shield" and "energy mills" that take advantage of the anticipated "chimney effect" are incorporated. Note how the base of the proposed structure is open, which would create visual corridors across the site.

10.28.02

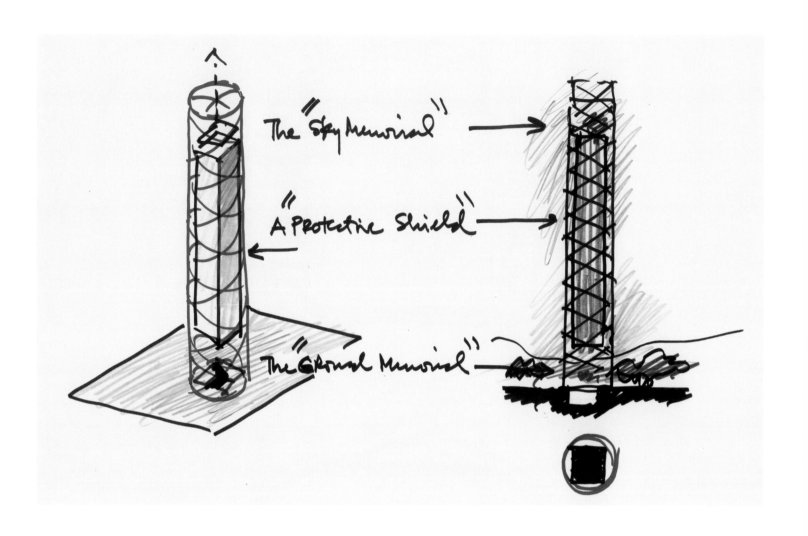

The "Sky Memorial"

"A Protective Shield"

The "Ground Memorial"

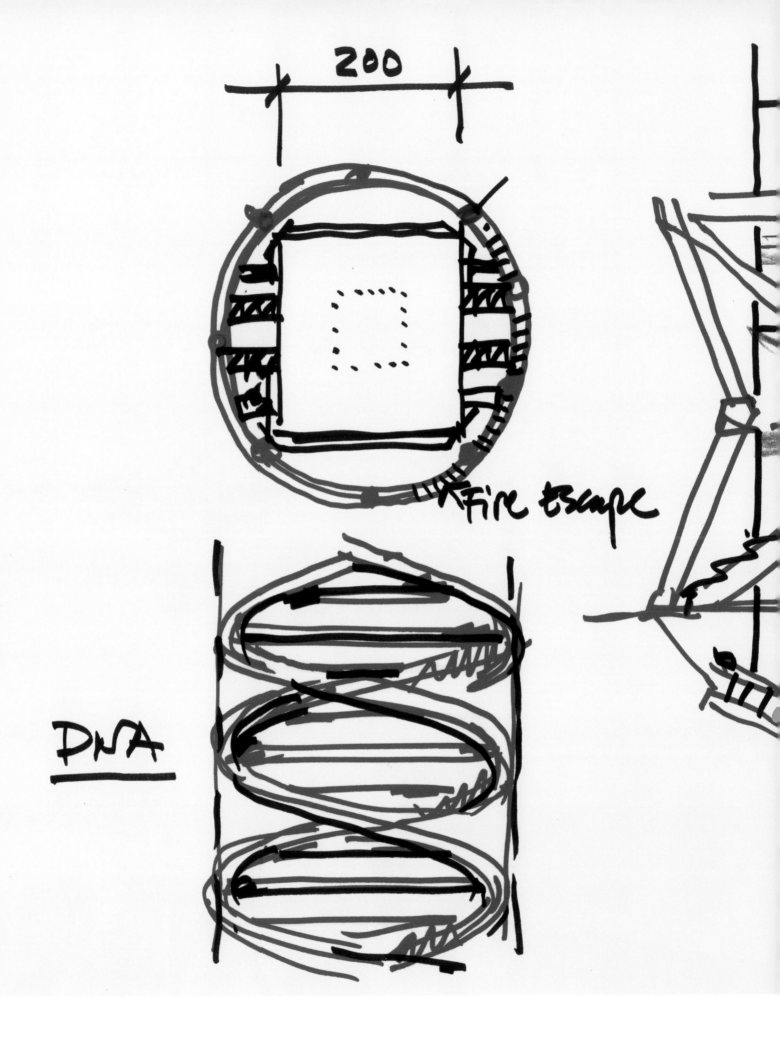

200

Fire escape

DNA

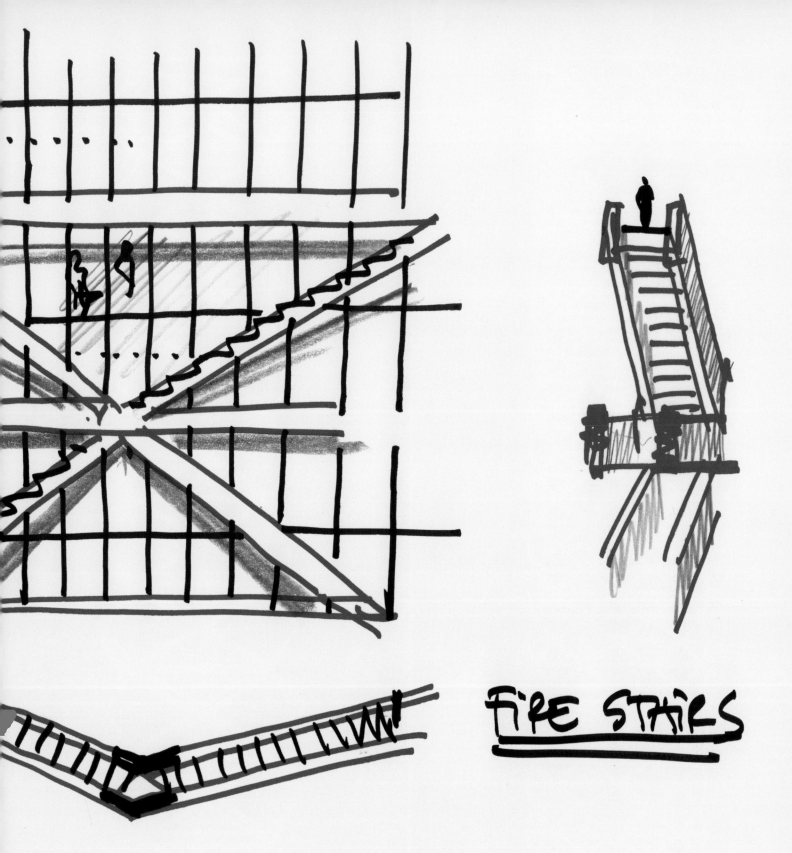

FIRE STAIRS

As a response to the shortcomings in emergency evacuation with the original towers, this design proposed using the external structure as a redundant system of interconnected fire stairs. In theory, this would allow the occupants of the building to find alternate routes around fires and obstructions in an emergency.

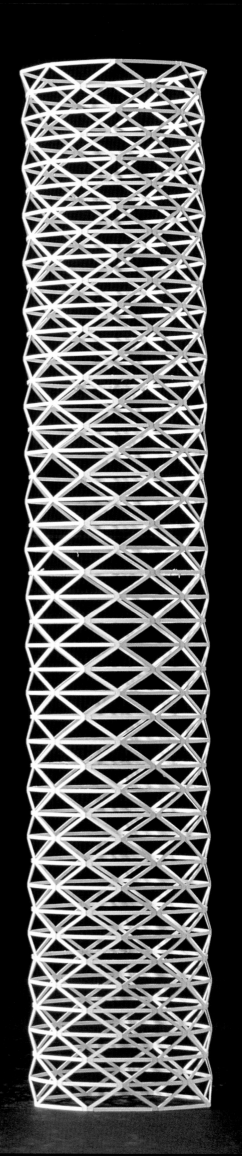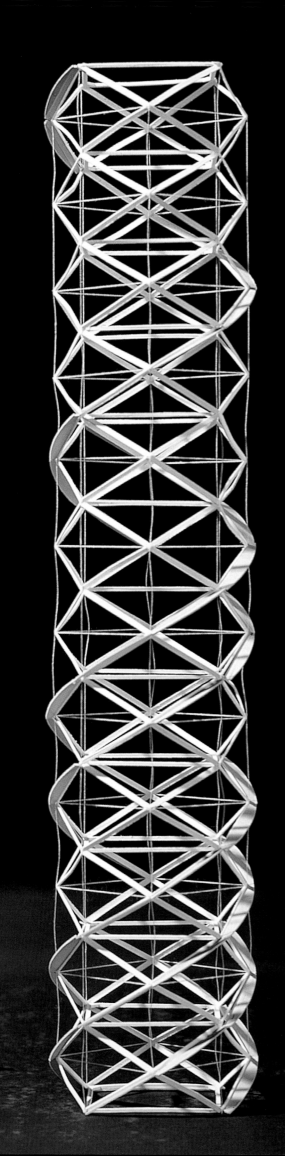

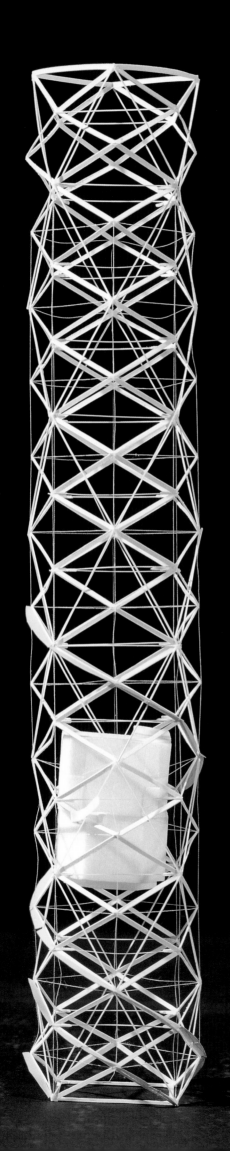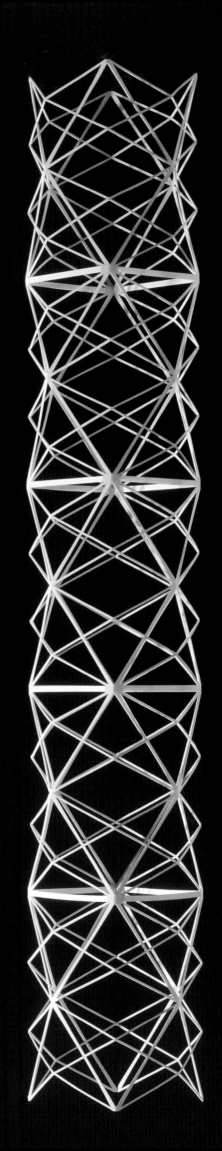

MODEL
SHOP

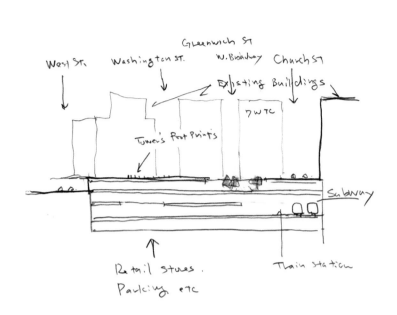

West St.　Washington St.　Greenwich St　W.Broadway　Church ST

Existing Buildings

Tower's Foot Prints

7WTC

Subway

Retail Stores.
Parking etc

Train Station

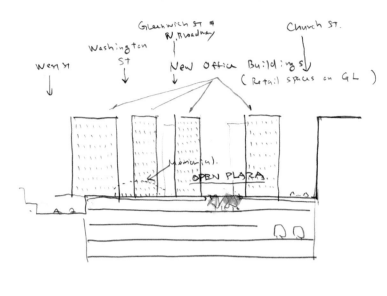

West St　Washington St　Greenwich St #
W.Broadway　Church St.

New Office Buildings
(Retail spaces on GL)

Memorial.

OPEN PLAZA.

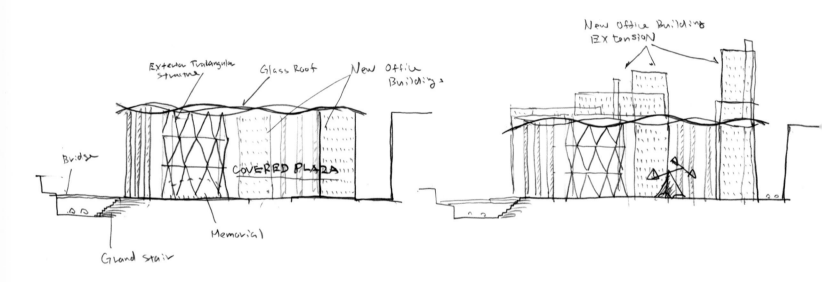

Exterior Triangular
Structure　Glass Roof　New Office
Buildings

Bridge

COVERED PLAZA

Memorial

Grand Stair

New Office Building
EX tension

10.29.02

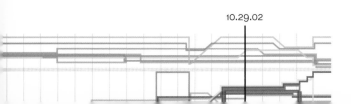

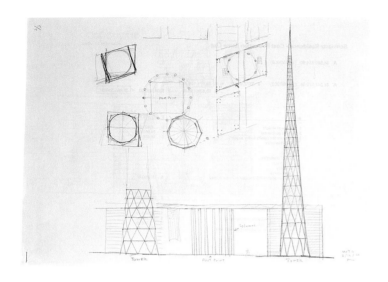

Shigeru Ban took the lead in the design of the **Great Hall** scheme. These drawings depict the scheme within the existing massing vocabulary and also an alternative vision of much taller structures. In early versions of this scheme calling for a covered public space, a conical tower with a small footprint would provide a striking skyline element.

10.29.02

AA

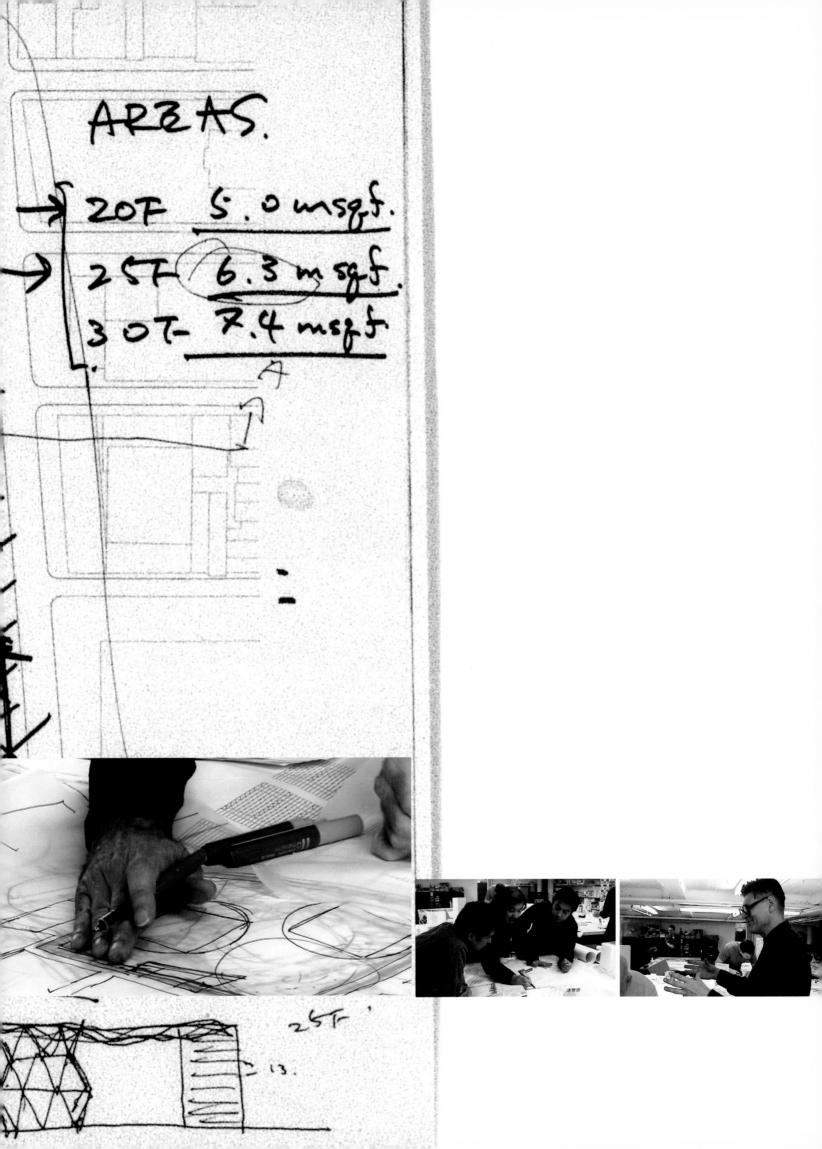

AREAS.

20F 5.0 msqf.

25F 6.3 msqf.

30T 7.4 msqf

Fresh from meetings at the LMDC, the THINK principals returned to the model shop at RVA yet again. The flow of work was constant. The drawing at near right shows the four schemes still under consideration (from top to bottom): the **Memorial Towers**, the **Great Hall**, the **Sky Park** and **Negative Space**. The **Great Hall** was introduced at this session and is detailed in the following pages.

At this moment it appeared that **Sky Park's** viability was in doubt—it is the only one lacking a check mark. The e-mail message from Schwartz to Viñoly shows how the team was constantly attempting to balance the client's expectations with THINK's understanding of what was actually possible. Schwartz addresses, among other aspects, the importance of the decision to create cultural space and the requirement to build office space.

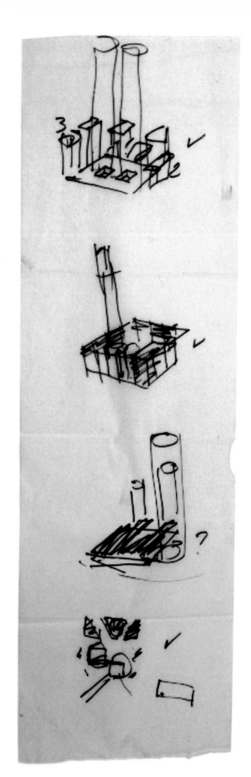

10.29.02

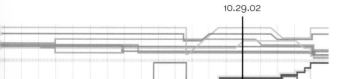

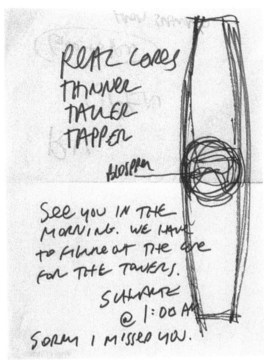

RV.
OPEN

Gve to RV

from Schwartz

REAL CORES
THINNER
TALLER
TAPPER

SEE YOU IN THE
MORNING. WE HAVE
to figure out the core
FOR THE TOWERS.

SCHWARTZ
@ 1:00 AM
SORRY I MISSED YOU.

Subject: Dear Rafael Viñoly
Date: 29 October, 2002
From: Frederic Schwartz
To: Rafael Viñoly

sorry I missed you tonight
I was at your office at 1:00am
I left a note and sketch at the front
desk

we need to make the cores real

we can help with that
perhaps the circle has to be bigger
in that case the towers have to be
taller and i think taper in perspective
they would appear even taller
yes the elevators would need a
transfer
maybe that is bad but they did that
before

we must in my thinking continue with
at least two of the other alternatives
because the two that you in
particular are focused on are based
on different but very specific buy ins

you must build office space and
maybe no one will now or much later

or you build culture at a great cost
when we know that less of that
money is available both public
and private and both the memorial
programmer and the winner of
the competition must agree that
the culture towers are the right
framework for a memorial

the other two alternatives to
continue with are the plug in vertical
street which makes sense to me
and leaves the memorial question
best framed and opened and the
open space idea which has phasing
potential both short and long term

Bill has some good new ideas and
we should discuss them and i have
one also
see you in the morning

Frederic Schwartz

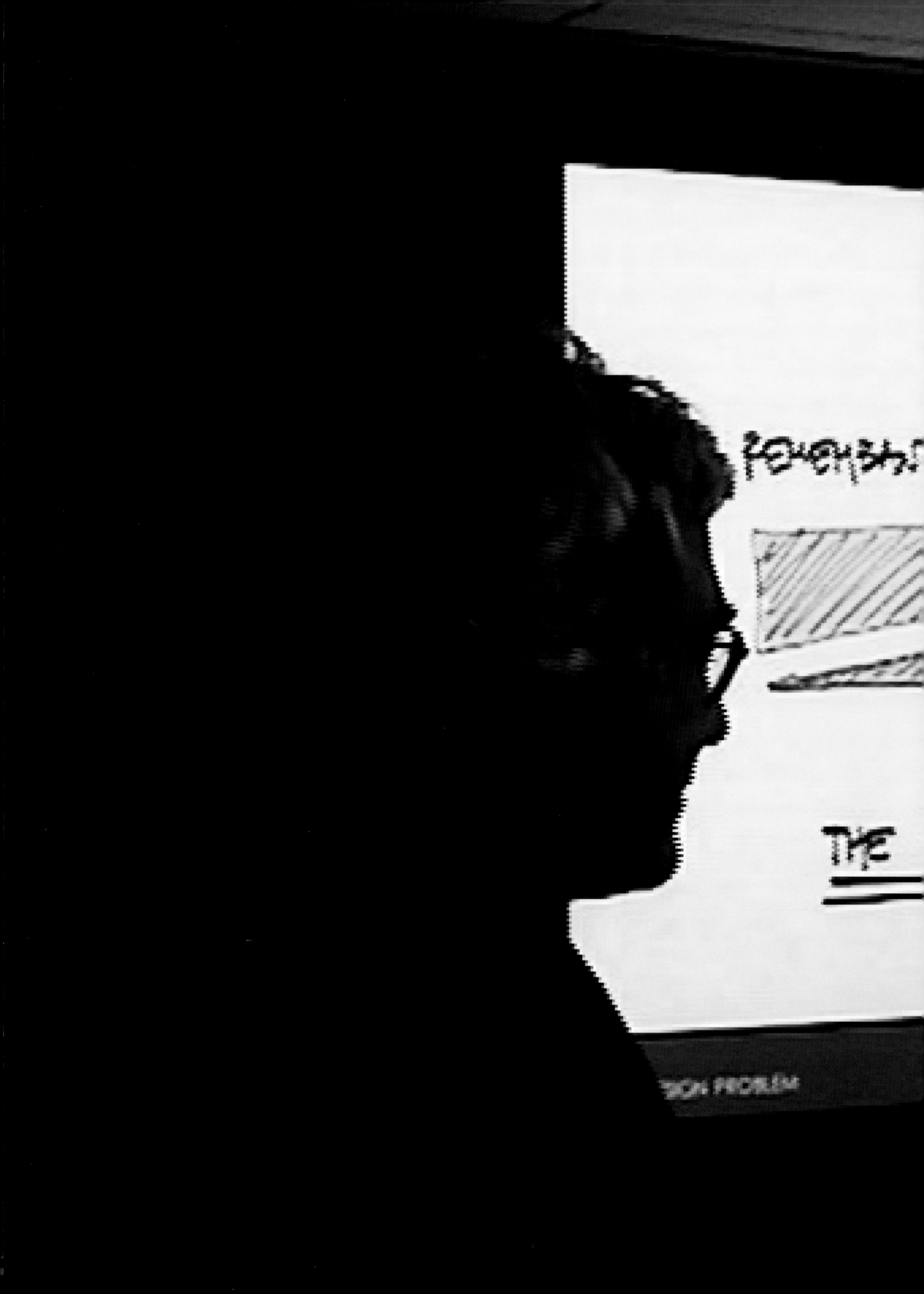
THE
SION PROBLEM

$\longleftarrow$ $\longrightarrow$ REDEVELOPMENT

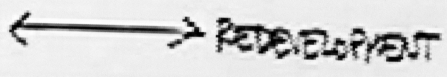

SPACE 2 MEANING

DESIGN CHALLENGE

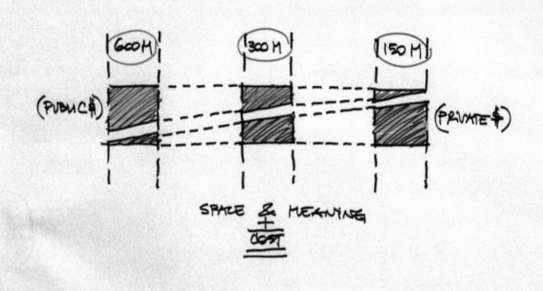

SPACE & MEANING

COST

11.08.02

In the previous spread, we see Rafael Viñoly presenting a key THINK concept to the LMDC at the second design review on November 8, 2002. Viñoly explores the tension between remembrance and redevelopment and states this is the key design challenge facing the LMDC. Remembrance, or the memorial function, is an essential component, despite the fact that the master planning teams had been asked to make room for a memorial, but not actually design one. Redevelopment, or the rebuilding of the lost commercial, retail and public space, is a core requirement, but in many ways at odds with the need for remembrance.

On this page, Viñoly takes this concept even further as he relates remembrance and redevelopment to the making of public and private space, adding the important factor of cost. He shows three scenarios with different proportions of public and private funding. Using examples that explore this dynamic, ranging from $150 million to $600 million (the numbers were for illustration only), Viñoly stresses the effect of increasing public expenditure on the possibilities of creating public space. Essentially, he was asking the LMDC to confront the realities of not only budget, but the source of funds. Private funding would certainly be focused on the creation of commercial and retail space, not areas for public use.

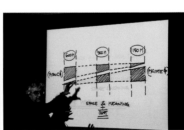

11.08.02

DEFINE 2 DISTINCT SITES

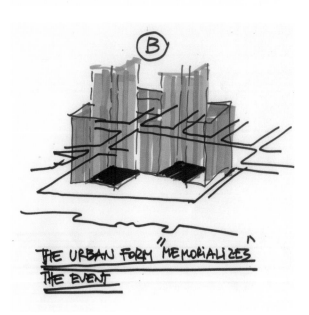

THE URBAN FORM "MEMORIALIZES" THE EVENT

On the next few pages, we see the same format used to present four different schemes by THINK. The images seen here show the **Negative Space** scheme, the only one that would not continue past this stage of development. Although the LMDC had requested that THINK continue work on **Negative Space**, THINK had already determined to drop it from consideration as this scheme was inferior to the other three alternatives.

This scheme concentrated massing at the center of the site, but left open the space that had once one been occupied by the former Twin Towers. THINK presented this concept originally to show the power of framing the absent towers with new structures and also in response to the team's understanding of the character of New York urbanism, which is very much about density. However, the team eventually concluded that this scheme lacked a sufficient buffer between the commercial development and the proposed memorial, which would challenge the emotional aspects of the site. Also, THINK had concerns about the design's ability to accommodate the phasing of development. The team used this opportunity to explain to the client the shortcomings of the approach and therefore make the argument for the other three alternatives.

The drawings marked "A" and "B" underscore the importance of creating an appropriate area for the memorial tracing the footprints of the former towers.

11.08.02

Here we see **Sky Park** as an alternative to the **Negative Space** scheme. Instead of presenting specific towers at the center of the site, **Sky Park** offers open public space that cleverly disguises development below. Access to the site is through a series of ramps that negotiate changes in elevation. The phasing of development is easily accommodated in this scheme, which shows generalized massing instead of precisely designed buildings on the site. These were intended to be developed at a later date by other architects.

One of the highlights of **Sky Park** is the ramp that integrates it with the LMDC's proposed landscaped promenade along West Street that leads to the waterfront. It is noted manually in the picture to the right. This scheme is especially appropriate in an economic environment that does not yet support large-scale building. **Sky Park's** other major street grid connection is via a ramp to Fulton Street.

11.08.02

The **Great Hall** scheme is similar to **Sky Park** in that it sets up two distinct sites, one for the public and the memorial, the other for commercial development. This contrasts with the **Negative Space** scheme, which melded these uses.

The extraordinary scale of the **Great Hall** can be understood from the model (below) and the rendering (upper left). Rising nearly 30 stories high and five blocks long, the 13-acre plaza would have been extraordinary, but perhaps overwhelming, an aspect that THINK willingly discussed with the client. In the rendering, the conical tower has been replaced by a simple massing envelope, in order to stress the option of having another architect design a structure at a later date.

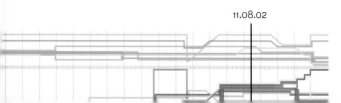

11.08.02

The final scheme presented to the LMDC at this meeting was the **World Cultural Center**, which featured twin towers that were to contain public uses, not commercial ones. This scheme was a natural extension of THINK's ongoing examination of the possibilities of vertical infrastructure; a direct follow-up to the ideas presented in the **Broadway Boogie-Woogie** scheme.

In the rendering on the left, we see color-coded structures that are inserted within and between the two towers. Commercial space is accommodated on the periphery of the site. The advantage of this scheme was the possibility of immediately rebuilding the skyline elements missing since the loss of the World Trade Center towers. The programming of the towers, which would contain structures such as a museum, conference and community facilities, viewing platforms, performing arts spaces and memorial functions, could take place at a later date. The funding schedule (and even basic decision-making concerning specific uses) is relieved of pressure in this scheme since the towers provide infrastructure as opposed to buildings.

November 15, 2002

Immediately following the LMDC meeting where THINK presented its four schemes, the team had to return to the studio and begin work on modifications to the three schemes still in contention. With only three days to prepare for the next round with the LMDC—the Steering Committee meeting on November 18, 2002—THINK's principals not only got back to the drawing boards, they labored "hands-on" in the model shop in order to incorporate the LMDC's feedback into the schemes.

Here we see Rafael Viñoly at work on the models of the **World Cultural Center** towers. THINK was concerned about the need for structural redundancy within these towers along with other technical issues. The result was a revised support system.

No Subject
15 November 2002
To: Rafael Viñoly
From Frederic Schwartz

the room
the tower
the park

must all have the very best public
space and the world's tallest and
most iconic building

right now the towers of culture is
both

the room's tower is tall but not
iconic

the park's towers are not iconic
at least one should be the both

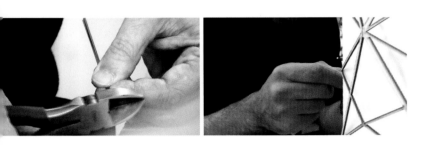

November 18, 2002

In this presentation, the first to the LMDC's Steering Committee, which included Chairman John C. Whitehead, Deputy Mayor Daniel L. Doctoroff and developer Roland Betts, THINK introduced the group to the three schemes that had been developed with the guidance of the Land Use Committee. Showing models, technical drawings, renderings and sketches of the **Sky Park**, the **Great Hall** and the **World Cultural Cente**r, the team encapsulated the thinking behind this diverse approach to the problems of the site and sought approval to proceed with the production of final presentation materials for the December 18 public unveiling.

11.18.02

Steering Committee meeting; attended by the **LMDC**, **PANYNJ**, representatives of the **city** and **state**, **Silverstein**, and the architectural teams.

Press reports possibility of a land swap between **PANYNJ** and **NYC** of WTC site and airport sites.

December 9, 2002

The video stills show the Steering Committee meeting where THINK's principals presented to the most significant decision-makers in the LMDC, including Whitehead, Thompson and Doctoroff. The image at the top highlights the transit hub and the connections to it. Shadows illustrate below-grade approaches and the overpass quality of Greenwich Street. The small sketches at the center of the page show a finer articulation of the floor plate for the suggested performing arts complex. The Interpretive Museum is placed at levels within the towers that correspond to the points where the planes struck the original towers on September 11. Other structures were not definitively programmed, but were intended to be conference centers, think tanks, and other noncommercial uses as needed or desired in the future.

12.09.02

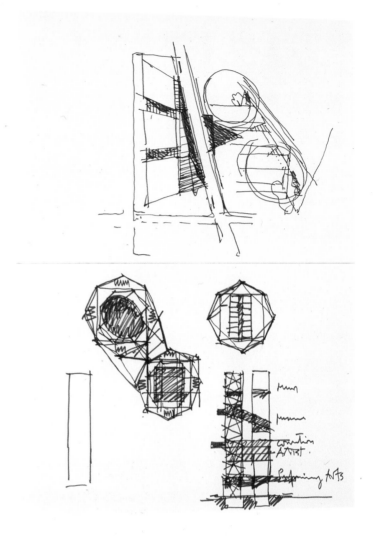

The meeting of the Steering Committee on December 9, 2002, brought some of the most important decision-makers involved with Ground Zero into the same room. The video stills below show Larry Silverstein, Roland Betts, Daniel Doctoroff, and John Whitehead in attendance. By the end of this meeting, THINK recognized far more strongly the importance of emphasizing a single scheme among the three it had pursued and just presented to the committee. This is despite THINK's long-standing belief that the team would best serve the client by assisting the LMDC to develop various options, rather than selecting a specific scheme.

Following this meeting THINK convened to reevaluate the team's strategy. The image to the right conveys THINK's review of the three schemes already presented to the LMDC, with "1" representing **Sky Park**, "2" referring to the **Great Hall** and "3" designating the **World Cultural Center**. At this time, the team considered dropping one, or even two, of the schemes, since by showing multiple schemes they were in essence competing with not only the other teams, but also themselves. Eventually THINK elected to present all three, albeit with different emphasis on each design, since they uniquely addressed issues of cost, public investment and symbolism.

While all three schemes had their respective advantages and disadvantages, it was determined that the **World Cultural Center** deserved to be showcased by the team as the ultimate expression of THINK's approach to the site.

12.09.02

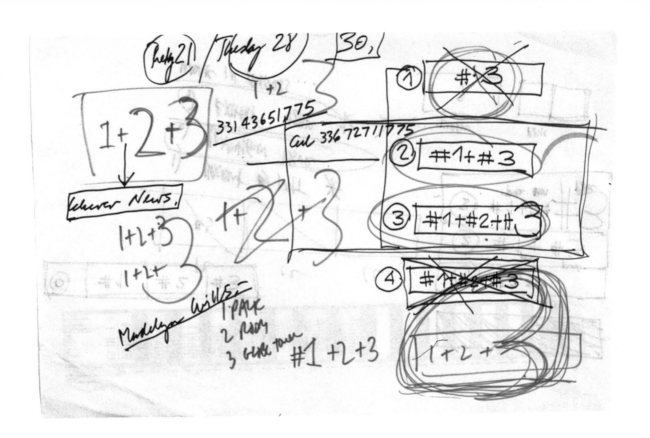

Román Viñoly

Two blocks from my father's studio in SoHo I heard the first plane streak by overhead and hit the north tower. Within minutes I was in a room full of architects and engineers already speculating about what would eventually be done. As we watched the building burn on television, someone wondered aloud if the damaged tower should be torn down, leaving a memorial at its base and the remaining tower in the skyline. It was 9:02 AM. Then the south tower was hit and we knew it would be more complicated than that. I went up to the roof of our building and took a picture of the view. It's the first image in this book.

Over the next two years my position at RVA and our participation in THINK afforded me a privileged view of the dynamic process that is still shaping the future of Ground Zero. The significance of the project and the excitement of the experience motivated me to document and preserve the development of our concepts. This book is intended as a record of our collaborative effort and of the particular kind of understanding that emerged from it; one that is not only about architecture and planning but also about the way in which information is handled and processed.

THINK's principals shared an enthusiasm for the project's intricacy and the conviction that its complexity could be mastered. From the start, they established an open creative process in order to get and integrate feedback from everyone on the team. Given the exploratory nature of the LMDC's "Innovative Design Study" and the implication of a public referendum, it seemed the right thing to do. It also proved inspiring and empowering to those who worked so intensely on the project, and was effective at enfranchising diverse constituencies within our team.

As we moved deeper into the competition, and saw our own progress, we realized that what we were doing could be extended to the public as well. So the team invested a significant amount of time and effort in developing the interactive education/polling system detailed in the pages corresponding to 10.26.2002. On that date we presented our public outreach initiative to the LMDC, which summarily rejected it. It might have been an indication of things to come...

We sought to develop and test leadership principles based on the conviction that information, gathered from a plurality of sources and used to educate the public, could result at least in a legitimate political direction.

Four years later, although people are still divided, most everyone agrees that incumbents at the site, Governor George Pataki, the Port Authority, and Silverstein Properties have successfully insulated themselves from real public involvement even while proclaiming transparency. Regardless, the underlying complexity still can be relied on to frustrate and delay what has been foisted on the public as a coherent and open process. But how could this happen?

More intractable even than the difficulty of the problem was the governor's appropriation of the project as a platform for demonstrating his leadership. Unfortunately, that obligated the redevelopment of Ground Zero to proceed according to a timeframe constrained by his political ambitions. The result was a condensed process characterized by arbitrary deadlines (just eighteen months from the time of the attacks to the selection of a master plan) and over-simplified rhetoric that diminished public understanding of fundamental planning issues when it should have been deepening it. Do we really want to build more surplus office space? Or could the whole site be used to add needed parkland and light to an area of Manhattan struggling to transform itself into a "vibrant 24-hour community"? These questions will have to be dealt with eventually and we can only hope that it won't be decades from now, after something else has been built and, like the Twin Towers before it, proven itself more of a burden than a boon.

This book is meant to contribute insights from THINK's process to the ongoing public discourse about the future of Ground Zero. It may help us avert the kind of large miscalculations that led to the original towers. After all, they neither supported themselves financially nor contributed as much as they could have to the quality of life in Lower Manhattan. At the time of this writing, the approved design for the skyline element of the trade center site is a single metal and glass tower that rises from a 200- by 200-foot base to a height of 1448 feet—the same height and base dimension of the original towers—and presiding over a huge memorial complex at grade. Sounds just like the idea that was floated at the RVA studio around 9:02 AM on September 11, 2001. It is ironic that after so much thinking about the great opportunities at Ground Zero, in some ways the conversation is still at square one.

12.18.02

Interviews done with *The New York Times* and other media outlets.

Sky Park

In order to present clearly the **Sky Park** concept to the public, THINK used this image to stress the scheme's ability to connect Ground Zero with New York's waterfront, create an urban park and relocate millions of square feet of new office space to the former World Trade Center site. Of course, protected areas are provided at the footprints of the former Twin Towers for a future memorial. The esplanade extends toward New York Harbor, punctuated here by the Statue of Liberty. The site is in fact idealized, since a view of Lady Liberty is not possible from this particular angle. As the other presentation images show, this image was designed to convey the central idea behind the scheme, not to depict specifically the actual design details that would only be developed once the client had selected an individual scheme.

Sky Park
Animated sequence

Sky Park

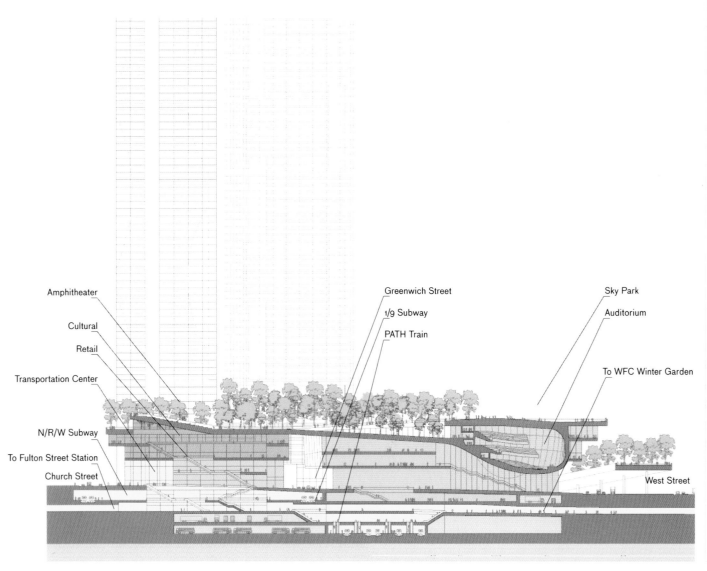

Amphitheater
Cultural
Retail
Transportation Center
N/R/W Subway
To Fulton Street Station
Church Street

Greenwich Street
1/9 Subway
PATH Train

Sky Park
Auditorium
To WFC Winter Garden

West Street

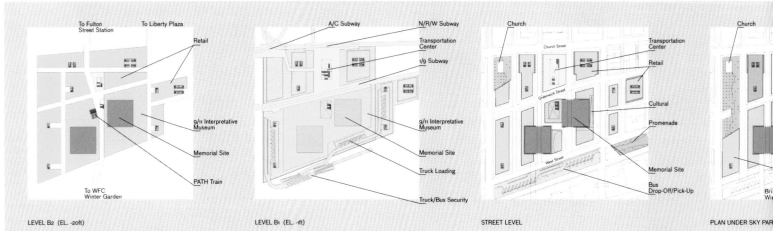

To Fulton Street Station
To Liberty Plaza
Retail
9/11 Interpretative Museum
Memorial Site
PATH Train
To WFC Winter Garden

LEVEL B2 (EL. -20ft)

A/C Subway
N/R/W Subway
Transportation Center
1/9 Subway
9/11 Interpretative Museum
Memorial Site
Truck Loading
Truck/Bus Security

LEVEL B1 (EL. -1ft)

Church
Church Street
Greenwich Street
West Street
Transportation Center
Retail
Cultural
Promenade
Memorial Site
Bus Drop-Off/Pick-Up

STREET LEVEL

Church

PLAN UNDER SKY PARK

12.18.02

A ten block, 16-acre rooftop Public Park floats above the familiar scale of the New York street grid, overlooking the City and beyond. Connecting to the Grand Promenade along West Street and beginning at street level across from St. Paul's Chapel, the Park gradually climbs to ten stories and culminates in a cantilevered three-acre lawn with sweeping views of the Hudson River and the New York Harbor.

The expansive Park includes groves of trees, an amphitheater, cafes, an ice-skating rink, fountains, community gardens and multiple Memorial sites located above, below, and around the WTC footprints. Ramps, pedestrian bridges (including one to the Winter Garden), escalators, and a "vertical pocket park" elevator provide convenient connections within the Park and to the street.

Located below the Park are cultural facilities, street level retail (in addition to retail on the concourse level), the Transportation Center, a hotel/conference center, and office space.

On the perimeter, three office towers (including the tallest building in the world) will complete the program in subsequent phases. The towers are designed by different architects and rise high above the Park to redefine the skyline of the city.

GREAT LAWN WITH CONNECTION TO WEST ST. PROMENADE

WORLD TRADE CENTER FOOTPRINTS ARE THE MEMORIAL SITES

OUTDOOR AMPHITHEATER AND PUBLIC ART

SKY PARK · AREA SUMMARY	TOTAL
Office	9,500,000 sf
Retail (street and concourse)	900,000 sf
Transit Center (above and below grade)	120,000 sf
Culture Facilities (above and below grade)	730,000 sf
Hotel	650,000 sf
TOTAL	11,900,000 sf
Park	17 acres
Total Open Space (Memorial, Park and Sidewalk)	26 acres

CONSTRUCTION PHASING

PHASE ONE   PHASE TWO   PHASE THREE   PHASE FOUR

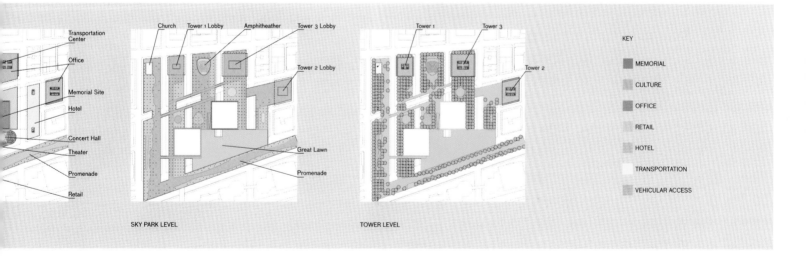

SKY PARK LEVEL

TOWER LEVEL

KEY

MEMORIAL
CULTURE
OFFICE
RETAIL
HOTEL
TRANSPORTATION
VEHICULAR ACCESS

12.18.02

Great Hall

The **Great Hall**'s extraordinary dimensions proved a challenge to THINK when it came time to present the scheme to the public. The goal was to create an urban-scaled room that gave an appropriate civic function to the site—a protected area for visitors to the site and footprints (and therefore the future memorial). Unlike the room, which is covered, the footprints are surrounded by cylinders open to the sky. The designers had to create an extremely tall interior in response to the overall dimensions of the room, which was dictated by the need to place so much square footage along the **Great Hall**'s periphery.

Due to this immense scale, THINK elected to show the space in this particular image filled with human figures that, if to scale or in proportion, would be 13 feet tall. Prepared to address this issue of scale with the client should the scheme be selected for further development, THINK nonetheless was concerned that the public would have difficulty imagining the experience of being within this monumental interior should THINK show humans at normal scale. Note the apparently demure size of Fritz Koenig's 1971 sculpture "The Sphere," which was originally located in the former plaza at the World Trade Center. Although damaged by the events of 9/11, it survived crumpled but intact and now serves a temporary memorial in Battery Park. The sculpture is 15 feet in diameter. Here it is shown at an enlarged scale.

Great Hall

Animated sequence

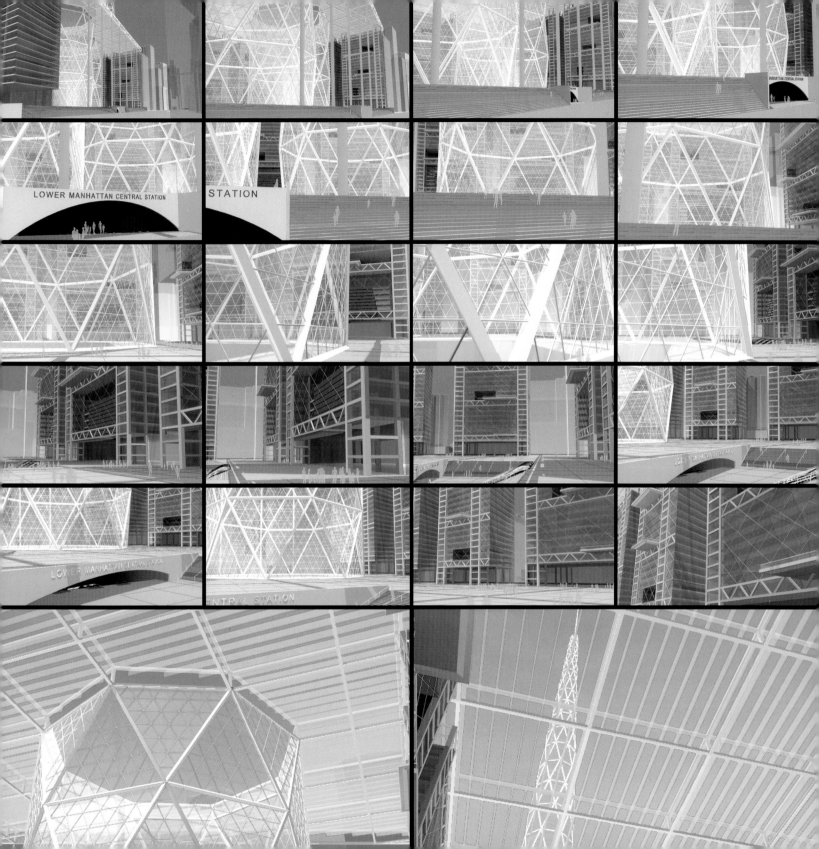

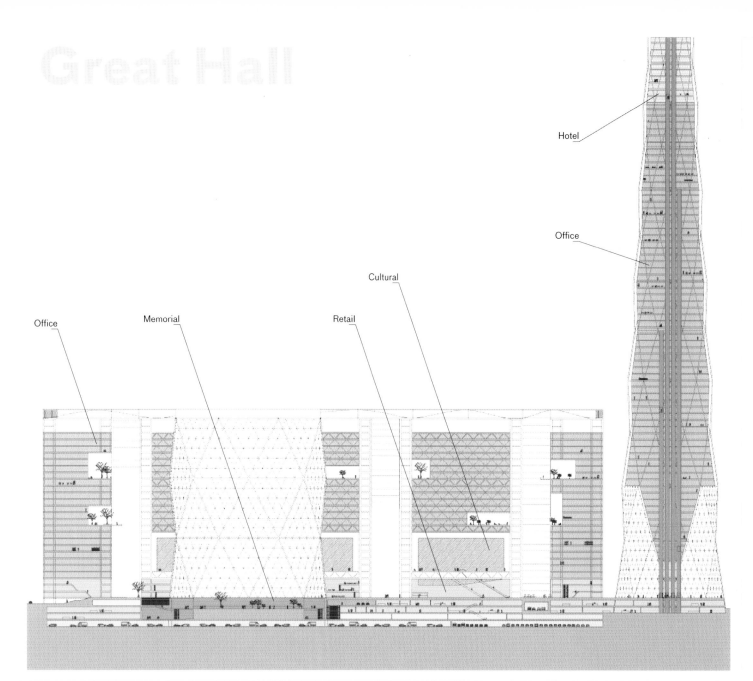

Hotel

Office

Cultural

Office

Memorial

Retail

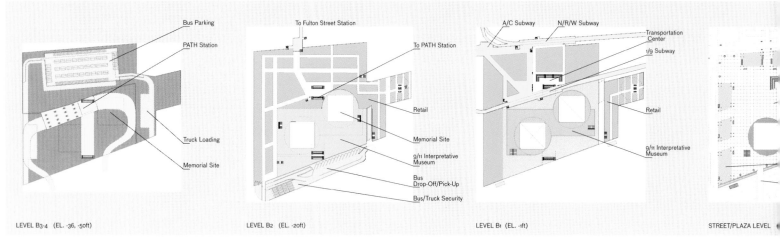

Bus Parking

PATH Station

Truck Loading

Memorial Site

LEVEL B3-4 (EL. -36, -50ft)

To Fulton Street Station

To PATH Station

Retail

Memorial Site

9/11 Interpretative Museum

Bus Drop-Off/Pick-Up

Bus/Truck Security

LEVEL B2 (EL. -20ft)

A/C Subway

N/R/W Subway

Transportation Center

1/9 Subway

Retail

9/11 Interpretative Museum

LEVEL B1 (EL. -1ft)

STREET/PLAZA LEVEL

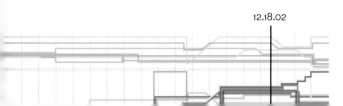

12.18.02

The Great Hall is a vast, enclosed public plaza. A soaring living memorial, the Hall connects all elements of the program under a great free-span glass ceiling. Encompassing 13 acres, the world's largest covered public plaza serves as the Gateway to the City and as the Great Hall of the Transportation Center — a magnificent place for arrival, celebration, memory, and civic events.

Two glass cylinders protect the WTC footprints as they surround and articulate the Memorial site and entrance to a 9/11 Interpretative Museum. Sustainable systems conserve energy and water consumption by creating a greenhouse, harvesting electricity and collecting rainwater. Stacking shutters open and close, moderating the plaza's temperature.

Phased mixed-use buildings define the perimeter and support the roof. The tallest structure in the world (2,100 ft), including offices, hotel and transmission tower, completes the program and redefines the skyline of the city.

SUSTAINABLE DESIGN FEATURES

NATURAL HEATING — WINTER
Stacking shutters in the closed position capture the **sun's solar rays** that radiate **heated air** in a green house effect that reduces dependency on fossil fuels.

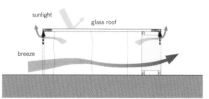

NATURAL VENTILATION — SUMMER
Stacking shutters in an open position permit river **breezes** to cool the plaza while translucent photovoltaic glass **screens** out a portion of the **sun's solar rays.**

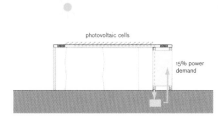

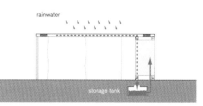

SOLAR ENERGY
Photovoltaic glass converts the sun's solar rays into electricity supplying 4 megawatts equaling 15% of the power demand.

WATER CONSERVATION
14 million gallons of rainwater collected and filtered from 18.5 acres of roof is used for plant irrigation and toilet flushing.

THE GREAT HALL· AREA SUMMARY	TOTAL
Office (9 buildings)	6,500,000 sf
Retail (street and concourse)	1,000,000 sf
Transit Center (above and below grade)	120,000 sf
Culture Facilities (above and below grade)	1,000,000 sf
Hotel	600,000 sf
TOTAL	9,220,000 sf
Plaza	13 acres
Total Open Space (Memorial and Plaza)	16.3 acres

CONSTRUCTION PHASING

PHASE ONE   PHASE TWO   PHASE THREE   PHASE FOUR   VIEW FROM WEST STREET

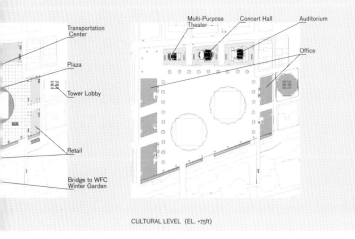

CULTURAL LEVEL (EL. +75ft)

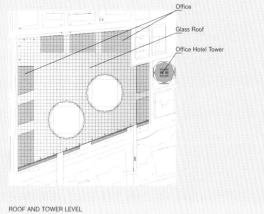

ROOF AND TOWER LEVEL

KEY

■ MEMORIAL
■ CULTURE
■ OFFICE
■ RETAIL
■ HOTEL
■ TRANSPORTATION
■ VEHICULAR ACCESS

12.18.02

World Cultural Center

The World Cultural Center scheme, particularly this image, resonated with the public, which voiced a positive opinion of the plan in a variety of media polls and interviews. Here, the central idea is the restoration of the Lower Manhattan skyline, dramatically demonstrated in this night view. Unlike the towers that once occupied the World Trade Center site, these were not to be used for offices, but for cultural programming, such as areas for the performing arts, museums and other nonprofit institutions, reclaiming a part of the skyline for the public realm. This program would have given the public access to high floors of the structures, a rarity among tall buildings in New York. Each tower would have spaces available—at the highest and lowest levels—for the construction of memorials. These images capture the essence of the idea behind the plan. The illumination of the towers suggests "Tribute in Light," the remarkable temporary memorial sponsored by Creative Time and the Municipal Art Society, and reminds the viewer that these towers would be special public structures, distinct from other commercial real estate development.

World Cultural
Center
Animated sequence

World Cultural Center

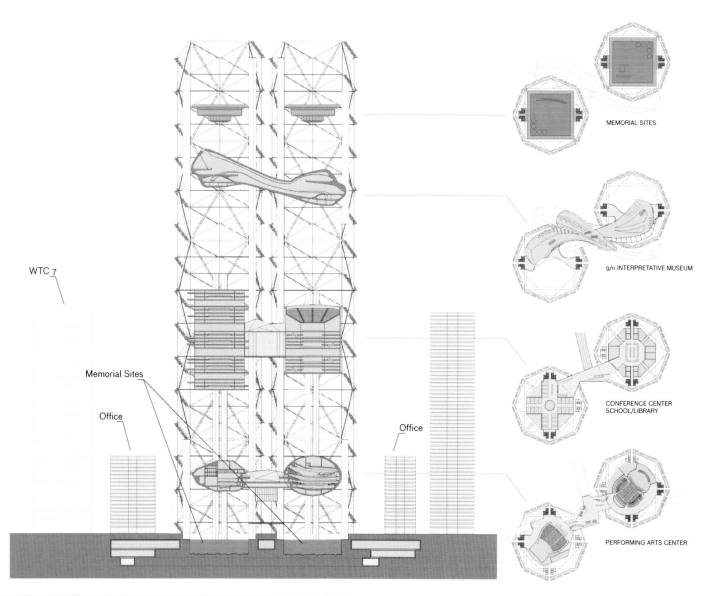

MEMORIAL SITES

9/11 INTERPRETATIVE MUSEUM

CONFERENCE CENTER
SCHOOL/LIBRARY

PERFORMING ARTS CENTER

WTC 7

Memorial Sites

Office

Office

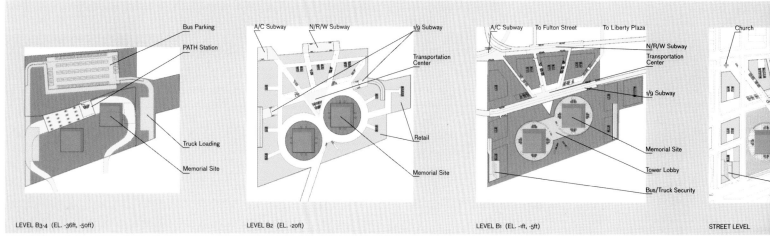

Bus Parking

PATH Station

Truck Loading

Memorial Site

LEVEL B3-4 (EL. -36ft, -50ft)

A/C Subway   N/R/W Subway   1/9 Subway

Transportation
Center

Retail

Memorial Site

LEVEL B2 (EL. -20ft)

A/C Subway   To Fulton Street   To Liberty Plaza

N/R/W Subway

Transportation
Center

1/9 Subway

Memorial Site

Tower Lobby

Bus/Truck Security

LEVEL B1 (EL. -1ft, -5ft)

Church

STREET LEVEL

12.18.02

The World Trade Center is reborn as the World Cultural Center. Built above and around the footprints of the World Trade Center towers, two open latticework structures create a "site" for development of the World Cultural Center. The global program of the World CulturalCenter will include: the Memorial (above and below), 9/11 Interpretative Museum, Performing Arts Center, International Conference Center, an amphitheater, viewing platforms and public facilities for exploration and discovery in the Arts and Sciences.

Within the soaring structures, distinctive buildings designed by different architects complete a program of innovative cultural facilities and memorial spaces while reconstructing the skyline with new icons for the public realm. The Towers emerge from large glass reflecting pools that bring natural light to the retail and transit concourse located below grade.

The Transportation Center occupies the memorable space between the towers. Retail space is located at both the concourse and street levels. Two large-scale turbines harvest wind to power the Center. Eight mid-rise office buildings and one hotel on the perimeter of the site fulfill the total program in subsequent phases.

THE WORLD CULTURAL CENTER - AREA SUMMARY	TOTAL
Office (8 buildings)	8,500,000 sf
Retail (street and concourse)	1,000,000 sf
Transit Center (above and below grade)	120,000 sf
Culture Facilities (above and below grade)	820,000 sf
Hotel	660,000 sf
TOTAL	11,100,000 sf
Total Open Space (Memorial, Park and Sidewalk)	14.3 acres

CONSTRUCTION PHASING

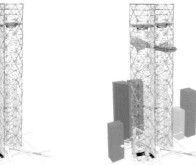

PHASE ONE   PHASE TWO   PHASE THREE   PHASE FOUR

VERTICAL TRANSPORTATION STRATEGY

Elevator service to each program element is separated into distict, dedicated cores distributed evenly around the perimeter of the structure. High-speed double-deck elevators will transport 8.5 million people per year to the memorial sites.

Memorial Sites and

9/11 Interpretative Museum

Conference Center
School/Library

Performing Arts Center

ESCAPE STAIRS   CONVENTIONAL LOADS   IMPACT LOAD

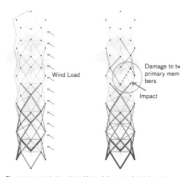

Wind Load

Damage to two primary members

Impact

Following the helical form of the secondary structure, multiple escape stairs spiral down the perimeter of each tower.

The structure is designed to withstand damages due to impact. Estimated weight of steel in each tower = 80,000 tons

TRANSPORTATION CENTER

GREENWICH STREET

MEMORIAL SITE ON TOP OF THE TOWER

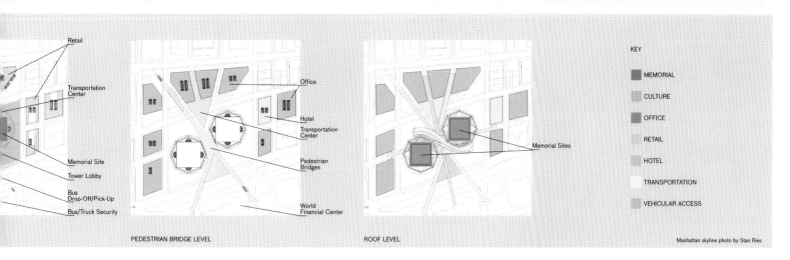

Retail

Transportation Center

Memorial Site

Tower Lobby

Bus Drop-Off/Pick-Up

Bus/Truck Security

Office

Hotel

Transportation Center

Pedestrian Bridges

World Financial Center

Memorial Sites

KEY

MEMORIAL

CULTURE

OFFICE

RETAIL

HOTEL

TRANSPORTATION

VEHICULAR ACCESS

PEDESTRIAN BRIDGE LEVEL   ROOF LEVEL

Manhattan skyline photo by Stan Ries

12.19.02

On December 18, 2002 the LMDC and the press viewed the finished versions of the competing teams' design suggestions at the Winter Garden in New York's World Financial Center. The following day the public had its chance to view the models, drawings and video animations of the much-anticipated designs. Situated on the edge of Ground Zero, the palm tree-filled public space at the Winter Garden is surrounded by sizable high-end office buildings—a similar mix of commercial and public uses to that suggested by the LMDC for Ground Zero itself.

The exhibition space was behind a curved glass wall that kept viewers from walking around the models. Above is the context model of THINK's three plans for the **World Cultural Center**. This model contained a robotic mechanism that transformed the model from **Sky Park** to the **Great Hall** and eventually to the **World Cultural Center**. This transformation was done in sync with a DVD animation that added another experience for the viewer.

Model of the **Sky Park**

In addition to the context model seen on the previous pages, THINK produced three additional models (at a larger scale), one for each of the schemes. The sketch to the right shows roughly THINK's exhibition design.

The challenge was how to show all three of the schemes and the context model, within the given space, originally allocated at a mere 20 feet of frontage. Since THINK wanted to show three times the number of models and drawings (in response to the requests of the LMDC), the team hoped it would have additional gallery space for its presentation (the team was granted some but not all of the requested area).

Part of the solution was to deploy a mechanical system that could alternate each of the three schemes within the single context model of Lower Manhattan. To control the mechanism, and to synchronize it with a loop of the three animations running nearby, THINK commissioned the NY technology company Control Group, which produced the electronics package seen here (near right). The robotic system was designed, built, programmed and deployed in one week.

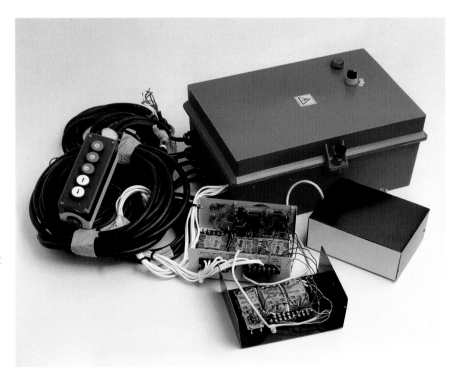

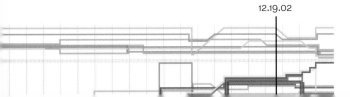

12.19.02

Model of the **Great Hall**

Model of the **World Cultural Center**

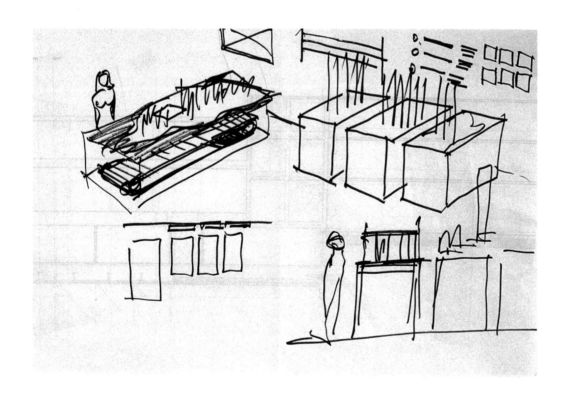

12.19.02

Architects' Proposals May Be Bold, But They Probably Won't Be Built

By CHARLES V. BAGLI

How will the plans presented yesterday by some of the world's most renowned architects be translated into concrete and steel on the site of the World Trade Center?

News Analysis
That question is being debated by urban planners, local residents, developers and public officials involved in rebuilding Lower Manhattan. With acres of vacant office space downtown, there is a consensus that five years or more will pass before the first commercial tower goes up on the 16-acre parcel of land where the twin towers once stood.

It is also likely that whatever is built there will not resemble what was unveiled yesterday in the Winter Garden at the World Financial Center: a bewildering array of crystalline towers, gardens in the sky, bedrock memorial parks 70 feet below street level, and the tallest and largest building in the world.

In the coming months, the Lower Manhattan Development Corporation and the Port Authority of New York and New Jersey, which owns the trade center site, will make a plan based on the work submitted yesterday. But officials say that the developer or developers who eventually build on the site will not be bound by, say, the proposal by Norman Foster for an oversized six-million-square-foot building.

"That's contingent on financing and the market," said Joseph J. Seymour, executive director of the Port Authority. "Whether it'll happen exactly as it was presented this morning or not, I don't think anybody can say at this time."

The architects' imaginative ideas will feed the public's desire to see what a restored skyline might look like. But the demand for office space, which is remarkably weak today, and the nature of the corporations, businesses and institutions that will move into any buildings on the site will have just as great an influence on what the buildings will look like and when they are built.

The value of an architect's conceptual plan, said Charles A. Gargano, chairman of the Empire State Development Corporation, is that "it will lay out a schematic plan for the size and location of the memorial and the reintroduction of the street grid. It also identifies the areas of the site for commercial development."

The development corporation could then proceed with an international competition for a memorial

---

Developers won't be bound to models of a future skyline.

---

design, Mr. Gargano said, and the state could start on transportation projects. Office buildings will be years down the line, he added.

In short, the architects' plans show how a memorial to the roughly 2,800 people who died at the trade center could work with office towers, museums, shops and housing. That is all the exotic models on display at the Winter Garden represent, said a director of the Lower Manhattan Development Corporation who spoke on the condition of anonymity.

"Fundamentally it's a sideshow because none of these things will be built," he said. "But they did show a variety of ways the site could have commercial development and a memorial without looking like a mess."

A major downtown landlord took a harsher view. "They should've stuck to urban planning, not architecture," he said. "A lot of it is abstract. You can't build that stuff. Ultimately, the market is going to dictate what's needed and when it's needed."

Douglas Durst, a developer who built the first of four skyscrapers in Times Square under a state-sponsored redevelopment plan for that neighborhood, said he had a pretty good idea how it would all work out, whether the developer is Larry A. Silverstein, who currently has the lease for the trade center site, or other builders. Although the Times Square design guidelines were not the result of an international architectural competition, Mr. Durst said he expected the process downtown to be similar to what happened on 42nd Street.

"The Times Square development guidelines had been discarded," he said. "At the trade center site, I would expect the developer will negotiate what the buildings will look like. Ultimately, it would resemble the conceptual plan only in spirit."

Mr. Durst said that no developer could build without a tenant, and the tenant will play an important role in determining the size and shape of an office tower. An investment bank usually wants huge, column-free floors for trading, while law and accounting firms prefer smaller floors with as many windowed offices as possible. Many developers believe that a building taller than 60 or 65 stories is both expensive and hard to market, given the public's current fear of tall buildings.

With as much as 17 million square feet of vacant or available office space in Lower Manhattan, no developer is rushing to build a new tower soon. The situation is even worse in the area surrounding the trade center, where one out of every four floors of office space is empty.

Think

Three concepts were developed by this team. One, the World Cultural Center, left, creates latticework structures enclosing buildings by different architects on a program of cultural facilities: the memorial, a museum, a performing arts center, an amphitheater and others. A second concept, the Great Room, top right, is a vast covered public plaza uniting many elements under an enormous glass ceiling. A memorial covering 13 acres is the entrance to the great hall of the transit center. Two glass cylinders protect the footprints of the twin towers. This concept includes a 2,100-foot-tall building, the world's tallest, that houses offices, hotel and a transmission tower. A third concept, the Sky Park, is a 10-block, 16-acre rooftop public park that floats above the street. The memorial is defined by the open squares of the footprints of the twin towers and including the space above, below and around them. The park also includes groves of trees, an amphitheater, cafes, a skating rink, fountains, gardens and sites for more memorials. Below the park are cultural facilities, retail space, a transportation center, a hotel/convention center and office space. On the edge of the park, three large office towers — including the tallest one in the world — are designed as independent buildings.

"It'll probably take a decade to fill the space that is currently vacant," said Robert D. Yaro, president of the Regional Plan Association. "We should spend the next decade building transportation improvements, public spaces, parks. Then the private sector will come because it's the most interesting and accessible business district in the world."

The architects' plans yesterday depicted anywhere from 6 million to 10 million square feet of office space. The Port Authority originally wanted to replace the 11 million square feet of office space at the trade center and include 600,000 square feet of retail space. But critics said that this was too much.

In a speech last week outlining his vision for downtown, Mayor Michael R. Bloomberg talked about investments in mass transit, tree-lined boulevards, parks and new housing, as well as a one-seat ride to the area's international airports. Those investments would justify the development of 10 million square feet of office space in Lower Manhattan, he said.

Mr. Bloomberg proposed the creation of a federal tax incentive zone to attract foreign multinational corporations to downtown.

Barry Gosin, vice chairman of Newmark & Company, a real estate firm, said that he agreed with the mayor's priorities.

"What downtown needs is a 24-7 environment: more housing, more retail, street life and better transportation," Mr. Gosin said. "The office buildings will follow."

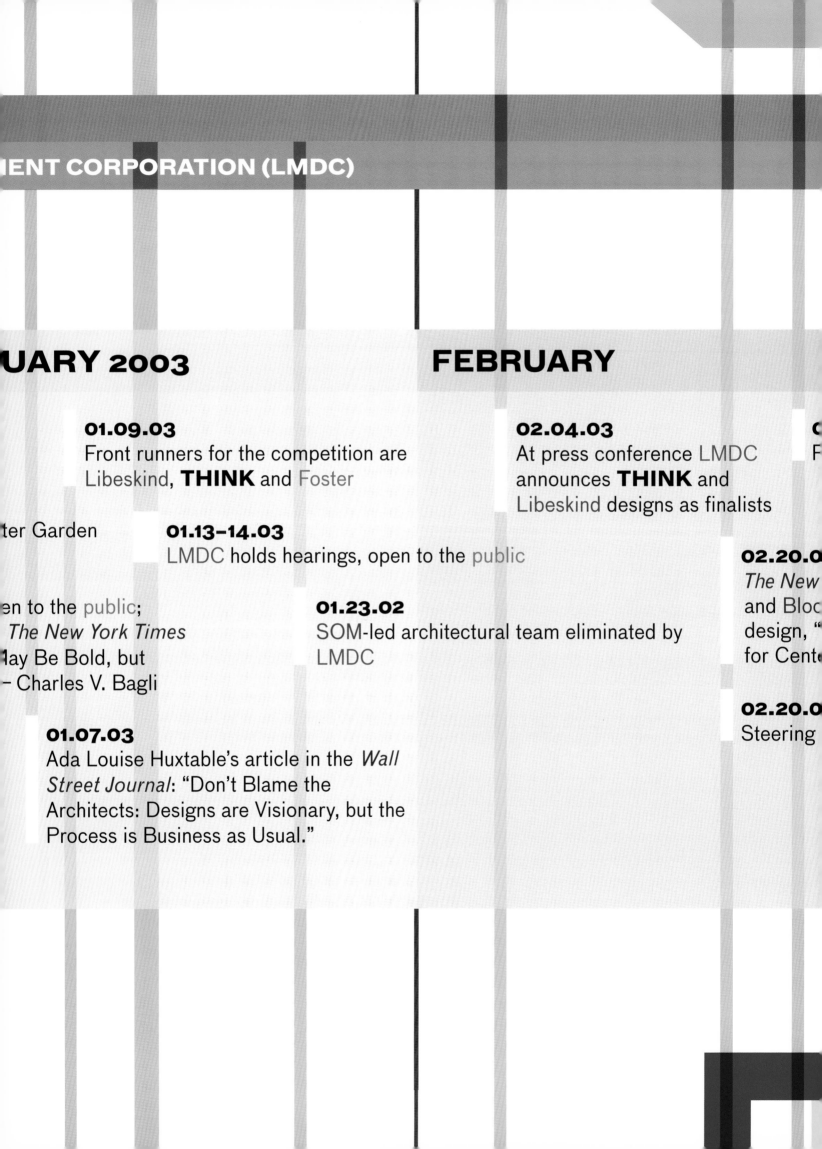

UARY 2003

FEBRUARY

01.09.03
Front runners for the competition are
Libeskind, **THINK** and Foster

ter Garden   **01.13–14.03**
LMDC holds hearings, open to the public

en to the public;
The New York Times
lay Be Bold, but
– Charles V. Bagli

01.23.02
SOM-led architectural team eliminated by
LMDC

01.07.03
Ada Louise Huxtable's article in the *Wall
Street Journal*: "Don't Blame the
Architects: Designs are Visionary, but the
Process is Business as Usual."

02.04.03
At press conference LMDC
announces **THINK** and
Libeskind designs as finalists

02.20.0
The New
and Blo
design, "
for Cent

02.20.0
Steering

25.03

steering committee meeting

02.27.03
LMDC, Pataki select Libeskind design

k Times reports that Pataki
rg support Libeskind
port Builds for One Plan
ite," Edward Wyatt

mittee meeting

02.26.03
HINK makes unscheduled presentation
o Bloomberg and Pataki

1.06.03
Schwartz and Viñoly speak at Architectural Record's "Waiting for Ground Zero" event

1.09.03
Gustavo Bonevardi meets with Rafael Viñoly to discuss his Tribute in Light

1.10.03
THINK consultant, Janet Marie Smith, meets with City Planning Commissioner, Amanda Burden

1.13.03
Viñoly and Schwartz attend Newsday Board meeting

1.13.03
Schwartz attends public hearing with Alex Garvin on the WTC designs

1.13.03
THINK retains Dan Klores Communications for public relations

1.14.03
Schwartz attends public hearing with Anita Contini regarding the memorial competition

1.15 — 1.16.03
Viñoly and Schwartz attend MoMA's and the New York Architectural League's round table discussion, "Redevelopment of Lower Manhattan" at Cooper Hewitt, moderated by Terry Riley

1.16.03
Schwartz and Viñoly represent THINK at a Town Hall meeting

1.16.03
Monika Iken, a member of September's Mission, a group representing victims' families, meets with Viñoly

1.17.03
Interview with Robin Finn of The New York Times for Public Lives column

1.21.03
THINK meets with Nikki Stern, Director of Families of September 11th

1.22.03
Newsweek interviews THINK

1.22.03
Turner Construction's World Cultural Center cost estimate meeting at RVA

1.23.03
Madelyn Wils of Community Board 1 meets with THINK

1.28.03
Edwin Heathcote of Financial Times, London, interviews THINK

01.09.0
Front runners for the competition are
Libeskind, THINK and Foster

nter Garden

01.13-14.03
MDC holds hearings, open to the p

en to the public;
. The New York Time
May Be Bold, but
s V. Bagli

01.23.02
SOM-led architectu
LMDC

01.07.03
Ada Louise Huxtable's article in the Wall
Street Journal : "Don't Blame the
Architects: Designs are Visionary, but the
Process is Business as Usual."

FEBRUARY

2.01.03
La Republica interviews
THINK

2.02.03
RTL-German TV interviews
THINK at Winter Garden

2.05.03
THINK meets with Silverstein

2.05.03
9/11 widow, Paula Berry, meets
with **THINK**

2.05.03
Viñoly appears with Libeskind
on NBC's Today Show

2.07.03
THINK meets with the Port Authority

2.07.03
Ban lectures at Cooper Union

2.08.03
Terry Riley meets with **THINK**

2.08.03
Schwartz and Viñoly
photographed for The New
Yorker at the Winter Garden

2.11.03
THINK meets with Port Authority

2.11.03
Ada Louise Huxtable of Wall Street
Journal meets with **THINK**

2.11.03
Viñoly interviewed by Charlie Rose

2.11.03
Viñoly lectures at Urban Center

2.09.03
THINK meets with Port Authority
to discuss planning issues

2.09.03
Cultural programming workshop
at RVA

2.13.03
THINK meets with Port Authority
at RVA regarding structural issues

2.16.03
THINK holds second meeting of
cultural programming workshop

2.17.03
Jorg Schlaich and Hans Schober,
engineering consultants, meet
with **THINK**

2.19.03
Rick Bell and twelve representatives
from New York New Visions at RVA

2.19.03
Kenneth Jackson of New York
Historical Society meets with **THINK**

2.24.03
THINK is interviewed by various
media outlets including BBC, CNN
and WNYC's Brian Lehrer

02.04.03
At press conference LMDC
announces **THINK** and Libeskind
designs as finalists

lic

al team eliminated by

02.25.03
Final stee

o
L

02.20.03
The New York Tim
Bloomberg suppo
"Support Builds f
Site," Edwart Wya

02.20.03
Steering committe

02.2
THIN
to Blo

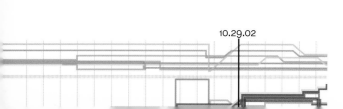

10.29.02

The Decision

On February 4, 2003, the LMDC unveiled the work of the two design teams still under consideration, THINK and Studio Daniel Libeskind. The next day *The New York Times* described the significant differences between the two competing concepts. Edward Wyatt, the author of the story, reported that Libeskind, "sees the foundations of democracy in the concrete walls surrounding Ground Zero," while THINK, "imagines New York's rebirth in soaring towers of culture." The last round of battle for public support had begun.

If media coverage had been intense during the earlier competition, it only grew further during the month of February, while the finalists continued to modify and refine their designs in response to various requests by the LMDC, as the organization readied to make its final decision. At the same time, newspaper, television, radio and internet coverage of each team's designs intensified, while the principal players were engaged in an elaborate media campaign that showcased the various personalities involved and their abilities to perform in front of the camera, on the radio and in print. In addition to seeing drawings, models and video animations of the proposed schemes, the public was also treated to an ongoing examination of the political and media skills of the contenders. This display of the figures behind the designs had the ability to sway the court of public opinion; however, its influence on those who would finally decide which design would go forward was less obvious.

Beyond the media circus, the pressure on the teams to perform at the drawing board, in the model shop and in presentations increased with each successive meeting with the LMDC. THINK, in discussions with the LMDC, had determined that of the three schemes it had proposed, the one to focus its energies on was the World Cultural Center, the DNA-inspired towers that would provide infrastructure for memorial spaces and cultural uses, and would quickly fill the void in the skyline created by the loss of the World Trade Center. Moving from the conceptual stage to a plan that truly could be built, complete with budgets, engineering details and production schedules was part of the challenge put forth by the LMDC. In order to accommodate a host of requests from the client, including concerns relating to construction, maintenance and access, THINK reworked its earlier concept. By the end of the month, THINK had significantly cut the cost of materials and construction through structural changes that improved the design and produced a much lighter and more elegant structure than the one presented to the public in December 2002. However, none of these refinements were ever seen by the public. This process is finely detailed in the following pages, culminating with the final presentation images produced by THINK, which show how the towers could assume their place as a powerful presence in Lower Manhattan and on the skyline.

What the public did see was a seemingly unending stream of articles and other media coverage on Libeskind and THINK. Prior to THINK's elevation to finalist status, *The New York Times* ran a piece on Viñoly in the paper's "Public Lives" column on January 22, 2003 titled, "A Visionary of the Skyline, with 3 Pairs of Glasses." The reporter suggested that THINK's tower scheme was not among the front-runners in the competition, an interesting interpretation considering THINK's selection as a finalist two weeks later. In response to this assertion, Viñoly spoke about the plan's essential optimism and its ability, "to regenerate the city's pride." He reminded the interviewer, "We see a skyline defined by culture and not by commerce."

Viñoly and Schwartz went on to speak publicly and use the media to explain the team's ideas and how its designs were appropriate, both specifically at Ground Zero and generally for New York. Both architects appeared frequently on television, locally and nationally. Viñoly made the case on NBC's "Today" and PBS's "Charlie Rose Show." Schwartz made repeated appearances on NY1's "New York Tonight," a major program on the local cable news station. Both designers were featured on the hit show, "Oprah." Britain's BBC chronicled the competition in a lengthy documentary, which underscored that this was not solely a New York story, but an international one.

Even architects no longer involved in the competition entered the debate. Richard Meier contributed an opinion piece entitled "Let Culture Soar at Ground Zero" to the *New York Daily News*, in which he voiced support for THINK's World Cultural Center. "The vertical framework of the open towers captures the still vivid memory of loss but also allows for evolution in the future." Meier tells his readers, "The Towers are elegant structures whose imaginative design complements their poetic conception, elevating culture to iconic status while restoring the skyline." On the same day, one day prior to the announcement of the winning design, *The Wall Street Journal* ran a piece with a very different slant that examined

Viñoly's former life in Argentina, and which suggested he had questionable links to the nation's former military junta. Julie V. Iovine reported in *The New York Times*: "Not since Gary Cooper appeared in 'The Fountainhead' has the public been so riveted by architecture and architects."

Of course, while the public was receiving a daily play-by-play via the press's constant investigation of the Ground Zero drama, in fact there was no mechanism for the public truly to play a role in the final decision on who should design the master plan, THINK or Libeskind. While in the past the LMDC had held sessions where the public could voice support, concerns or disdain for the many designs created by the original seven participants in the competition, no such public forums were available during this final, crucial stage. That did not mean that media outlets, from newspapers to websites, shied away from requesting the public's input. There were polls and questionnaires people could respond to, but how influential these would be was anyone's guess. It appeared that the LMDC would be the final arbiter on the next phase of the master plan.

Then again, the LMDC was beholden to other political forces. An amalgam of city, state and federal representatives, the organization eventually presented its recommendations both to the Mayor and Governor before a final decision could be made. Perhaps more of a client representative than an actual client, the LMDC was asked to do most of the work, but was not bestowed with complete authority. As reported in *The New York Times* on February 26, 2003, the day before the selection was to be announced, the LMDC was then leaning toward THINK's towers over Libeskind's slurry wall-focused plan. However, the same article stated that Mayor Bloomberg and Governor Pataki were then more partial to Libeskind's concept. At this point, it was not the public, but their elected representatives that would have the final say on the largest development project in New York in decades.

On this same day, THINK and Libeskind met for the last time with the LMDC and Bloomberg and Pataki. Encouraged by their prior experiences with the LMDC, the members of THINK felt positive about their chances to win the competition. However, they were concerned that the Governor did not share the LMDC's enthusiasm for the towers. They were right to be wary.

On February 27, 2003, the decision was announced at a press conference at the Winter Garden in the World Financial Center. Studio Daniel Libeskind had gotten the nod from the decision-makers, contrary to the

PUBLIC LIVES

A Visionary of the Skyline, With 3 Pairs of Glasses

By ROBIN FINN

Deep in the modernist bunker at 50 Vandam Street that serves as the main office of the architect Rafael Viñoly, a leader of the "Think Team" that contributed a fabulist, Eiffel Tower-inspired confection to the World Trade Center design competition, sits a bronze bust of Napoleon.

Besides being the only old-fashioned touch in an otherwise cutting-edge sort of room, it is, Mr. Viñoly says, a gift from his wife, Diana, an interior designer with whom he collaborates on hipper-than-thou hangouts like Bungalow 8 and Lot 61. And with whom he raised three sons. Hence Napoleon occupies a position of honor and influence, or perhaps irony, by the computer.

"I hate the man!" sputters Mr. Viñoly, clearly the excitable type. "I think she sees some parallels in my life to what that other dwarf did with his."

Surely he's referring to the developer of empires part of Napoleon's résumé, not the despot part? Mr. Viñoly, who could run a charm school in his spare time, if he had any, smiles mischievously beneath black crescent eyebrows.

Maybe his spouse simply means he is a little self-starter with a grand capacity for reinvention: of himself (he fled persecution in Argentina for New York City in 1979 with little more than a suitcase) *and* of architecture (he once defined architecture as the art of dealing with heaviness, and he was the first architect in Buenos Aires to live in a house that brought exposed concrete indoors as a decorative touch).

He is fresh off a plane from Maryland, where his firm, Rafael Viñoly Architects, is designing a research center for the Howard Hughes Medical Institute.

"We make the thing where they do their thing," he says, dumbing it down — not condescendingly.

Ask him about the Kimmel Center for the Performing Arts in Philadelphia and he describes it as curvaceous, a veritable cello; as for his $34 million transformation of a decrepit City College library into the School of Architecture, Urban Design and Landscape Architecture, he speaks of an atrium that embraces the building "like a doughnut."

Inquire about the Princeton football helmet in plexiglass on his desk and he practically jumps out of his turtleneck: "That stadium may be our greatest success! Everybody loved this thing!" He is hoping everyone, especially musicians, will love his $128 million Jazz at Lincoln Center

Alan Chin for The New York Times

"This is a great moment for architecture. It's gone from being marginal to a way to truly regenerate the city's pride."

RAFAEL VIÑOLY

colossus, scheduled for a fall 2004 unveiling.

"Meeting Wynton Marsalis was like a revelation," he gushes. "You feel like what you are building is connected to something spiritual: what he does, it's not just a profession, it's a mission in life."

Mr. Viñoly, 58 and stoked by black coffee even at sundown, is a black-clad wraith with a madcap nimbus of silvery hair that serves as a nest for one of the three pairs of eyeglasses he keeps tethered to his neck at all times. This is no affectation: this is a security blanket. He gets hysterical if he loses his glasses. Architects, he says, are only as good as their vision. And his

vision is all over New York City.

"I've got buildings in every borough — this is informational; I'm not bragging," he says. "I've always felt the city was an extraordinary client."

His take on what should happen at ground zero is informed by what he says happened to him decades ago in Argentina, first when a 1966 coup resulted in raids, and murders, at his university, and later when the military, no friend to intellectuals, raided his home and suspected him of Communist ties because of his Larousse dictionary. To them, Larousse was code for La Russie. To him, it was time to leave, and with help from Rabbi Marshall Meyer of Amnesty International, he did.

"The World Trade Center project made me rehash all these things that happened 30 years ago in a very powerful way, and it reinforced an attitude I find completely unique to this town, which is its ability to overcome tragedy not only with pain but with celebration," he says, gesturing at his elaborate model of two soaring latticework towers that "protect" the airspace once filled by the twin towers. Suspended at various heights are parks, performance facilities and restaurants. Commercial office space is relegated to peripheral buildings.

That his team's proposal has not emerged a front-runner among the plans on display at the Winter Garden does not vex him. "This is a great moment for architecture," he says. "It's gone from being marginal to a way to truly regenerate the city's pride. And our plan does that best. We see a skyline defined by culture and not by commerce."

A floor-length black scarf flutters from his neck as he dashes around the room. The huge black Steinway grand piano (he owns eight pianos and has a miniconcert hall at his Hamptons place, in Water Mill) is a reminder of the career he gave up, at 17, to study architecture at the University of Buenos Aires. His father was director of Montevideo's opera house and later a filmmaker in Buenos Aires; Mr. Viñoly sat down at the keyboard at 3. But as an architect, he was a prodigy. He won the first competitions he entered, designing a college cafeteria and a woodworking shop.

At 18, he started a firm, Estudio de Arquitectura, with a group of elders; at 34, he moved here and started over.

"In New York City," he says, "there is only one way to do things, the New York way: you affirm your spiritual connection to this tragedy, but you reaffirm your optimism. You make something positive out of this outrageous crime."

reporting the day before. The following day *The New York Times* announced the selection that stressed the pragmatic over the aesthetic. "In the end, it was not so much about architecture, about solemn memorial pits or soaring gardens in the sky," Edward Wyatt wrote in "Practical Issues For Ground Zero: Politics and Economics Figure in Choice of Renewal Plan." Wyatt surmised, "Instead, the decision announced yesterday to choose Daniel Libeskind's design for the World Trade Center site revolved mainly around politics, economics and engineering, people close to the selection process said."

What really happened is open to interpretation. One can argue that THINK's was the more practical plan, requiring a modest expenditure to repair the skyline and accommodating long-term development, while not requiring large-scale building for the short term. Nonetheless, it seemed inarguable that Wyatt was correct to focus on the political angle. It appeared that the LMDC had been overruled by politics.

The period following September 11, 2001, but especially the timeframe of the design competition from late September 2002 through late February 2003, was intense for all those involved with planning the coming phases for Ground Zero. Once the decision was announced on February 27, 2003, the entire team at THINK could finally take a well-deserved rest following the hectic pace of all those late nights, intense meetings and elaborate design sessions. Reflection on all that had gone on could wait—for a bit.

Both Schwartz and Viñoly maintained their passionate interests in the fate of Ground Zero. Schwartz went on to participate in and win two major memorial competitions, for Westchester County and New Jersey; Viñoly returned to his full schedule of major commissions, including the redesign of the Kennedy Center in Washington, D.C., but also continued his effort to speak out on New York's approach to development in Lower Manhattan. In December 2003, he published a prominent piece on the Op-Ed page of *The New York Times*, "Master Planner or Master Builder?" In this, Viñoly spoke about the essential differences between master planning and architecture and the confusion that arose over the two during the Innovative Design Study process: "The corporation reacted to the public outrage by creating the Innovative Design Study, a sort of 'noncompetition' that was supposed to identify one or more consultants to help the agency further develop the master plan for the site. This process resulted in the most exciting architectural event in years. It was from this competition that Mr. Libeskind's rendering was chosen. But instead of portraying the exercise as one step along a more deliberative path, the corporation created the impression that this was the final result."

Viñoly went on to say it was not too late to treat the chosen plan for what it really was, a plan, not a complete architectural design and reminded readers that the point of a plan is to accommodate later development, including the upcoming memorial. He argued for the need to take some time to think through the next steps, returning to his earliest instincts that the rush to rebuild was not necessarily the wisest course of action. He also chided the LMDC: "In my view, the Lower Manhattan Development Corporation has consistently failed to educate the public—and perhaps even the governor—as to what to expect (and not to expect) from a master plan."

In this statement, Viñoly raised an even larger topic than that of the essential difference between planning and building, he touched on the issue of the public's involvement, or lack thereof. If not fully educated, how could the public really participate? Then again, given the process, how could they participate at all? There was no true public referendum, no vote.

Subject: We are in
Date: 30 Jan 2003 8:04am
From: Rafael Viñoly
To: Cecilia Arca,
Maria Aviles,
Jay Bargmann,
Carolyn Hill,
Mateo Paiva,
Mark Sarosi,
Joseph Schollmeyer,
Román Viñoly

we are in
stay put
the real battle starts now
its going to be a long tiring month
congratulations

True, there were public meetings and the dissension that emerged at the "Listening to the City" events, but in fact, there was no direct instrument by which the public could specifically engage in the debate. Viñoly was right in mentioning that the LMDC needed not only to increase the public's understanding, but also that of the Governor. How did Governor Pataki make that final decision and on what did he base his choice? Why was his vote (and perhaps that of the Mayor) the only one(s) that mattered?

In New York's desire to move forward—move forward quickly—much was pushed off the table. Imagine what would have happened if the timetable had been different, or if the financial arrangements had been more flexible. By buying into the necessity of working with Larry Silverstein, the one player who brought money and entitlement to the table—and specific requirements to rebuild office space—the entire set of options was never available. This is not to fault Mr. Silverstein, who in many ways had become the key to rebuilding swiftly, but it needs to be noted that the public, the politicians, the architects and the LMDC never had an open slate upon which to work. That knowledge should have been part of the public's architectural education as well.

rafael vinoly
architect

Photographs by Reuters

Officials are down to two competing concepts for the redesign of the World Trade Center site, one by the Think team, left, and the other by Studio Daniel Libeskind.

Two Finalists Are Selected For the Void at Ground Zero

By EDWARD WYATT

Two teams of architects, one that sees the foundations of democracy in the concrete walls surrounding ground zero and another that imagines New York's rebirth in soaring towers of culture, have been selected as finalists in the competition to create the design for the World Trade Center site, rebuilding officials said yesterday.

Each of the designs includes what would be the tallest building in the world, though in both plans, the towers' upper reaches are not occupied by offices. Rather, there is a memorial observation deck in one case, and a hanging garden in the other.

The two teams, Studio Daniel Libeskind, the firm headed by the Berlin-based architect Daniel Libeskind, and the Think team, headed by the architects Frederic Schwartz, Rafael Viñoly and Ken Smith of New York, and Shigeru Ban of Tokyo, will now work with rebuilding officials on refinements to their designs. One team is to be selected as the winner by the end of the month.

The winning design will include the layout and conceptual vision for the trade center site's buildings, transportation terminals and a memorial to the victims of Sept. 11, 2001 — an architectural project like no other and one that is already among the most watched in the world.

Rebuilding officials from the Lower Manhattan Development Corporation, the Port Authority of New York and New Jersey, and the offices of the mayor and the governor were effusive yesterday in their praise for the two plans, which they said stood out in their excellence from the plans by five other teams of architects that were also unveiled

Continued on Page B4

Two Finalists Are Selected For the Void at Ground Zero

Continued From Page B1

in December.

And they vowed that while each of the designs selected yesterday would require modifications, those changes would not alter the architects' central vision. Among possible changes, an official said, is raising the level of the floor of the memorial space in the Libeskind design and adjusting the height of the Think team's towers downward.

"No plan in its current configuration is perfect," said the official, Roland W. Betts, a development corporation director who oversaw the task force that selected the two plans. "Rest assured that whatever the modifications, the core idea of each plan will be preserved. The goal of the next few weeks is not to compromise the plans but to make them better."

Even after a single team is chosen to complete a plan for the layout of the site, the office buildings that will be constructed there over the next 10 to 12 years could look significantly different from the renderings created by the two teams.

That is because these two plans, unlike some of those that were rejected, have the memorial, rather than office towers, as their centerpiece. The architects themselves have acknowledged that the design of the office buildings in their drawings are subject to change.

The final site plan will include parcels where office buildings will eventually be located, including the size and shape of each building's footprint and the anticipated height. But the design of the office buildings' actual skin will depend on when they are built and by what developer.

There are also several other forces competing for control of the site and for the authority to develop it. Among those forces is Larry A. Sil-verstein, the lead representative of the firms that hold the lease to the site. In a letter Friday to rebuilding officials, Mr. Silverstein asserted that the lease gave his group the right to rebuild the site as the group sees fit and to choose the architecture firm that will design it.

In response to a question yesterday, Mr. Betts said that "in spite of what he said in his letter," Mr. Silverstein has been involved in discussions and decisions about the site. "We had a number of consultants looking at all the issues that were raised in that letter and we came to different conclusions," Mr. Betts added.

But other, possibly conflicting forces are also at work. The city is seeking to negotiate a land swap that would give it authority over the trade center site, while transferring ownership of the city's two major airports to the Port Authority, the agency that now owns the trade center property.

Officials from the Port Authority and the development corporation have clashed in recent weeks over priorities for the site, people involved in the process said. The Port Authority has been primarily focused on infrastructure, encompassing everything from the layout of a new transportation complex to the location of truck ramps into the basement levels of the site.

Development corporation officials, meanwhile, have often been more interested in aesthetics, including which architect's concept makes a more significant impact on the skyline and on the memorial.

Some officials of the Lower Manhattan Development Corporation, half of whose directors are appointed by the governor and half by the city, have also maintained that regardless of who owns the land at the trade center site, the development corporation will continue to oversee the

Rafael Viñoly, left, and Daniel Libeskind and his wife, Nina, with renderings of their designs for the World Trade Center site. Each plan includes soaring towers, memorials and cultural and office space.

Joyce Dopkeen/The New York Times

Each competing design includes what would be the world's tallest building.

development.

The decision announced yesterday had been expected, because the Libeskind and Think plans had won wide acclaim from architects, design professionals and the general public.

Mr. Libeskind's plan includes an open pit on the western portion of the trade center site, where the memorial to victims would be located.

The pit, including the footprints of the trade center towers, would be outlined by the concrete slurry walls designed to hold back groundwater from what were formerly the concourse and basement levels of the trade center.

It is within those walls that most of the remains of the victims were found. Mr. Libeskind has said that the walls "withstood the unimaginable trauma of the destruction and stand as eloquent as the Constitution itself, asserting the durability of democracy and the value of individual life."

A museum that would cantilever over the pit would serve as an entrance to the ground zero memorial. In addition, two large public spaces at ground level would commemorate the victims; the park areas would be located to catch rays of sunlight each year on the morning of Sept. 11, from the time of the first attack to the collapse of the north tower.

Additionally, a series of office and cultural buildings would surround the memorial site, including a 1,776-foot spire inhabited in its upper half by hanging gardens.

Mr. Libeskind estimated that the public spaces and reinforcement of the bathtub walls would cost $280 million to $330 million.

The second semifinalist, the Think team, originally designed three options, but the team began in recent weeks to promote its "World Cultur-al Center" design almost exclusively. The design includes two 1,665-foot latticework towers, inspired by the Eiffel Tower. Within them, various buildings would be constructed to hang seemingly in midair. They would include a museum, a performing arts center, a conference center, educational facilities, viewing platforms and other public spaces.

The towers would surround the footprints of the twin towers and would themselves be surrounded by large glass-bottomed reflecting pools, which would bring natural light to the underground retail and transit concourse.

As many as eight commercial office buildings and a hotel would surround the towers on the site's perimeter. Mr. Viñoly estimated that the public spaces and the framework of the cultural towers would cost $750 million to $800 million.

"Each of these plans breaks new ground literally by creating new ground," John C. Whitehead, the chairman of the development corporation, said yesterday. "They have the audacity and faith, on the one hand, to suspend buildings in midair, and on the other to make meaning of the void."

An exhibit of the two semifinalists' designs is to reopen at the World Financial Center's Winter Garden on Friday.

The two plans, each with a distinct focus on the memorial, have enjoyed general support from family members of many of the victims of the attacks, although each design also has drawn criticism for some of its elements.

More pointed has been the criticism of the development corporation, the Port Authority, and their process for arriving at the designs. Yesterday, officials of the Regional Plan Association, a planning advocacy group, repeated criticisms that the process seemed to be made up as it has progressed.

"Public agencies owe something to the public: a process that they can follow along with, know when they will be asked to participate and know when decisions will be made," said Jeremy Soffin, a spokesman for the planning group.

The media had a constant presence during this stage of the competition. Here a film crew documents THINK's frenetic work schedule at RVA's offices in downtown New York.

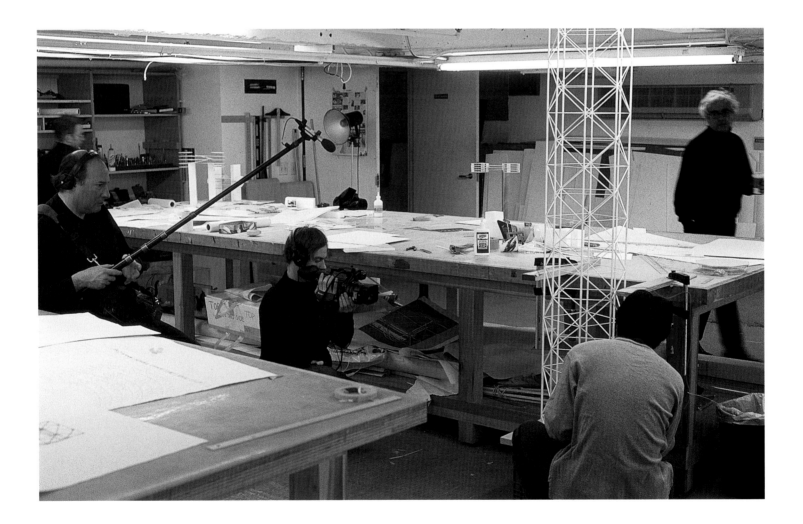

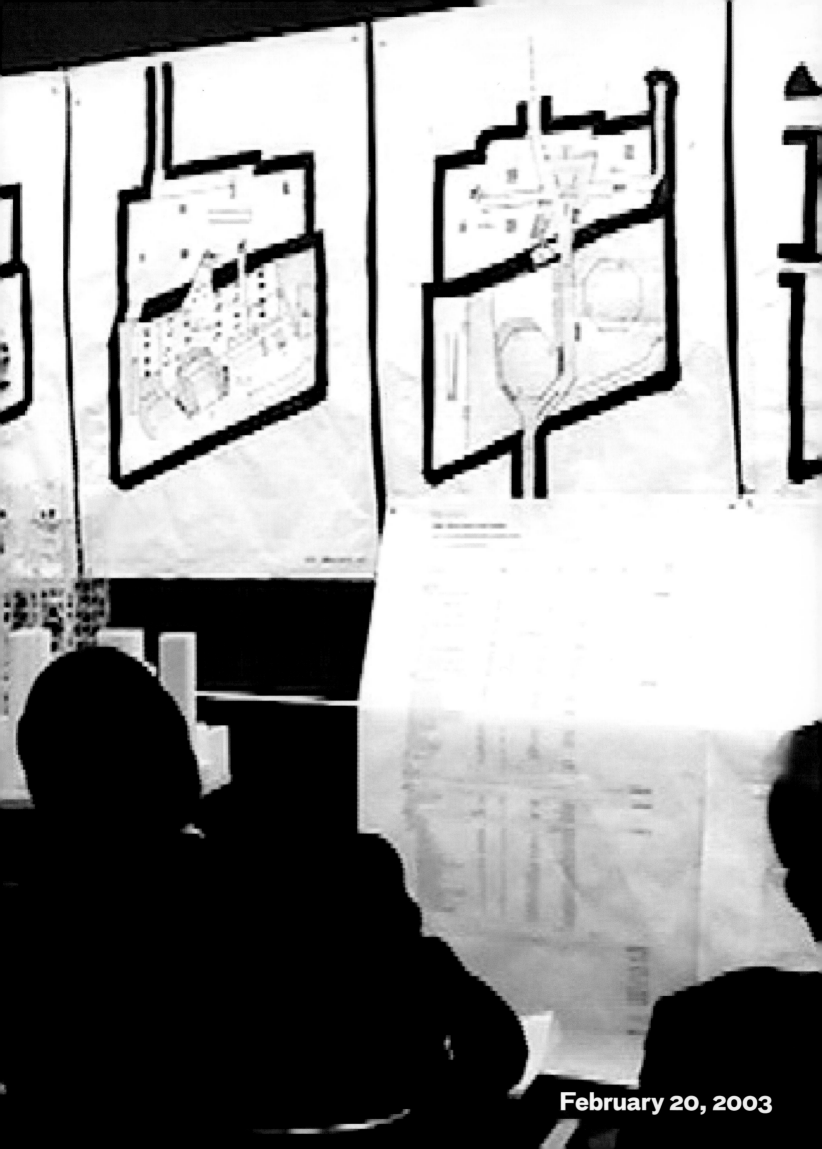

February 20, 2003

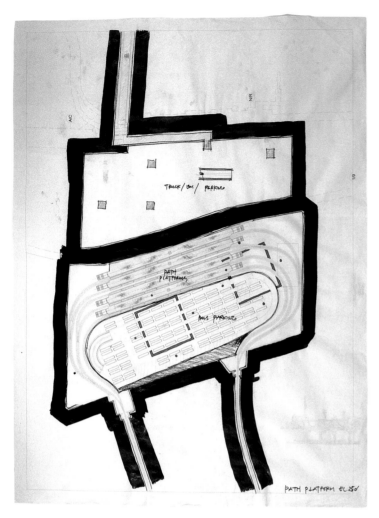

PATH PLATFORM EL.250'

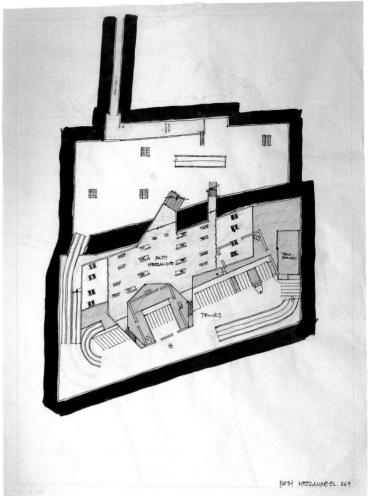

PATH MEZZANINE EL. 264'

In the presentation to the Land Use Committee of the LMDC on February 20, 2003, THINK presented several concepts including the detailed plan for the below grade conditions of the **World Cultural Center**. This plan addressed structural aspects, access issues and transportation connections. THINK worked on specific elements concerning the PATH train platform and parking areas for bus use, both of which would need to traverse the foundations of the proposed **World Cultural Center** towers.

The four drawings represent the complexity of accommodating the PATH and subway lines, the Con Edison electrical substation, the connection between the Winter Garden at the World Financial Center and the transportation hub, as well as the required access routes onto the site for buses and trucks.

02.20.03

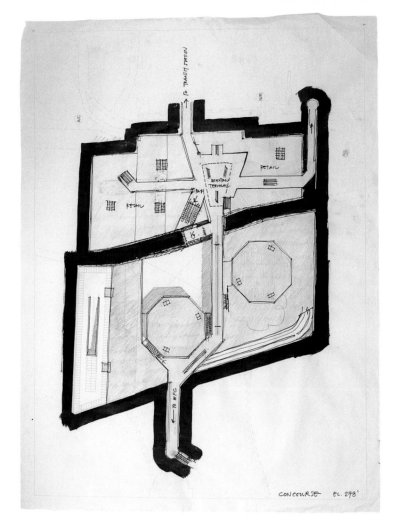

CONCOURSE   EL. 278'

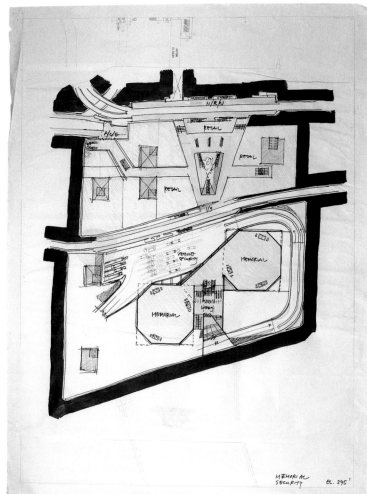

MEMORIAL
SECURITY   EL. 295'

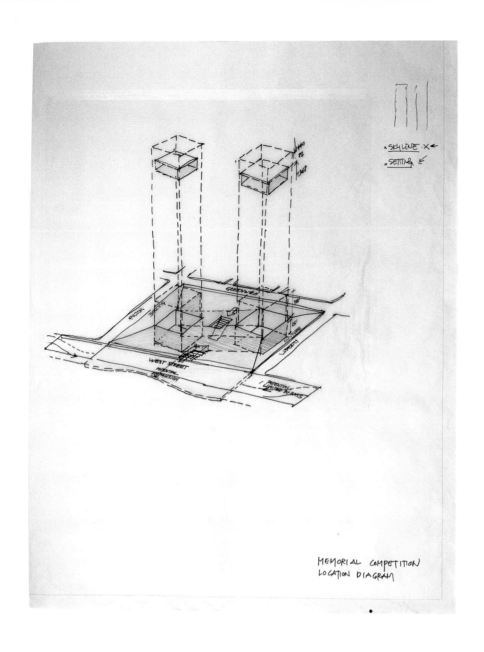

MEMORIAL COMPETITION
LOCATION DIAGRAM

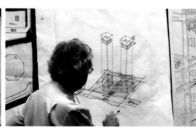

02.20.03

THINK presented a sketched section of the entire site along the east–west axis. This illustration explores connections at various levels—note that not all levels connect throughout the site. THINK also detailed issues concerning the flow of visitors through the secured lobby at the entrances to the proposed memorial areas. A model representing the same conditions shown in the drawing can be seen in the video stills below.

The smaller drawing to the right shows the shift to a new design for the towers' structure. THINK proposed a smaller footprint for the towers and therefore structures of smaller volume and proportionately lower height with the towers connecting to the ground at eight points instead of four. Although of smaller diameter, the towers still avoid touching the original footprints; this time they straddle the footprints instead of surrounding them.

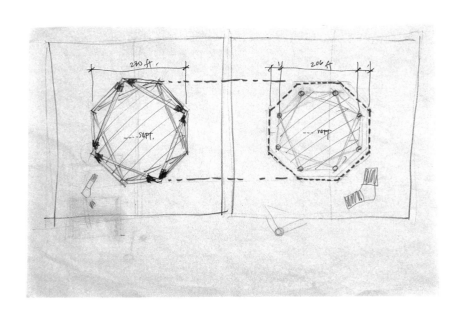

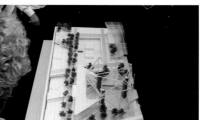

02.20.03

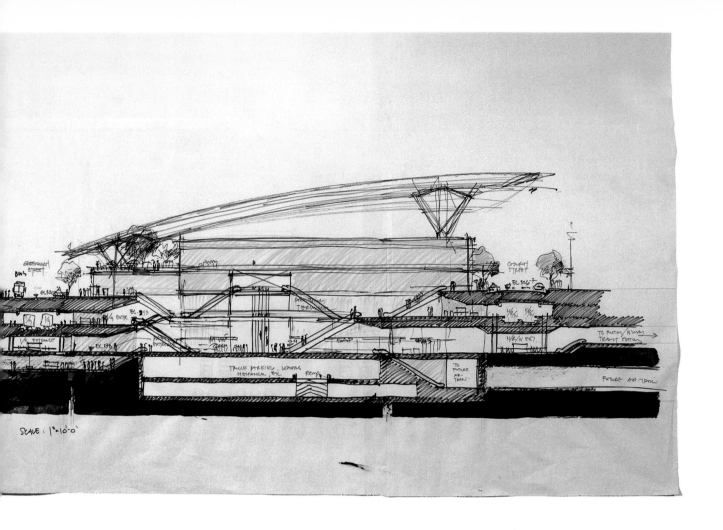

SCALE: 1"=10'-0"

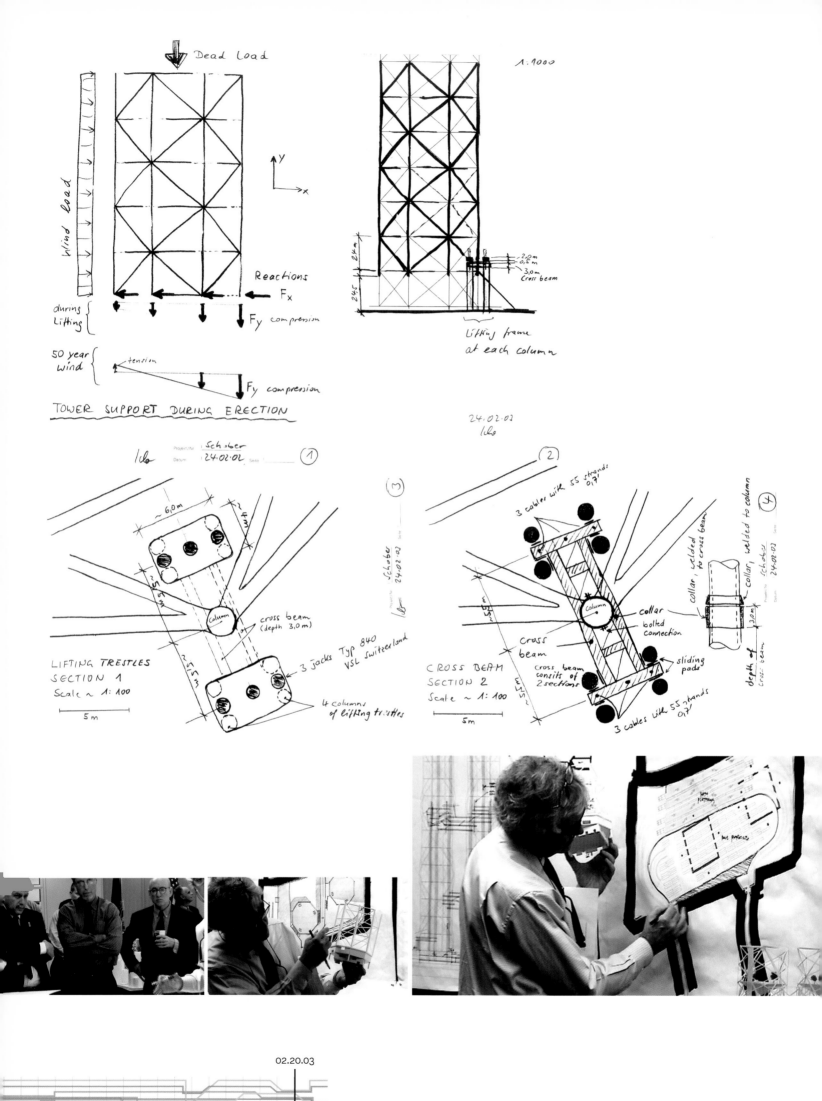

Dead Load

Wind load

$\uparrow y$ $\rightarrow x$

Reactions F_x

during Lifting

F_y compression

50 year wind

tension

F_y compression

TOWER SUPPORT DURING ERECTION

1:1000

24m

245

2,0 m
0,5 m
3,0 m
Cross beam

Lifting frame at each column

24.02.03
Iko

Iko   Projekt/Nr : Schober
Datum : 24.02.02   Seite ___ ①

~ 6,0 m

~5,5 m

Column

cross beam
(depth 3,0 m)

3 jacks Typ 840
VSL Switzerland

LIFTING TRESTLES
SECTION 1
Scale ~ 1:100

5 m

4 columns
of lifting trestles

②

③

Projekt/Nr : Schober
Datum : 24.02.03   Seite ___

3 cables with 55 strands 0,7"

collar, welded to cross beam

Column

collar

bolted
connection

Cross
beam

cross beam
consits of
2 sections

sliding
pads

CROSS BEAM
SECTION 2
Scale ~ 1:100

5m

3 cables with 55 strands 0,7"

④

Projekt/Nr : Schober
Datum : 24.02.03   Seite ___

collar, welded to column

depth of
cross beam   3,0m

02.20.03

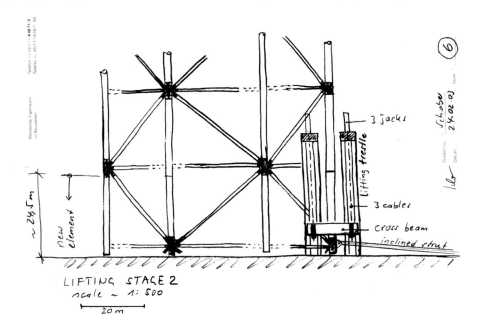

LIFTING STAGE 2
scale ~ 1:500

20 m

3 jacks

lifting trestle

3 cables

cross beam

inclined strut

new element

~ 24.5 m

By this time, THINK had developed its own concerns about the scale, cost, and structural feasibility of the proposed towers. In response, the team developed a simpler, lighter design for the towers. Structural engineer Jörg Schlaich played an essential role in the engineering of these new tower structures and presented his ideas directly to the LMDC on behalf of THINK.

The revised design greatly simplified the geometry of the towers and allowed for a more robust, safer structure with twice as many columns now touching the ground. Because the new design's eight columns now carried the loads more efficiently—vertically, instead of diagonally—it required less steel overall and smaller welds for smaller structural connections. A streamlined, more rational and safer construction process was the result.

The sketches opposite top show the structure's dead loads and wind forces during the erection sequence. The sketches opposite below and on the left detail the system of powerful hydraulic jacks that would be used to sequentially lift each structural module after it has been assembled on grade. During construction, sixteen copies of each one of these six-jack assemblies, one for each column of the two towers, would be required.

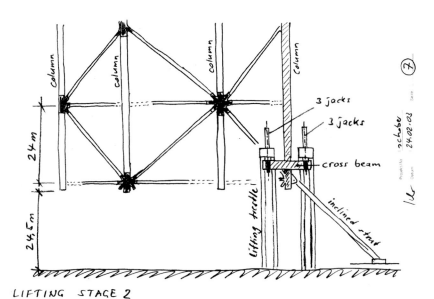

column   column   column   column

3 jacks

3 jacks

cross beam

lifting trestle

inclined strut

24 m

24.5 m

LIFTING STAGE 2

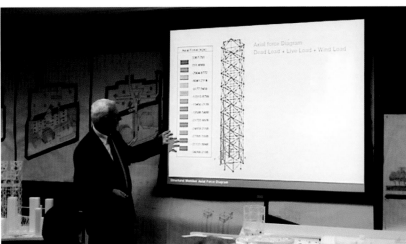

Step 1: Construct Module #1

A Controlled Environment for Construction at Grade
· Tightest Erection Tolerances
· Easiest to Access Construction Area
· Best Finish Quality
· Lowest Cost

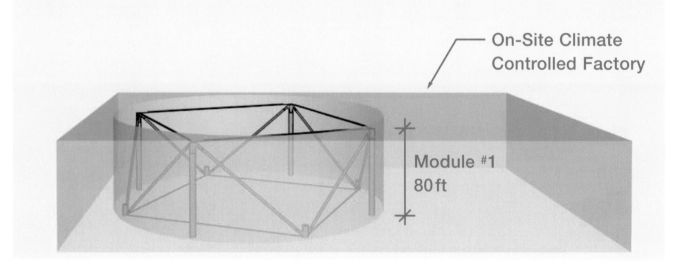

On-Site Climate
Controlled Factory

Module #1
80 ft

Construction of the towers' 80-foot-tall structural modules was
planned to take place on the ground in a temporary enclosed
factory. Each completed section would then be sequentially
lifted out of the factory's roof by the system of hydraulic jacks
(described on the previous page), and in the now-vacant
factory below another module would be constructed and
welded to the structure. The factory idea and resulting erection
strategy was a response to THINK's concern for achieving
the highest safety and quality control standards during
construction. As the construction strategy was being developed
the team recognized that welding two pieces of 4-foot-thick
steel 1,400 feet up in the air would be unacceptably difficult,
dangerous and prone to welding defects arising from variations
in temperature and humidity.

02.20.03

Step 2: Lift Module #1

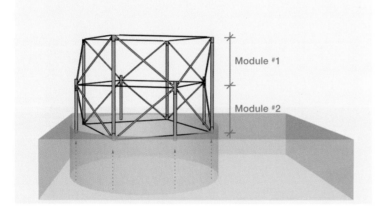

Module #1

Step 3: Construct Module #2

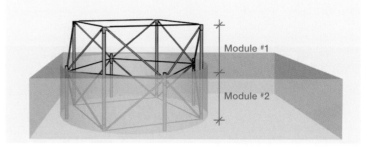

Module #1

Module #2

Step 4: Lift Module #1 and #2

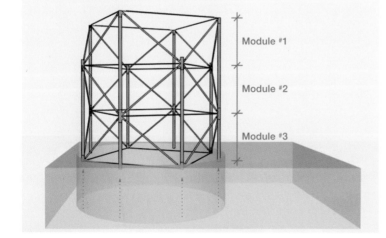

Module #1

Module #2

Step 5: Construct Module #3

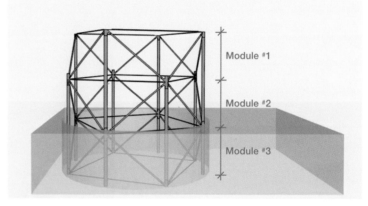

Module #1

Module #2

Module #3

Step 6: Lift Module #1, #2 and #3

Module #1

Module #2

Module #3

Step 7: Construct Module #4

Module #1

Module #2

Module #3

Module #4

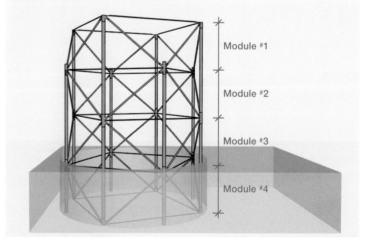

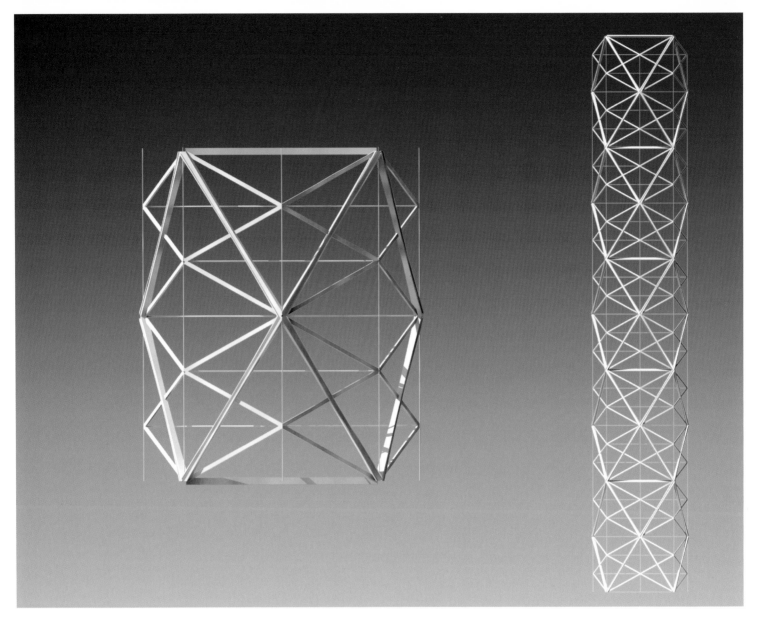

World Cultural Center towers as presented on December 18, 2002.

02.20.03

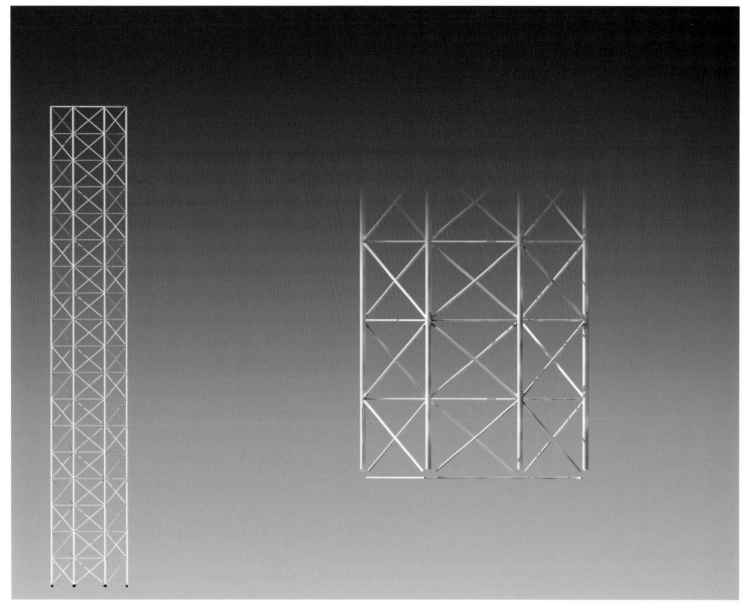

World Cultural Center towers as presented on February 20, 2003

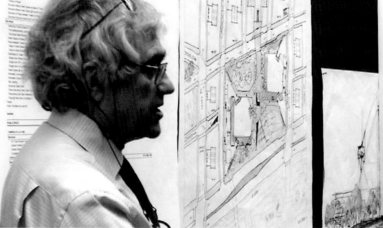

The LMDC was concerned that there be traditional double-loaded street frontage on Liberty and Fulton Streets. Therefore, the LMDC asked for specific changes at this point in the competition.

In response to this request THINK showed this draft of the site plan on February 20, 2003. The drawing shows the development of additional buildings at the northern and southern borders of the site at Liberty and Fulton streets. These buildings were designated for cultural uses, but also would be used as staging areas and for access to the proposed funicular, which would rise along the towers. These buildings would also serve as street frontage.

This plan shows another major change in the master plan that THINK was developing. Whereas the dramatic water feature surrounding the towers in the plan from December 18 had created a super-block condition, THINK now altered the design to a grass-covered expanse that made it easy for pedestrians to get across the site.

02.20.03

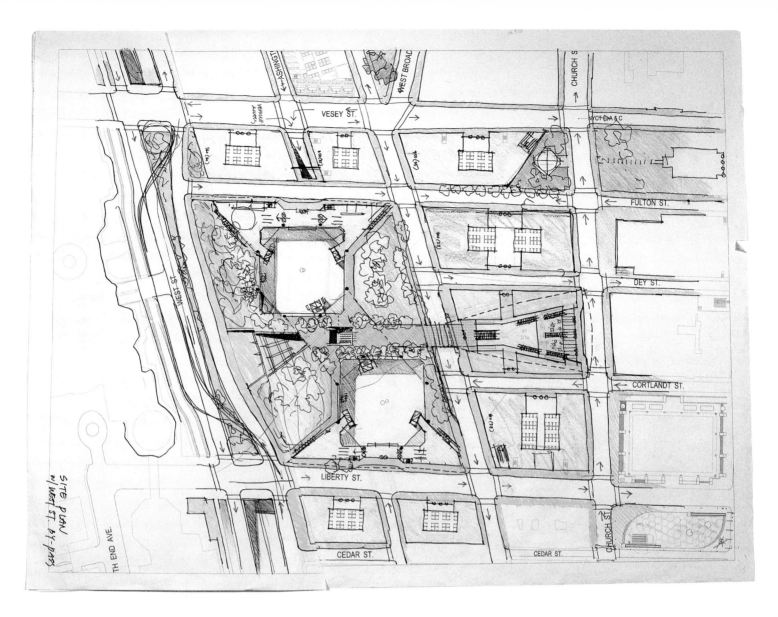

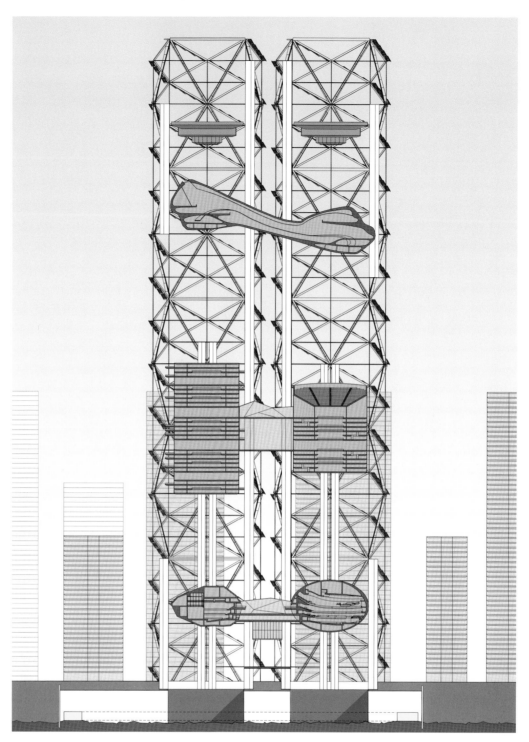

Earlier version of **World Cultural Center**—1665 feet high.

02.20.03

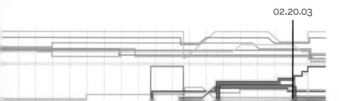

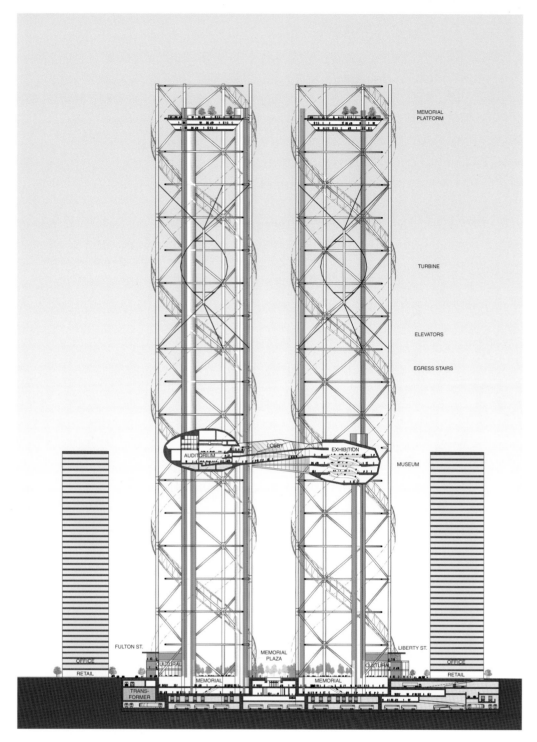

Revised version of **World Cultural Center**—1440 feet high.

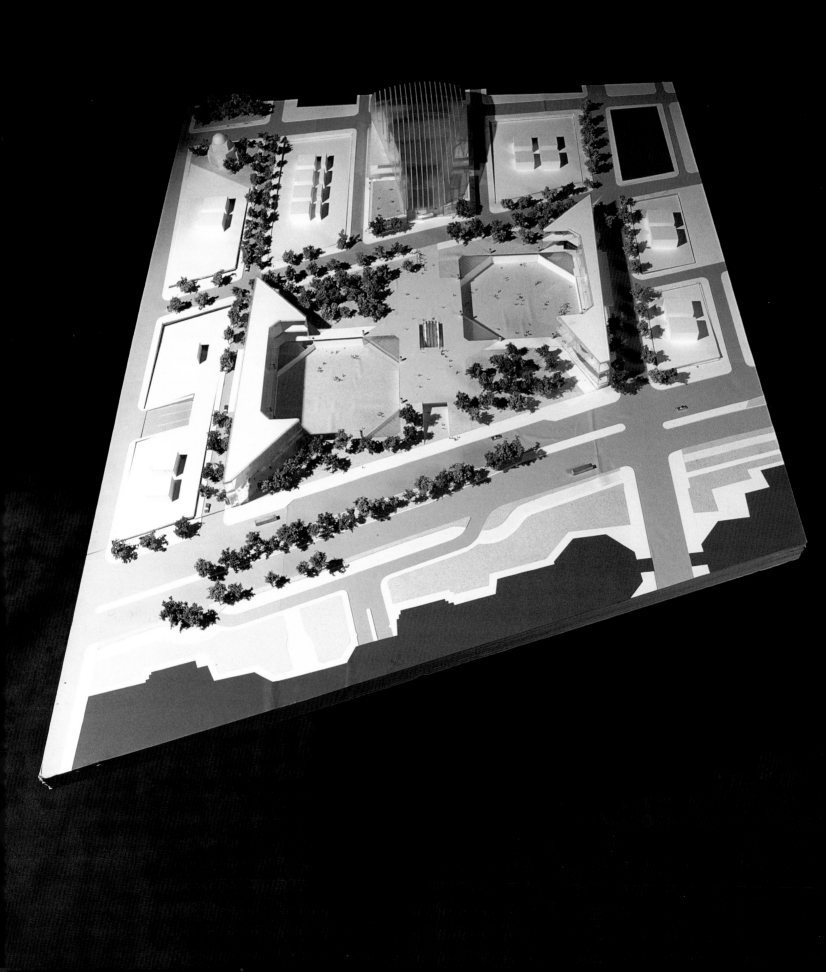

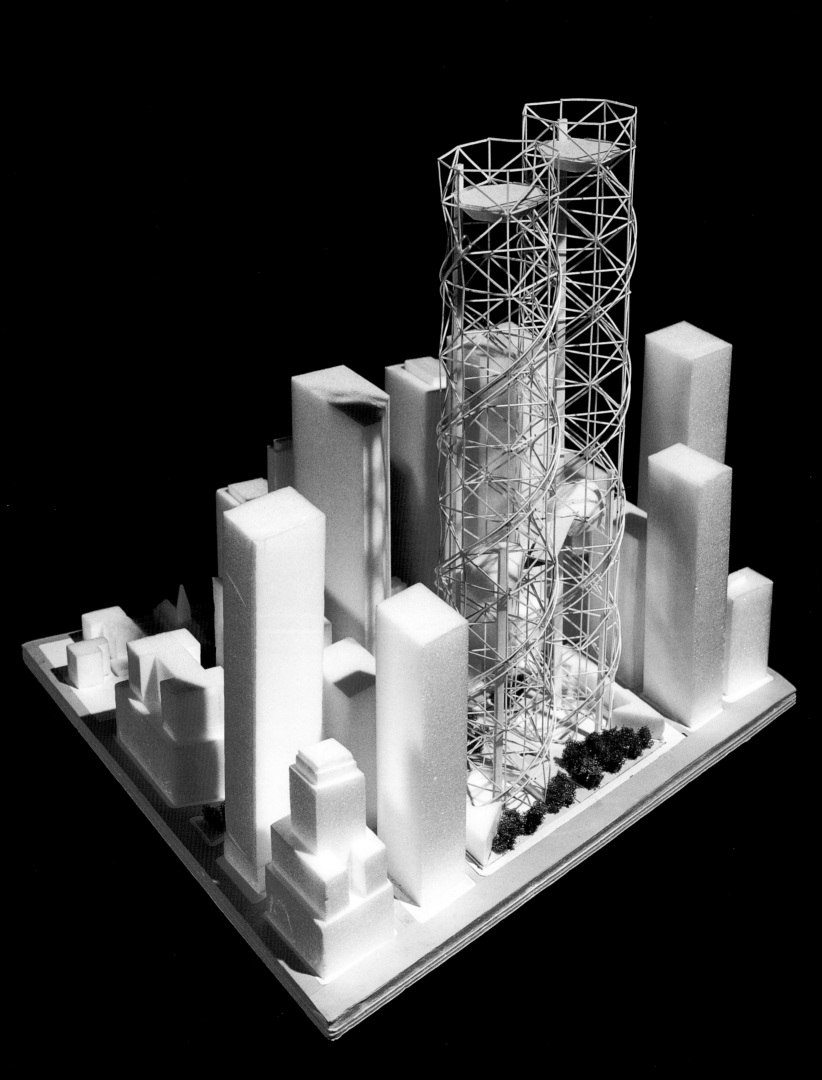

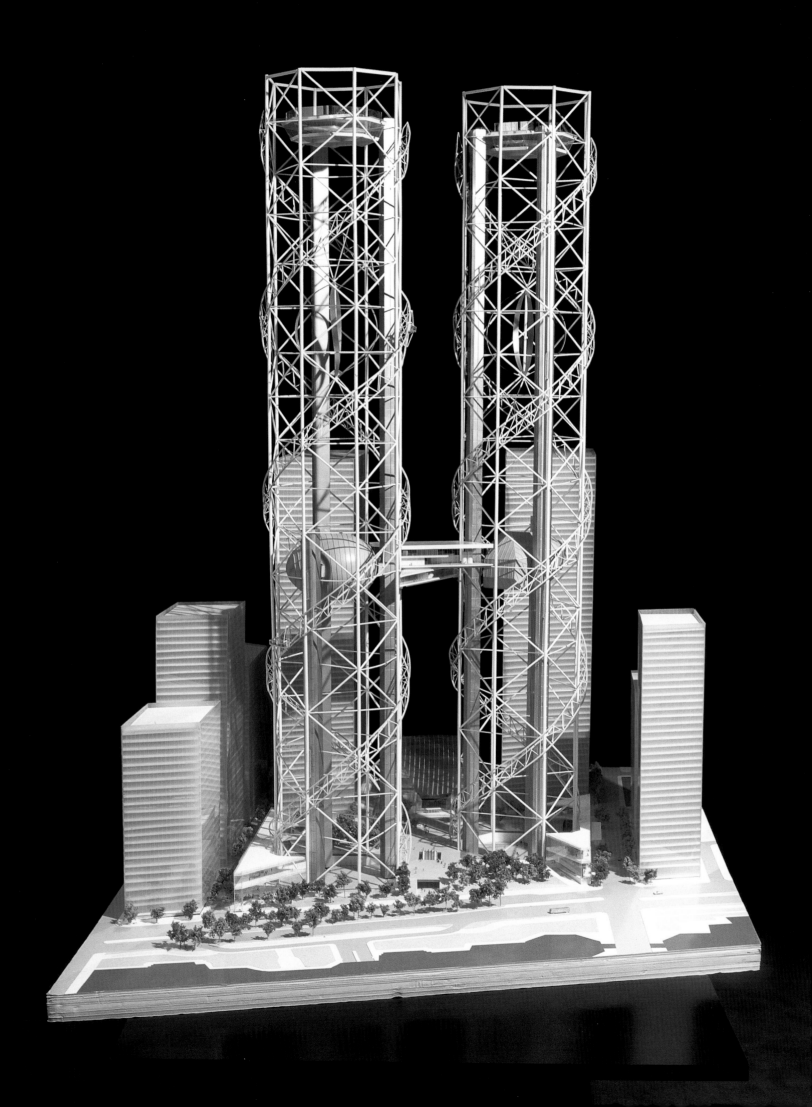

February 25, 2003

THINK frequently reiterated the LMDC's mantra: Remember Rebuild Renew. The image on this page and those on the following spread address these three essential requirements of the master plan as part of the presentation to the LMDC Steering Committee on February 25, 2003.

As noted, THINK's **World Cultural Center** towers accommodated future memorial uses in several locations. The image titled "Remember" spells out the way in which the towers will do this. At the base of the footprints and at the tops of the towers, space was allocated for public access and memorial programming. All areas including the surrounding park and plaza are associated with the future memorial.

In the following spread "Rebuild" and "Renew" are addressed by images of the two distinct, yet connected, components of the master plan. The master plan's treatment of the street grid, reintroduction of retail, new insertion of cultural uses, and establishment of the new transportation hub all are part of the rebuilding of this portion of Lower Manhattan. The monumental presence of the towers in the New York skyline would have had a symbolic value associated with renewal. THINK anticipated topping out the structure on July 4, 2006, to coincide with Independence Day.

02.25.03

Civic Alliance general meeting

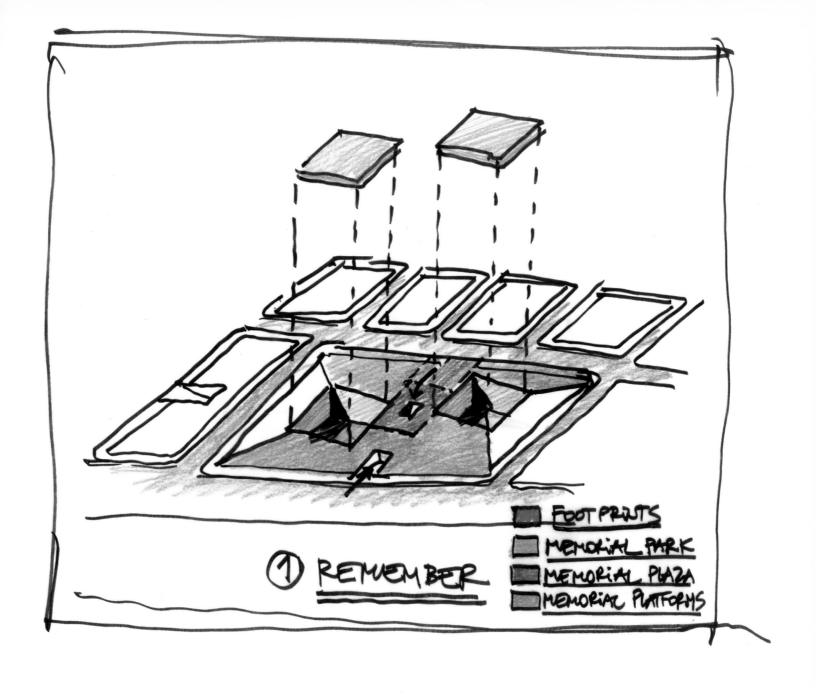

① REMEMBER

- ■ FOOT PRINTS
- ■ MEMORIAL PARK
- ■ MEMORIAL PLAZA
- ■ MEMORIAL PLATFORMS

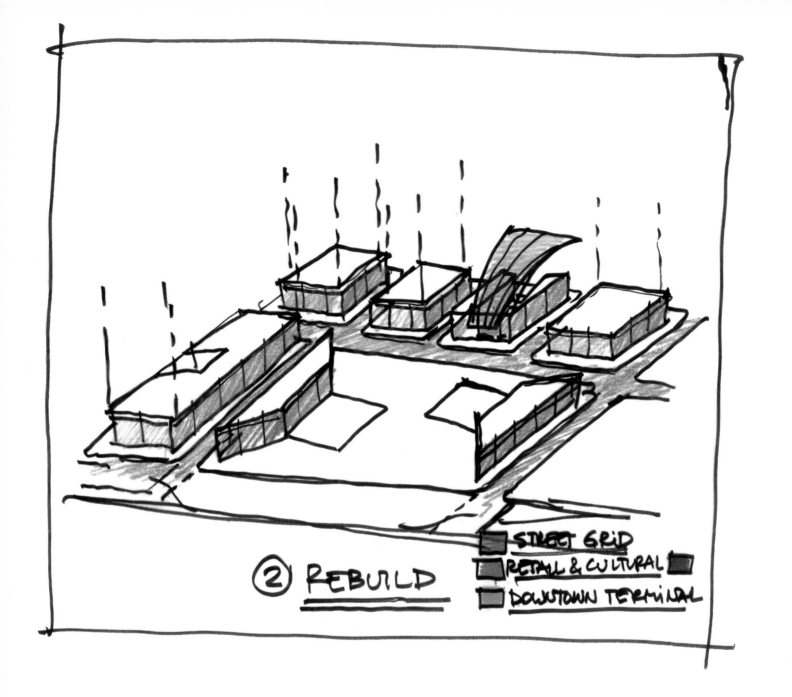

② REBUILD

■ STREET GRID
■ RETAIL & CULTURAL ■
■ DOWNTOWN TERMINAL

02.25.03

③ RENEW

LOWER MANHATTAN

JULY 4TH 2006

On February 25, 2003, THINK produced this far more refined
image of the plan.

02.25.03

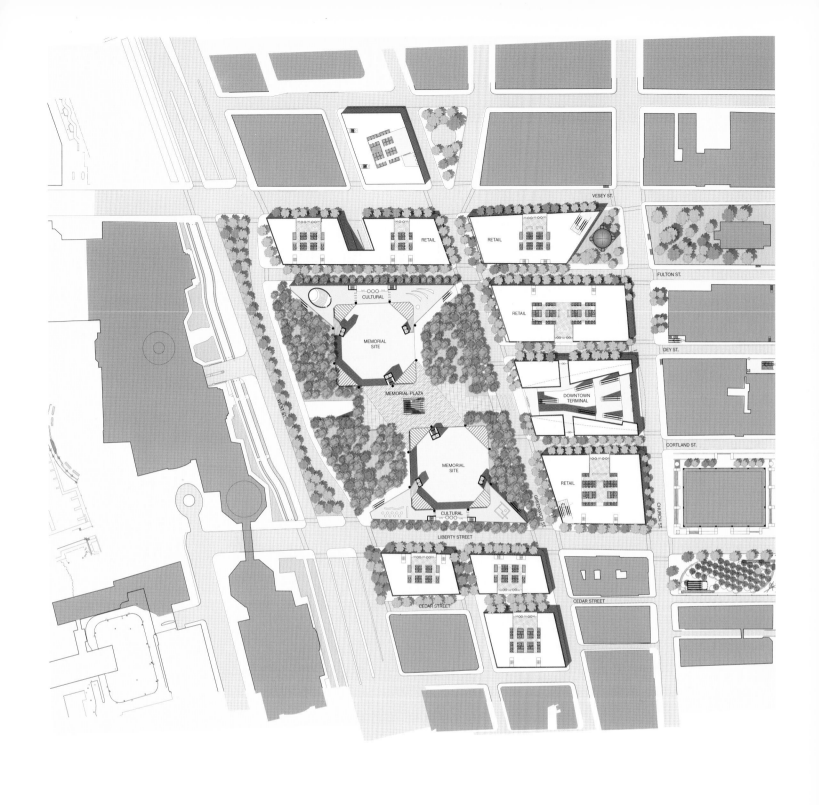

VESEY ST.

RETAIL   RETAIL

CULTURAL

RETAIL

MEMORIAL
SITE

FULTON ST.

DEY ST.

MEMORIAL PLAZA

DOWNTOWN
TERMINAL

WEST ST.

CORTLAND ST.

MEMORIAL
SITE

RETAIL

CULTURAL

GREENWICH ST.

CHURCH ST.

LIBERTY STREET

CEDAR STREET

CEDAR STREET

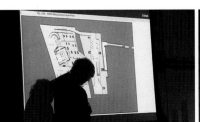
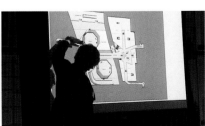
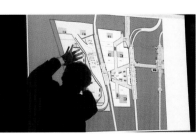

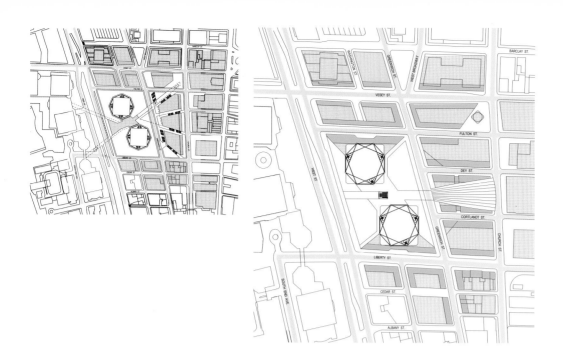

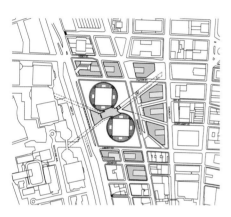

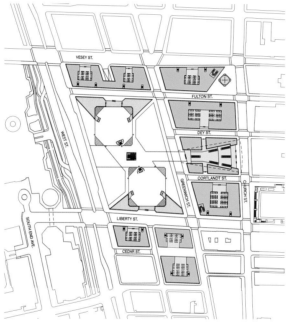

These drawings offer a comparison of the differences at various elevations between the earlier version of the **World Cultural Center** (here shown at a smaller scale) and final revised iteration. By this time, THINK has also added a significant amount of detail to these plans that address retail, frontage, the street grid, connections to the transportation hub and access to the memorial.

02.25.03

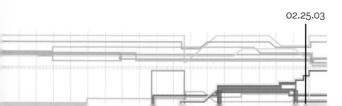

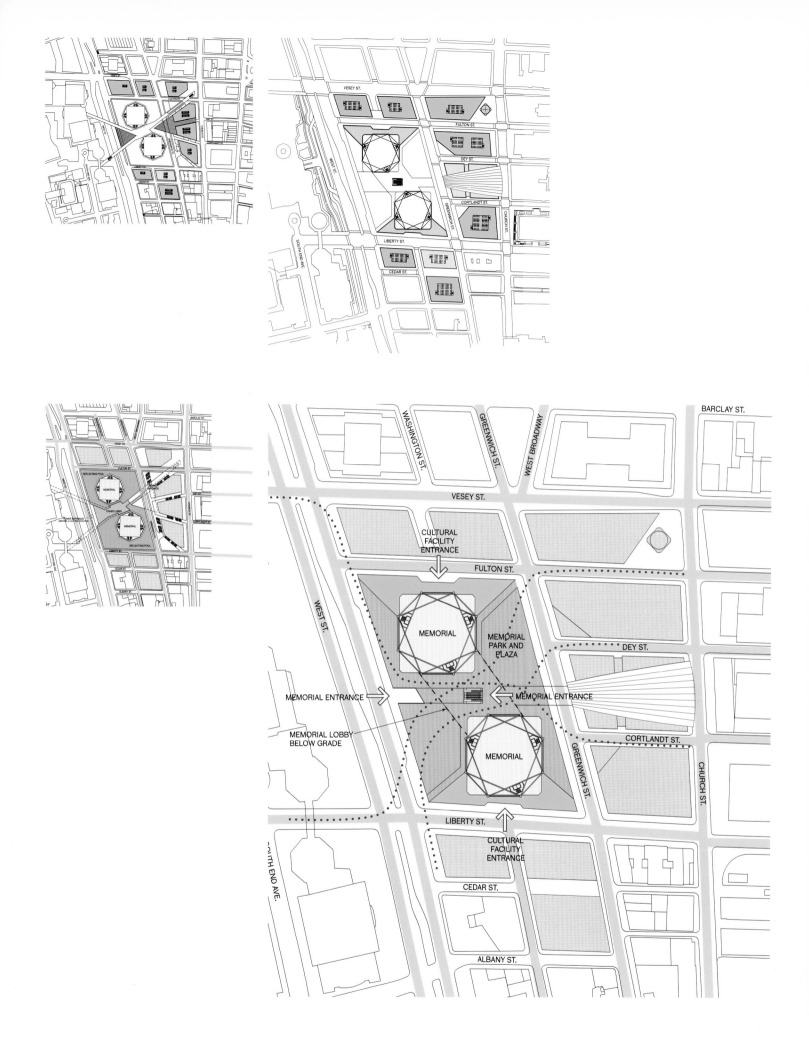

The LMDC expressed its concerns about placing structures above 40 stories within the towers. In response to this, THINK adjusted its design and placed the suggested cultural buildings at a lower elevation within the structures. These images show the revised design, including the elevators and platforms. One symbolic element that is lost in this new design is what in the December 18 plan had been the Interpretive Museum, which had been poorly received by the majority of people whose opinions were solicited. Its fluid design had sought to connect the positions where the original World Trade Center towers were damaged in the attacks of September 11.

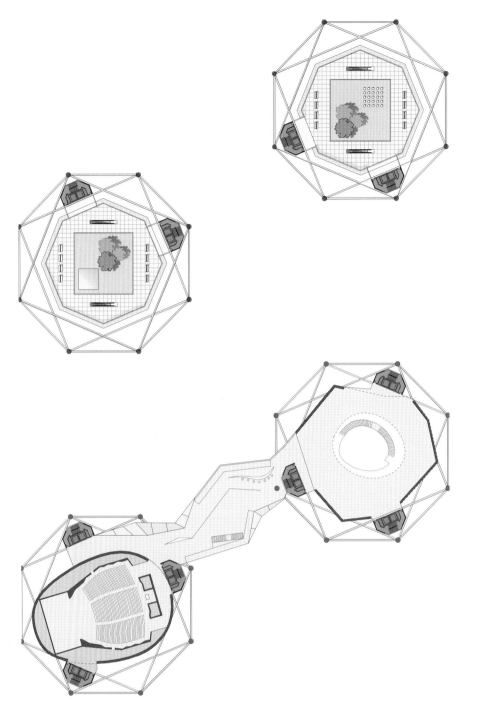

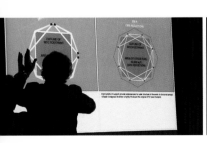

02.25.03

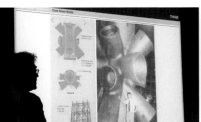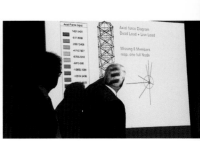

This detailed east–west section of the final master plan shows access to the memorial, security-controlled access for buses and trucks, pedestrian access between the World Financial Center to the west and the Transportation Hub to the east, and connections to the transportation infrastructure.

As THINK developed its design, more attention had to be paid to the manufacturing and construction process required for the towers. The images below show a presentation by structural engineer Jörg Schlaich. Solutions to issues concerning quality control, construction feasibility, cost and other technical aspects were detailed for the benefit of the steering committee at this meeting.

Schlaich shows a detail of the structural nodes that indicate the scale of the members. Also, the shape of these elements was specifically designed so as not to accumulate water (and therefore potentially ice, which could not only damage the structure, but also pose a threat to visitors). Once again, Schlaich explained the advantages of an on-site factory at grade, (especially concerning the welds, which would require extensive quality control efforts). The ground-level factory would have made it easier to check and X-ray the welds, as well as control for humidity and temperature—enabling a round-the-clock, all-weather construction effort.

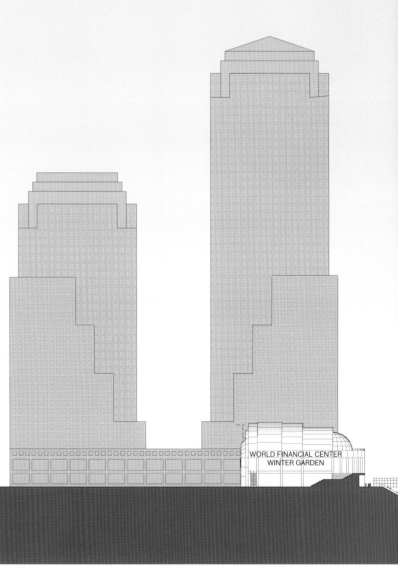

WORLD FINANCIAL CENTER
WINTER GARDEN

02.25.03

WEST
STREET

MEMORIAL PLAZA

GREENWICH
STREET

DOWNTOWN TERMINAL

CHURCH
STREET

MUSEUM

MEMORIAL LOBBY
CONCOURSE

SECURITY

TRUCK LOADING

TRUCK LOADING

N/R

CONNECTION TO NYCT

PATH MEZZANINE

BUS PARKING

FUTURE AIR TRAIN BEYOND

Comparison of construction phasing.

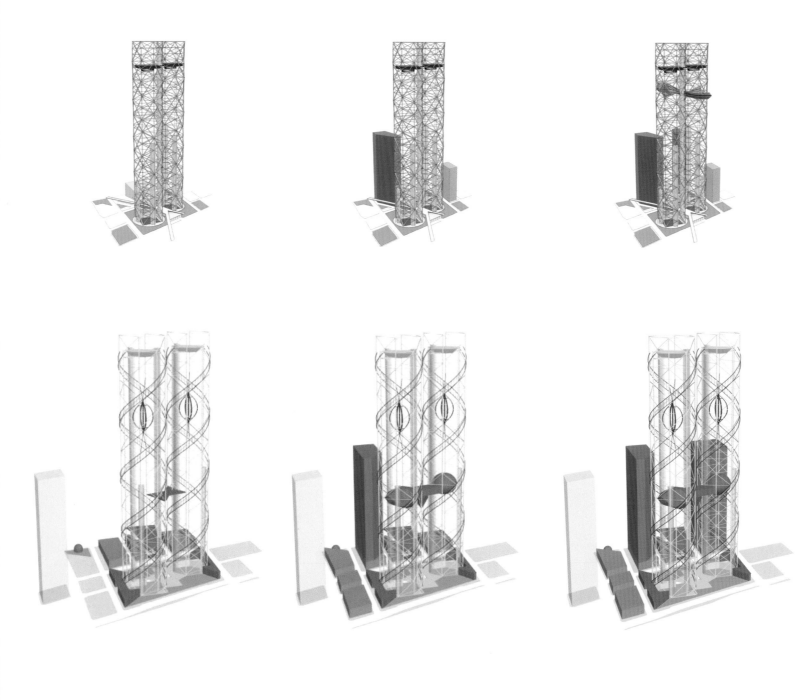

02.25.03

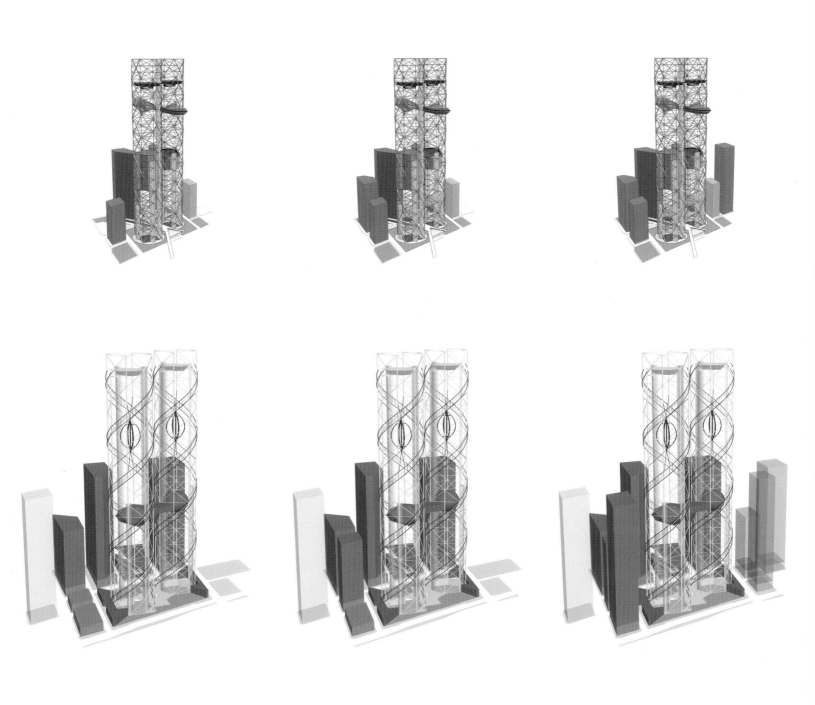

The video stills below show Peter Davoren, the President and Chief Operating Officer of Turner Construction, one of the major construction firms in New York. Before the Steering Committee, Davoren committed Turner to enter into a contract as "construction manager at risk" on the THINK towers. This meant he was prepared to guarantee that his firm would construct the project on time and on budget, including the proposed deadline of July 4, 2006 for the topping-out of the structural steel. His commitment and confidence added significant credibility to THINK's claims concerning the feasibility of the plan and schedule.

02.25.03

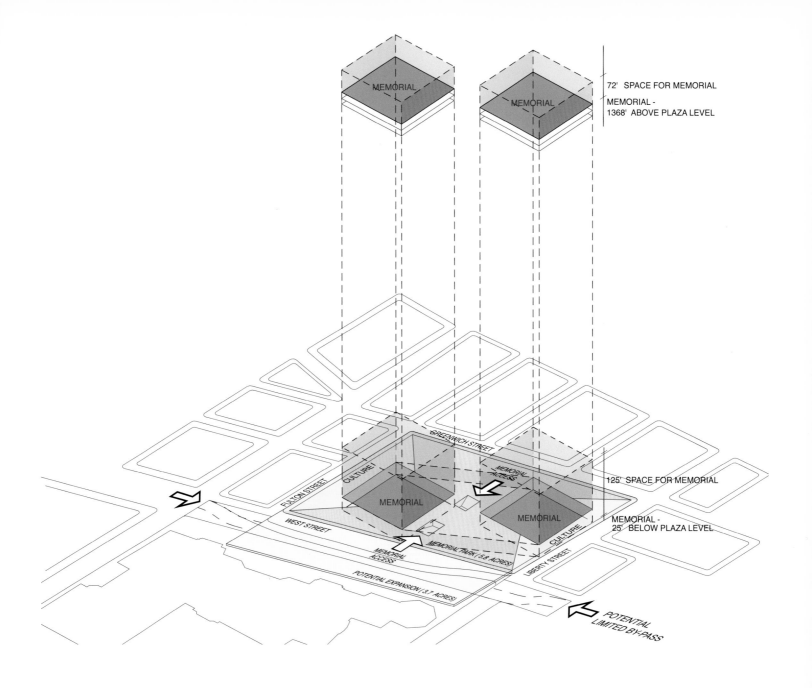

72' SPACE FOR MEMORIAL

MEMORIAL -
1368' ABOVE PLAZA LEVEL

125' SPACE FOR MEMORIAL

MEMORIAL -
25' BELOW PLAZA LEVEL

GREENWICH STREET

FULTON STREET

CULTURE

MEMORIAL ACCESS

MEMORIAL

WEST STREET

MEMORIAL ACCESS

MEMORIAL PARK (5.8 ACRES)

MEMORIAL

CULTURE

LIBERTY STREET

POTENTIAL EXPANSION (3.7 ACRES)

POTENTIAL LIMITED BY-PASS

02.25.03

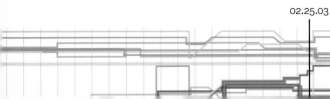

On the right, a series of sketches show the development of Viñoly's final presentation image of the funicular below.

02.25.03

Views of the footprint memorial areas from plaza level and
below grade.

02.25.03

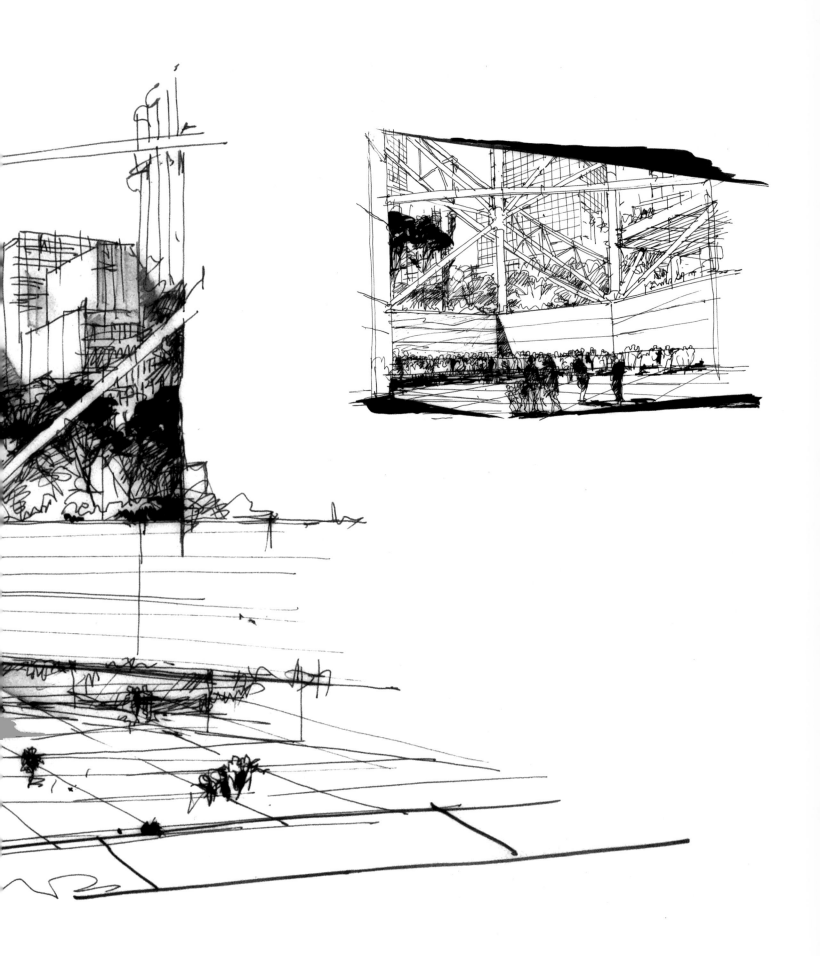

World Cultural Center

Construction :: Cost Estimate

BUILDING SYSTEM	Quantity	Unit		Unit Cost	Estimate	Intermediate Totals	CURRENT SYSTEM TOTALS
PUBLIC SPACE							
Infrastructure							$41,233,487
Rebuild Greenwich St between Vesey/Liberty							
Structure for Road	30,000	SF		$187.10	$5,613,000		
Structure above 1/9 Subway Tunnel	30,000	SF	Not Included				
Paving above 1/9 Subway Tunnel	30,000	SF		$43.37	$1,301,000		
Paving of Road	30,000	SF		$43.37	$1,301,000		
Rebuild Fulton St between Church/West							
Structure for Road	38,500	SF		$187.10	$7,203,300		
Paving of Road	38,500	SF		$43.37	$1,669,600		
Rebuild Washington between Vesey/Fulton							
Structure for Road	10,500	SF	Not Included/Bus Ramp				
Paving of Road	10,500	SF	Not Included/Bus Ramp				
Rebuild Dey between Greenwich/Church							
Structure for Road	10,900	SF		$187.10	$2,039,400		
Paving of Road	10,900	SF		$43.37	$472,700		
Rebuild Cortlandt between Greenwich/Church							
Structure for Road	9,600	SF		$187.10	$1,796,200		
Paving of Road	9,600	SF		$43.37	$416,300		
Structure Below Green Space at Base of Towers	92,500	SF		$187.10	$17,306,700		
Structure Below Green Space @Church/Fulton	12,900	SF		$187.10	$2,413,600		
Structure of Plaza between Towers at Street Level	47,800	SF		$187.10	$8,943,400		
Eliminate Structure above Bus/Truck Secure Area	(49,400)	SF		$187.10	($9,242,713)		
Site Work							$38,227,800
Reflecting Pools at Base of Towers							
Pool waterproofing, pumps	148,700	SF		Not Shown			
Structural Glass Bottom	148,700	SF		Not Shown			
Green Space at Base of Towers	92,500	SF		$154.88	$14,326,700		
Plaza between Towers at Street Level	47,800	SF		$154.88	$7,403,400		
Steps to West Street from Plaza				Not Shown			
Ramp to West Street from Plaza	10,500	SF		$154.88	$1,626,300		
Skybridges to Tower Lobby above Pool					Not Included		
Bridge from Winter Garden to Tower Lobby over Pool							
Bridge from WFC South to Tower Lobby over Pool							
Bridge from Church/Fulton to Tower Lobby over Pool							
Green Space @Church/Fulton	12,900	SF		$154.88	$1,998,000		
Perimeter Concrete Sidewalks	103,800	SF		$18.59	$1,929,200		
Perimeter Granite Curbs	5,400	LF		$105.32	$568,700		
Site Lighting	895,600	GSF		$7.43	$6,658,300		
Structural Glass Walk	12,000	SF		$309.77	$3,717,200		
Plaza Area along West Side Church St	22,550	SF		Not Shown			
Plaza along East Side Greenwich St	30,300	SF		Not Shown			
Plaza @ West Side of Building 3	30,000	SF		Not Shown			
Chapel	2,300	SF			Not Included		
Public Circulation at Level B2	271,400	SF			w/Retail		
Subtotal						$79,461,287	
PUBLIC SPACE							$79,461,287

PUBLIC SPACE $ 79,461,287

TOWER COST, PAINTED STEEL $ 384,630,200

TOTAL CONSTRUCT COST $ 464,091,487

02.25.03

TOWERS OF CULTURE						
Structure						$251,550,100
3-D Truss Structure (Two Towers)	48,000	TONS	$4,000.00	$192,000,000		
Exterior Painted Finish on Trusses	48,000	TONS	$300.00	$14,400,000		
Painted Steel Egress Stairs				w/3-D Truss Structure		
Foundations	15,000	CY	$826.05	$12,390,700		
Hoisting	$327,594,100	LS	10.00%	$32,759,400		
Services						$133,080,100
Interior Paritions				w/Program Space Fitout		
Vertical Transportation	16	EA	$1,032,557.71	$16,520,900		
Shaftwall/Enclosure	776,000	SF	$77.44	$60,094,900		
Mechanical Systems	68,000	SF	$55.76	$3,791,600		
Plumbing	68,000	SF	$58.24	$3,960,100		
Plumbing Riser	3,330	LF	$1,100.00	$3,663,000		
Fire Protection	68,000	SF	$42.13	$2,864,700		
Fire Protection Riser	3,330	LF	$1,100.00	$3,663,000		
HVAC Systems				w/Program Space Fitout		
HVAC Chilled Water Riser	3,330	LF	$2,500.00	$8,325,000		
Electrical-Building Feeders	3,330	LF	$750.88	$2,500,400		
Electrical-Lighting & Distribution At Public Area	68,000	SF	$24.78	$1,685,100		
Electrical -Top of House Sub Station	2	LS	$867,348.48	$1,734,700		
Electrical -Elevator Power	8	EA	$154,883.66	$1,239,100		
Electrical -Stair Lighting	400	EA	$24,781.39	$9,912,600		
Electrical-Emergency Power	2	LS	$1,239,069.26	$2,478,100		
Electrical-Fire Alarm	3,300	LF	$371.72	$1,226,700		
Electrical-HVAC Power	2	LS	$309,767.31	$619,500		
Electrical-Communications Empty Conduit Risers	3,300	LF	$526.60	$1,737,800		
Electrical-Security System	2	ALLOW	$619,534.63	$1,239,100		
Electrical-Building Illumination	64	EA	$29,043.78	$1,858,800		
Electrical-Roof Lighting	80	EA	$23,232.55	$1,858,600		
Electrical-FAA Top of Building Lights	2	LS	$123,906.93	$247,800		
Electrical-Lightning Protection System	2	LS	$929,301.94	$1,858,600		
Subtotal					$384,630,200	
TOWERS OF CULTURE						$384,630,200
SUB TOTAL:				$464,091,487	$464,091,487	$464,091,487
DESIGN CONTINGENCY (5%)						INCLUDED ABOVE
CONSTRUCTION CONTINGENCY						NOT INCLUDED
TOTAL: DIRECT COST						$464,091,487
SUBCONTRACTOR BOND						INCLUDED ABOVE
GENERAL CONTRATOR BOND						INCLUDED ABOVE
GENERAL CONDITIONS & FEE						INCLUDED ABOVE
GENERAL LIABILITY AND INSURANCE						INCLUDED ABOVE
SUBTOTAL						
ESCALATION						INCLUDED ABOVE
TOTAL CONSTRUCTION COST						$464,091,487

PUBLIC SPACE $ 79,461,287

TOWER COST, STAINLESS STEEL $ 415,630,200

TOTAL CONSTRUCT COST $ 494,091,487

These spreadsheets detail the cost of constructing the World Cultural Center Towers in painted steel. The two summaries above compare that cost to a stainless steel option. While the stainless steel scenario was more expensive, it would have produced structures requiring far less maintenance and therefore lower costs over the long term.

Frederic Schwartz and Rafael Viñoly show the models of the revised towers to a television crew. THINK would opt not to bring these large models to the final presentations at the LMDC due to the restricted dimensions of the room used for that presentation. THINK determined that it would only be appropriate to show the models if they could be raised on plinths and therefore, allow their audience to experience them appropriately as buildings by being able to see them from below. This would have been impossible in a room with only 8-foot ceilings.

02.25.03

February 26, 2003

On February 26, 2003, *The New York Times* reported that THINK's design was preferred by the LMDC over that of Studio Daniel Libeskind. However, the paper also noted that Governor George Pataki and Mayor Michael Bloomberg were leaning toward the work of Libeskind.

That same day, the LMDC and the master planning teams met for the last time prior to the agency's decision in an impromptu meeting that was scheduled that morning—a surprise to the principals of THINK who had understood that the February 25 meeting was to be the last presentation and had planned finally to rest on February 26. THINK presumed that this additional meeting was a perfunctory one for the VIPs in attendance, Governor George Pataki and Mayor Michael Bloomberg.

02.26.03

LMDC reported by *NY Times* to support **THINK**, "Panel Supports 2 Tall Towers at Disaster Site," by Edward Wyatt.

Julie Iovine's "Turning a Competition into a Public Campaign".

Designers' Dreams, Tempered By Reality

By HERBERT MUSCHAMP

The decision on who will redesign the World Trade Center site is expected to be announced later this week. Both finalists, Studio Daniel Libeskind and Think, a team led by Rafael Viñoly, Frederic Schwartz, Shigeru Ban and Ken Smith, have extensively revised their plans at the request of the Lower Manhattan Development Corporation.

The Libeskind plan originally specified that most of the so-called bathtub, the sunken area enclosed within the concrete retaining walls of the World Trade Center, be used for a mix of cultural purposes. Much of that area, however, has since been claimed by the Port Authority's decision to build a major transportation hub within the retaining walls. This would leave only a marginal portion of the site to be used as the Libeskind team had planned. It would also substantially diminish that plan's architectural strength.

The most significant change required of the Think team was the reduction of the elevated platforms originally intended for cultural uses. As now envisioned, a museum would be between the 30th- and 35th-floor levels of the two 110-story towers of

---

Less room in trough and towers for cultural uses.

---

steel lattice. Observation platforms would be at the summits of the towers. The platforms originally designed for other cultural uses have been eliminated, diminishing the plan's vitality as a cultural center. Officials of the development corporation said it would be impossible to ensure construction on higher platforms after the museum was built.

Yet even the revised designs cannot be considered final. As is the case with many competitions for major building projects, the steering committee will be choosing a team of architects, not a completed design. Further design development is contingent on the framing of an architectural program: the precise mix of uses that the buildings will contain. An outline for a proposed program could be released as early as tomorrow.

The plans of both finalists call for incremental development, with new office buildings, designed by different architects, that would be constructed as market demand dictates. Thus we may not get a complete picture of what ground zero will look like until a decade from now.

For now, development corporation officials remain committed to realizing the core concepts of whichever plan is chosen. The composition of the corporation's board will undoubtedly change with time, however, as will the agency's mission. City officials are likely to assume more substantial representation. The position of Larry Silverstein, leaseholder of the World Trade Center site, will remain unclear pending the outcome

Continued on Page 5

Photographs by Joyce Dopkeen/The New York Times

Daniel Libeskind, a finalist in the design competition for ground zero, talking to reporters.

Rafael Viñoly of the Think Team discussing its design after the finalists were announced.

Turning a Competition Into a Public Campaign

Finalists for Ground Zero Design Pull Out the Stops

By JULIE V. IOVINE

Packed meetings at Town Hall, get-out-the-vote e-mails and head-to-head chats with Charlie Rose may not be as rugged and ritualized as photo-ops in the South Bronx, but in many ways the architects proposing designs for the World Trade Center site have been acting like media-age politicians.

The two finalists from an original pack of seven design teams — Daniel Libeskind from Berlin and Rafael Viñoly and Frederic Schwartz, the two front men on the Think team — grasped the political nature of the selection process from the start, playing straight to the public as if the citizens of New York City themselves were the clients for the job.

With talk of truth and beauty, memory and monument, these architects have been selling themselves like movie stars. They have hired publicists, been hosts of mini-salons for journalists and well-wishers at the Odeon bar and the Four Seasons Hotel, raved about their foot and eye wear in print and made presentations to any civic or cultural

group that would have them. Not since Gary Cooper appeared in "The Fountainhead" has the public been so riveted by architecture and architects.

"Usually, it's the client in the lead orchestrating the media and managing the political situation," said Robert Ivy, the editor in chief of Architectural Record magazine. "But in the absence of a strong client and with an ad hoc political entity acting as developer, it has fallen to the architects."

It has been 10 weeks since kickoff at the Winter Garden, where the highly orchestrated presentation of architectural designs for rebuilding at ground zero was as widely televised as any national convention. Since then stops along the campaign trail have included the quiet resignation of key members of one team, Skidmore, Owings & Merrill, under the cloud of conflict of interest (the firm was already working for the developer Larry Silverstein); a profile of Mr. Libeskind in The New York Observer and regular appearances by Mr. Schwartz on New York Tonight, a cable program on New York One. On Monday, the finalists appeared on the Oprah Winfrey show. Richard Kahan, the former chief

Continued on Page 5

Let culture soar at Ground Zero

By RICHARD MEIER

It has been a privilege for me to play a significant role in the critical and highly publicized debates over the future architecture at Ground Zero. My involvement — in collaboration with Peter Eisenman, Charles Gwathmey and Steven Holl, in the Lower Manhattan Development Corp.'s Innovative Design Study — has given me an intimate perspective on an extraordinary process.

Considering the emotional and logistical complexity of this project, it is remarkable that we have come this far in such a short period of time.

As we approach the day for choosing the architectural team that will proceed, we should remember that a great opportunity has been born of the horrors of 9/11 — an opportunity to reassert our deep beliefs in the values of freedom, diversity, education, creativity and the hope for a better future.

This is a pivotal moment in the history of our city, our nation and the world. Whatever we construct on this intensely symbolic site will be interpreted through the lens of that traumatic day and its persistent echoes in our hearts and minds. It is critical that we transcend raw emotion and focus on what it means to live, work and create in New York City and reassert our leadership as citizens of the world.

We will rebuild at Ground Zero, and we will remember the 2,998 lives that were lost. But we also must look forward to a day and a place where the creative energies of the whole world will be allowed to flourish and grow. For architects, the response to 9/11 should not simply be to enshrine the memory of violence. It should be to reaffirm the belief that culture and learning are the best responses to the tyranny of ignorance and hatred.

The design team THINK has proposed a sensitive and uplifting concept called the World Cultural Center. Its focus on culture as an engine of economic renewal in lower Manhattan is sensible when you consider the depressed real estate market, the lack of cultural facilities in the area and Mayor Bloomberg's vision for a vibrant residential community downtown.

The THINK scheme provides an open framework — open to incremental commercial development, to an unconstrained memorial design competition, to evolving ideas about a cultural program and to the work and ideas of other architects, not only on designated commercial parcels but also in the cultural buildings that could exist within the design's latticed towers.

The team has resisted the temptation to design the whole project. It has provided two frameworks on which the future of Ground Zero can be determined over time.

The horizontal framework of the restored street grid encourages pedestrian circulation throughout the site to create a vibrant street life.

The vertical framework of the open towers captures the still vivid memory of loss but also allows for evolution in the future. The towers are elegant structures whose imaginative design complements their poetic conception, elevating culture to iconic status while restoring the skyline.

The THINK team is operating on the assumption that we should act while the public continues to be the driving force behind this process. I agree that we have a responsibility to put the long-term public interests — art, music, performance, learning and new types of public pro-

The THINK group's model for the WTC site.

grams that we have yet to imagine — above everything else.

If the proposal's core concepts prevail, in two years they may begin to fill the void with life, memory, beauty and creative expression. What more fitting testament to memory and hope?

Meier is a recipient of the Pritzker Prize, architecture's highest honor, and the architect of the Getty Center in California, the City Hall and Central Library in the Hague, Netherlands, and the soon-to-be-completed Jubilee Church in Rome.

02.26.03

Architect Richard Meier expressed his views on the master plan for Ground Zero in an opinion piece in the *New York Daily News* on February 26, 2003. Meier endorsed the THINK plan.

Below are images of a book specially prepared by the LMDC for its outgoing President, Lou Thompson. On a page in this volume containing a drawing by THINK, Rafael Viñoly inscribed: "To Lou: Who has proven that public service is an Art." In part, the tight schedule of the design competition had been determined by Thompson's desire not only to serve on the LMDC board but also to return to retirement by March 2003.

That afternoon, THINK was to receive the final word from the LMDC. At this time, THINK's principals were somewhat concerned about their chances of being selected by the LMDC to move forward with the master plan. The governor and the mayor had been especially unresponsive during the final presentation.

Also on the crucial day of February 26, *The Wall Street Journal*
ran a piece on Rafael Viñoly that reported other people's
unflattering characterizations of the architect's professional
accomplishments during the period of military regimes in
Argentina in the 1960s and 1970s.

02.26.03

THE PROPERTY REPO

Ground Zero Finalist's Past Draws Questions

Argentine Architect's Work For Junta Emerges as Issue As Trade-Center Plan Gains

By Jess Bravin

When Argentina's military junta needed someone to design major structures for soccer's 1978 World Cup, it turned to a brilliant young architect named Rafael Viñoly. Just 33 years old, he already had built offices for the national Chamber of Deputies, as well as housing projects, bank buildings and other impressive works throughout the country.

For the junta, a diplomatic pariah because of its ruthless repression of political dissent, the World Cup was a propaganda opportunity to claim international legitimacy. For Mr. Viñoly, it was the opportunity to showcase his talent before a world-wide audience.

Tomorrow, Mr. Viñoly could be awarded a project of even greater significance: His plan is one of two finalists to fill Ground Zero, where the World Trade Center stood before its destruction by terrorists. Although Mr. Viñoly's entry has won acclaim, his past association with one of South America's most brutal regimes is raising questions among dissidents.

Some say Mr. Viñoly hasn't been forthright about his activities in the 1970s, particularly after recent newspaper profiles suggested that he came to the U.S. to escape persecution. The agency responsible for selecting the Ground Zero finalists, the Lower Manhattan Development Corp., says it was unaware that Mr. Viñoly had worked for the junta. A spokesman, Matthew Higgins, says the agency plans now to ask Mr. Viñoly for further information.

Mr. Viñoly, now 58, says he hasn't hidden his past. He wrote in a compendium of his architecture published this month of being "co-opted" by the military regime and in a "state of denial" over its crimes. No one has suggested the architect supported the junta's politics, much less its campaign in which as many as 30,000 people disappeared. He left Argentina in 1979 for New York, where, over two decades, he earned recognition as a visionary architect.

Some dissidents say these ambiguities should be resolved before the award is made in New York. "It's important not to allow misrepresentations," says Juan Mendez, a lawyer who was tortured by the junta and today heads the Center for Civil and Human Rights at the University of Notre Dame in Indiana. After a Jan. 22 article in the New York Times—in which some of Mr. Viñoly's

remarks suggest he is a victim of persecution—one dissident sent an e-mail to Mr. Viñoly praising his design but accusing him of reinventing his past. "Inexplicably for someone of your sensitivity and intelligence, you humiliated everybody who knows you," wrote Rolando Epstein, a former architect and a producer of the movie "The Official Story," set during the Argentine military regime.

The team Mr. Viñoly headed, called Think, proposed two latticework towers that would soar over Ground Zero. His competitor, Studio Daniel Libeskind, offered a plan centering on an open trench that remains unfilled to recall the devastation of Sept. 11. The competition for perhaps the 21st century's most symbolic building has been intense and personal.

Mr. Viñoly and Mr. Libeskind have been promoting their designs on "Oprah" and the "Today Show." Much has been made of Mr. Libeskind's link to projects that touch on war and repression such as the Jewish Museum in Berlin, and he often raises his background as a son of Holocaust survivors.

In an interview, Mr. Viñoly said he left Argentina for a combination of personal and professional reasons. He said he was attracted by opportunities in New York, and that several revelations made him unable to stomach further work for the regime, which overthrew President Isabel Peron in 1976.

In "Rafael Viñoly," just published in the U.S., Mr. Viñoly describes outmaneuvering rivals to win the World Cup project. He was chauffeured to work by military escort, and, he says, enjoyed the fruits of success—"a huge house, a boat, a practice with 75 people." He designed a soccer stadium

Rafael Viñoly's *design, one of two finalists for rebuilding at Ground Zero*

and the broadcast center for the government-run network known as ATC.

But soon thereafter, he says, he had misgivings. He was moved, he says, by an article on the conductor Bruno Walter, who left Germany in 1933 rather than work under the Nazi regime. Mr. Viñoly said he met with Marshall Meyer, an American-born rabbi and human-rights activist in Argentina. Mr. Viñoly says the rabbi showed him documentation that a friend, a leftist philosophy professor, had been taken away and secretly killed.

Mr. Viñoly says Mr. Meyer helped him secure a visa to the U.S. Mr. Viñoly's wife and child are Jewish, and the junta was known for its anti-Semitism. After the police searched his own library looking for

subversive books, Mr. Viñoly says he realized that no one was above suspicion.

"People who are trying to achieve something they consider important often find room in their ethical framework to excuse many things," he writes in "Rafael Viñoly." "You can be corrupt; you can pay bribes," to get ahead, "but working for murderers was too great a contradiction." Another dissident, Hector Timerman, says he dined with Mr. Viñoly at the expensive Palm restaurant shortly after his arrival in New York and that the architect "never mentioned any reason for his move to New York" other than work.

The New York Times profile, which described him as fleeing persecution "with little more than a suitcase," quotes him as saying: "The World Trade Center project made me rehash all these things that happened 30 years ago in a very powerful way." Asked about the assertions, Mr. Viñoly now says he arrived with more than $40,000 and had properties in Argentina, and that there was no specific way his experiences there affected his Ground Zero design. He says after hearing from concerned Argentines, he realized the article "could be misconstrued," but has not sought a published clarification.

A Feb. 25 Los Angeles Times profile also omits his association with the junta, saying only that he left because he "found himself working in an increasingly authoritative and oppressive society."

The result "makes you believe he was a freedom fighter or something like that, which he certainly wasn't," says Mr. Epstein. (Several years ago, the two had a falling out over an architecture project.) Mr. Viñoly replied to Mr. Epstein's e-mail by saying "there is nothing further from the truth" than that "I'm trying to pass as a martyr—which I never was."

Panel Supports 2 Tall Towers At Disaster Site

But Mayor and Governor Favor the Rival Proposal

By EDWARD WYATT

A key committee recommended yesterday that Lower Manhattan be rebuilt along the lines of a plan that had seemed out of favor, a proposal by the Think architectural team for two soaring latticework towers as the centerpiece of a memorial area. The unexpected decision appeared to set the stage for a showdown today among city and state officials.

In the last two weeks, Gov. George E. Pataki and Mayor Michael R. Bloomberg had expressed support for the other finalist plan, by Studio Daniel Libeskind, which features an excavated pit on the site of the former World Trade Center towers.

But The Associated Press reported that Mr. Pataki, when asked yesterday if he had a favorite, said that he did, but then refused to say what it was. "The mayor and I are going to be talking about that this week," Mr. Pataki said. The final choice is to be announced tomorrow.

The group that made the recommendation yesterday, the site planning committee of the board of the Lower Manhattan Development Corporation, acted after a four-hour meeting at which the seven committee members reviewed the architects' revisions

---

Rebuilding officials challenge the politicians who appointed them.

to their plans for the trade center site, according to people involved in discussions about the designs.

The committee's preference is not binding on a broader group of rebuilding officials who will meet today to decide whether to select the Think plan or the Libeskind plan. But the committee's move represents a direct challenge to Mr. Pataki and Mr. Bloomberg, who now face a choice of following or rejecting the recommendation of the people they appointed to the rebuilding effort.

That broader group includes officials from the development corporation, the governor's office, the mayor's office and the Port Authority of New York and New Jersey, which owns the trade center site.

The committee's action yesterday reflects a vigorous lobbying effort by Roland W. Betts, a director of the development corporation, who has been leading both the site-planning committee and the broader rebuilding steering committee.

"It's going to be a close one," a director of the development corporation said yesterday following the meeting. "It could simply come down to how the governor and the mayor feel."

Mr. Pataki and Mr. Bloomberg are scheduled to be briefed on the final plans of the

Continued on Page B6

Panel Supports 2 Tall Towers For the Former Trade Center Site

Continued From Page B1

two architecture teams this afternoon. After those briefings, the eight-member steering committee will meet to agree on a winning design, and its decision will be announced tomorrow morning at a press conference at the World Financial Center's Winter Garden, which overlooks ground zero.

Several people involved in the rebuilding process said they remained uncertain about which way the decision would go. But one member of the committee that recommended the Think plan yesterday, who spoke on the condition of anonymity, said several committee members believe that the mayor and the governor should pay heed to their preference.

"We don't expect anyone to overrule us," the committee member said.

The members of the steering committee are Mr. Betts; John C. Whitehead, the chairman of the development corporation; Louis R. Tomson, the corporation's president; Charles Kushner and Anthony J. Sartor, directors of the Port Authority; Joseph J. Seymour, executive director of the Port Authority; Diana Taylor, deputy secretary to Mr. Pataki; and Daniel E. Doctoroff, the deputy mayor for economic development and rebuilding.

People involved in yesterday's meetings said much of the discussion focused on the revisions proposed by the two teams. The Think team, which originally planned to make its latticework towers of forged steel, now plans to build the towers of stainless steel, making them far lighter, according to people who have been briefed on the plan.

That change could address a primary concern of Port Authority engineers, who previously said the towers would be too heavy to be support-

NEW HORIZONS FOR ARCHITECTS

Finalists campaign for their ground zero designs, as political reality tempers their dreams. Articles in The Arts, Page E1.

ed in their proposed location — directly above the rebuilt PATH station at the trade center site.

It also reduces the expected cost of the design, which according to estimates released by the development corporation was at least $800 million, far more than the $330 million estimate for the Libeskind plan. One official said that the revisions make the plans approximately equal in cost.

The Think team, led by Rafael Viñoly, Frederic Schwartz, Ken Smith and Shigeru Ban, also agreed to alter the cultural components of their design, lowering a proposed museum from the 85th floor to about the 30th floor of the towers.

The museum would be built within the latticework so that it appeared to be suspended within the towers. But many rebuilding officials objected to the original proposal, saying that placing the tower so high would present engineering problems and discourage visitors who might fear another attack on an occupied portion of the buildings.

The Libeskind team also made changes to its plan, agreeing to raise the level of the pit that would serve as the site of the memorial to the victims of the 9/11 attack. It was originally designed to be 70 feet below ground, at the level of bedrock. Mr. Libeskind's revised design has the pit about 30 feet below ground level. Below it would be mechanical and electrical systems for the PATH station and, perhaps, a bus parking area to serve visitors to the memorial.

02.26.03

During the afternoon of February 26, Rafael Viñoly receives the telephone call from Lou Thompson on behalf of the LMDC informing him that THINK has not been selected to proceed with the master plan.

On February 28, 2003, *The New York Times* reports
the February 27 announcement by the LMDC of the
competition results at a special event at the Winter Garden.
Daniel Libeskind had been selected as master planner for
Ground Zero.

The New York Times

"All the News That's Fit to Print"

Late Edition

VOL. CLII...No. 52,408   NEW YORK, FRIDAY, FEBRUARY 28, 2003   ONE

Daniel Libeskind, whose design for the trade center site was named yesterday as the competition's winner.

Pentagon Contradicts General On Iraq Occupation Force's Size

Democrats Demand Estimates of Cost of a War

By ERIC SCHMITT

PRACTICAL ISSUES FOR GROUND ZERO

Politics and Economics Figure in Choice of Renewal Plan

By EDWARD WYATT

NASA Pressed on When Officials Learned of E-Mail About Shuttle

By KENNETH CHANG and RICHARD A. OPPEL Jr.

Hearing War Drums, Iraqis Still March to Their Own Beat

By NEIL MacFARQUHAR

BAGHDAD, Feb. 27 —

"IN PRINCIPLE AGREES TO D FORBIDDEN M

SECURITY COUNC

Inspector to Report
Response on Dis
Has Been 'Very'

By PATRICK E.
with FELICITY BA

Terrorism Al Is Lowered

Mister Rogers, TV's Fr For Children, Is Dea

INSIDE

A Shift on Drug Benefits

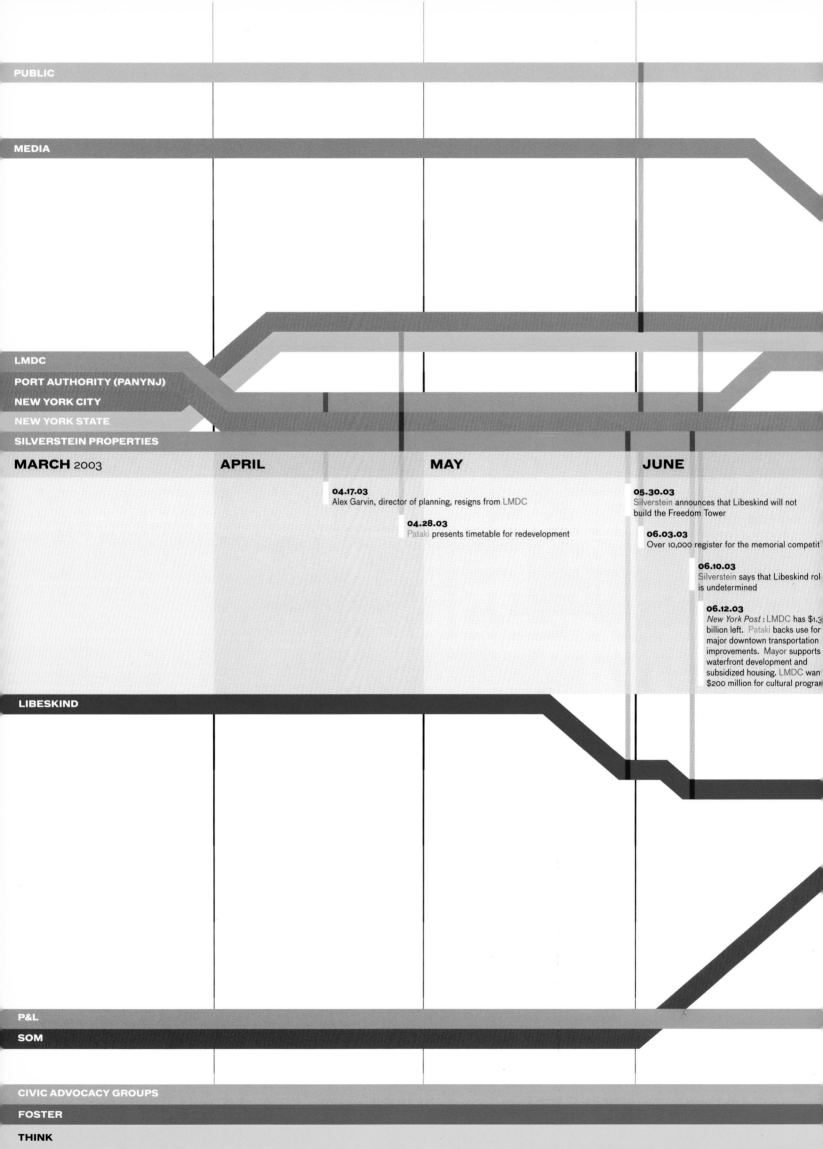

PUBLIC

MEDIA

LMDC
PORT AUTHORITY (PANYNJ)
NEW YORK CITY
NEW YORK STATE
SILVERSTEIN PROPERTIES

MARCH 2003   **APRIL**   **MAY**   **JUNE**

04.17.03
Alex Garvin, director of planning, resigns from LMDC

04.28.03
Pataki presents timetable for redevelopment

05.30.03
Silverstein announces that Libeskind will not
build the Freedom Tower

06.03.03
Over 10,000 register for the memorial competit

06.10.03
Silverstein says that Libeskind rol
is undetermined

06.12.03
New York Post : LMDC has $1.3
billion left. Pataki backs use for
major downtown transportation
improvements. Mayor supports
waterfront development and
subsidized housing. LMDC wan
$200 million for cultural progra

LIBESKIND

P&L

SOM

CIVIC ADVOCACY GROUPS

FOSTER

THINK

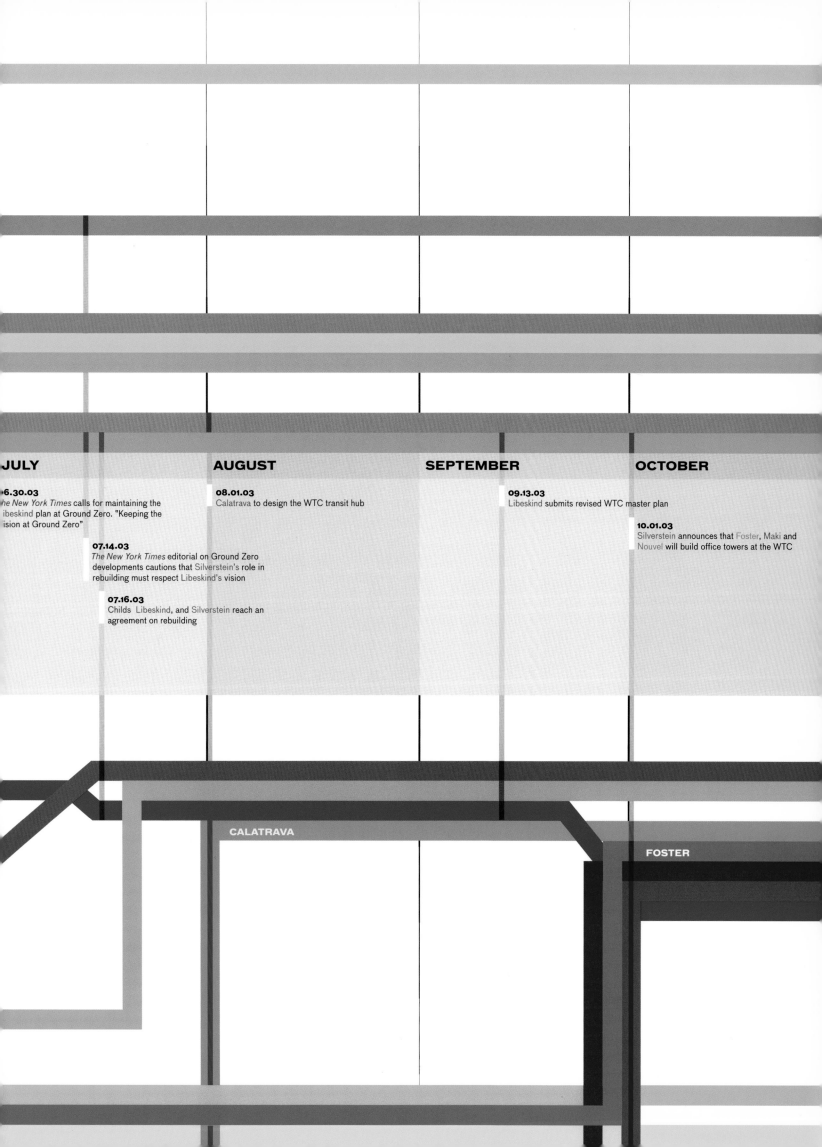

JULY

06.30.03
The New York Times calls for maintaining the Libeskind plan at Ground Zero. "Keeping the Vision at Ground Zero"

07.14.03
The New York Times editorial on Ground Zero developments cautions that Silverstein's role in rebuilding must respect Libeskind's vision

07.16.03
Childs Libeskind, and Silverstein reach an agreement on rebuilding

AUGUST

08.01.03
Calatrava to design the WTC transit hub

SEPTEMBER

09.13.03
Libeskind submits revised WTC master plan

OCTOBER

10.01.03
Silverstein announces that Foster, Maki and Nouvel will build office towers at the WTC

CALATRAVA

FOSTER

NOVEMBER   **DECEMBER**

11.19.03
WTC memorial finalists named

Master Planner or Mas

By Rafael Viñoly

As Gov. George E. Pataki prepares to unveil the latest design of the "Freedom Tower" at ground zero, the long-simmering dispute between Daniel Libeskind, the master planner for the site, and David M. Childs, the architect chosen by Larry Silverstein, the commercial leaseholder at the site, to design the tower has come to a boil. Although this is unfortunate and unprofessional, it will probably pale in comparison to the struggle for symbolic control of the rebuilding after the designer of the World Trade Center memorial is chosen next week. That is the way things will go if certain crucial points are not clarified now.

As a member of the team that was the runner-up to Daniel Libeskind as master planner of the World Trade Center site, I am familiar with the trajectory of the process. As a New Yorker, I care deeply about the future of Lower Manhattan, and how the rebuilding will honor the memory of those lost on 9/11 and shape our future as a dynamic metropolis.

Much of the confusion that reigns today centers on the public's — and apparently Governor Pataki's — mis-

Rafael Viñoly is an architect.

understanding of what constitutes a "master plan." Master planning, although usually done by architects, is not the same as architectural design. The planner decides where buildings go, how big they are, the kind of urban form they create and the purposes they serve. A planner marks out roads and figures out how the underground infrastructure relates to the surface infra-

---

How to straighten out the mess at ground zero.

---

structure. What a master planner does *not* do is design the buildings themselves.

None of this is to say that a master plan should not have an enormous impact on a site's development. (After all, I too wanted the job.) A master plan is an important tool in a city's overall evolution, even if it does not mandate specific designs. Paris and Washington were shaped by master plans; on a smaller scale, so was Battery Park City. The outlines were set by a planner and then the details were filled in, to varying degrees of success, by individ-

ual architects.

The trouble at ground zero began with the governor's decision to support Mr. Libeskind's "vision" (what his rendering looked like) rather than the master planning ideas behind it. Unfortunately a vision is not a master plan, it is simply a version of what one particular architect would do within that plan.

Mr. Libeskind's master plan is a spiral of rising towers around the site where the twin towers were. This is a powerful urban form that can and should be respected. However, the detailed design that Mr. Libeskind incorporated into his rendering has too often been treated by the governor and others as a design guideline, which it is not.

This problem is particularly apparent when it comes to the memorial. In his rendering, Mr. Libeskind essentially designed the memorial itself. After all, the exposed slurry wall, the waterfall and the names of the public spaces he specified all had a commemorative function. What's wrong with this? Well, the task of creating a memorial was intentionally removed from the master-plan competition because it was supposed to be the subject of the memorial design competition. I think that the weaknesses in the finalist designs for the memorial are a consequence of having to design a memorial within a memorial.

In my view, the Lower Manhattan

12.12.03
"Master Planner or Master Builder?" op-ed piece by RV appears in *The New York Times.*

12.19.03
First WTC "Freedom Tower" design unveiled.

ter Builder?

Development Corporation has consistently failed to educate the public — and perhaps even the governor — as to what to expect (and not to expect) from a master plan.

How so? First the corporation asked Beyer Blinder Bell and other firms to put together six master plans. These weren't building designs. Rather, they were geometric shapes meant to give people the sense of what Lower Manhattan's cityscape might look like. These plans encountered public opposition not just because they were not very inspirational in themselves, but primarily because they were mistaken for architectural designs.

The corporation reacted to the public outrage by creating the Innovative Design Study, a sort of "noncompetition" that was supposed to identify one or more consultants to help the agency further develop the master plan for the site. This process resulted in the most exciting architectural event in years. It was from this competition that Mr. Libeskind's rendering was chosen. But instead of portraying the exercise as one step along a more deliberative path, the corporation created the impression that this was the final result.

No matter. There is still time to clarify the process and allow it to move forward in a fair, constructive and logical manner. For this to happen, though, the governor, the development corporation, Mr. Libeskind, Mr. Silver-

stein and the other parties need to agree to the following basic points, which any first-year architecture student would be able to derive from a textbook on master planning.

- Define the basic idea of the master plan as a spiral of structures around the footprints of the towers. This is Mr. Libeskind's vision — and it should be accepted.
- Assure the developers that the design of the buildings is the responsibility of their chosen architects.
- Prompt Mr. Libeskind to see to it that there is a set of precise design guidelines — guidelines that can preserve his urban form without restricting the architectural design of those buildings.
- Give control of the memorializing functions of the plan to the winner of the memorial design competition.
- Specify where cultural facilities will be placed and outline where the money for them will come from (and make sure that money is not diverted to other uses).
- Build more time into the project. To coordinate the laying of the Freedom Tower cornerstone with the Republican National Convention in New York next summer is an unrealistic goal that will compromise the success of all our efforts. Would it not be better to disappoint a few conventioneers than to let down all New Yorkers and the 9/11 families? □

Video Glossary

Shigeru Ban
Shigeru Ban Architects

Roland Betts
Chelsea Piers Management, LLC

Anita Contini
LMDC

Tony Cracciolo
Director of Priority Capital
Programs, PANYNJ

Bob Davidson
Port Authority of NY & NJ

Peter Davoren
Turner Construction (President)

Daniel Doctoroff
Deputy Mayor for Economic Development

Stan Eckstut
Ehrenkrantz Eckstut & Kuhn Architects

Robert Eisenstadt
Port Authority

Alex Garvin
LMDC

Chan-Li Lin
Rafael Viñoly Architects, PC

William R. Morrish
UVA School of Architecture

David Rockwell
Rockwell Group

Jörg Schlaich
Schlaich Bergermann und Partner

Fred Schwartz
Frederic Schwartz Architects

Larry Silverstein
Silverstein Properties

Ken Smith
Ken Smith Landscape Architect

Rafael Viñoly
Rafael Viñoly Architects, PC

John C. Whitehead
Chairman of Board of Directors/LMDC

Andrew Winters
LMDC

Acknowledgments

We are deeply indebted to Anne Lebleu for her great efforts in assembling and organizing the materials for this book as well as her creative and editorial contributions to its form and content. We also wish to thank Maria Aviles-Lebron for her invaluable input on content and design and for her support and championing of the project from the start. The book's design is the result of the intelligent and talented people of the design firm Pure+Applied—Urshula Barbour, Paul Carlos, and Andy Pressman—who always shared our objectives and our enthusiasm for the project.

Obviously, this book would not have been possible without the extraordinary participation of the principal design firms of THINK: Ken Smith Landscape Architecture, Frederic Schwartz Architects, Shigeru Ban Architects, and Rafael Viñoly Architects, whose particular generosity and support was the foundation upon which we were able to produce this book. We are also grateful for the contributions and assistance of Schlaich Bergermann und Partner, Buro Happold Engineers, Ove Arup & Partners, Professor William Morrish, and Robert Greenberg and the staff of R/GA.

We are thankful to Takeshi Miyakawa, Derek Conde and the RVA model shop, which restored all of the models that were photographed for this book, to Tracey Hummer who not only edited the texts but also helped us "corral" the talent, and to Robby Stein who provided support and perspective throughout. Edward L. Smith kindly contributed wise legal counsel in the securing of rights and permissions for this publication.

THINK

Shigeru Ban

Shigeru Ban Architects & Dean Maltz

Principals
Shigeru Ban
Dean Maltz

Personnel
Hirosugi Mizutani
Ken Ishioka
Andrew Lefkowitz

Frederic Schwartz

Frederic Schwartz Architects

Principal
Frederic Schwartz

Project Manager
Taizo Yamamoto

Personnel
Tomas Bauer
Felicity Beck
Patrick Evans
Arvin Flores
Heike Heister
Tracey Hummer
David Mann
Franziska Michel
Gali Osterweil
Henry D. Rollmann
W. Douglas Romines
Jason Warren

Ken Smith

Ken Smith Landscape Architect

Principal
Ken Smith

Personnel
Annie Weinmayr
Judith Wong
Elizabeth Asawa
Tobias Armborst
Joanne Davis Rose
Johanna Ballhaus
William Morrish
Janet Marie Smith

Rafael Viñoly

Rafael Viñoly Architects

Principal
Rafael Viñoly

Personnel
Ute Bessenecker
Derek Conde
Yoko Fujita
Miwa Fukui
Laura Gelso
Frances Gretes
Kevin Kleyla
Timo Kuhn
Asaka Kusuma
Chan-li Lin
Alda Ly
Takeshi Miyakawa
Yoshinori Nakamura
Hiroshi Nakayama
Harold Park
Diego Petriella
Andrés Remy
Kazimierz Rzezniak
Mark Sarosi
Joe Schollmeyer
Anna Shtobbe
Jeffrey Timmins
Rei Tokunaga
Konstantin Udilovich
Román Viñoly

Rockwell Group

Principals
David Rockwell
Marc Hacker
Diego Gronda
Edmond Bakos
Designers
Charlotte Macaux
Jean Pierre Fontanot

ARUP

Principal
Leo Argiris
Personnel
Jonathan Drescher
Fiona Cousins
Markus Schulte
Al Palumbo

Buro Happold

Principal
Tony McLaughlin
Engineer
Byron Stigge

Schlaich Bergermann und Partner

Prof. Dr.-Ing. Jörg Schlaich
Dr.-Ing. Hans Schober

Stan Reis Photography

Stan Reis

Photo Credits

Introduction
Endpaper: ©Space Imaging
Circular pavilion: ©Max Protech
Sky memorial rendering: ©Ken Smith Landscape Architects
Tall structures drawings: ©Frederic Schwartz
DNA towers: ©Frederic Schwartz
London Eye sketches: ©Rafael Viñoly
London Eye: ©Anne Lebleu
Tower ride sketches: ©Rafael Viñoly
Eiffel Tower: ©Martin Sañudo
Rebuild the Towers billboard: ©urban75.com

7.16.02
Herbert Muschamp meeting: ©Richard Leslie Schulman
West Street images: ©Frederic Schwartz

7.22.02
West Street models: ©Frederic Schwartz
The New York Times Magazine meeting: ©Richard Schulman

08.24.02
Transportation Center renderings: ©Rafael Viñoly Architects

09.08.02
The New York Times Magazine cover: ©*The New York Times*
Venice biennial guide: ©Anne Lebleu

10.15.02
Landscape drawing: ©Ken Smith Landscape Architects
Elevation sketches: ©THINK
Yellow trace sketch: ©THINK

10.20.02
Tower sketches: ©Shigeru Ban
Tower renderings: ©Shigeru Ban
Japanese lanterns: ©Corbis

10.26.02
Typologies tracing paper: ©THINK
Website screen grabs: ©R/GA
"My Kind of Town": ©*Architecture Today*
"The Man Who Dared the City...": ©*The New York Times*

10.27.02
Piet Mondrian, 1872–1944
Broadway Boogie Woogie, 1942–43
Oil on Canvas, 50" x 50"
© 2006 Mondrian/Holtzman Trust
c/o HCR International, Warrenton, VA

10.29.02
Great Hall sketches: ©Shigeru Ban

12.09.02
Frederic Schwartz and Román Viñoly: ©Takeshi Miyakawa

12.19.02
Winter Garden: ©Whirlwind Creative
"Brave New World": ©*Daily News*
"Rising from the Ashes": ©*New York Post*

02.05.03
Charlie Rose stills: ©*Charlie Rose Show*
Today Show stills: ©NBC Universal
"A Visionary of the Skyline...": ©*The New York Times*
"Two Finalists are Selected...": ©*The New York Times*

02.26.03
"Turning a Competition...": ©*The New York Times*
"Let Culture Soar at Ground Zero": ©*Daily News*
"Ground Zero Finalist's Past...": ©*The Wall Street Journal*
"Panel Supports 2 Tall Towers...": ©*The New York Times*

02.28.03
"Practical Issues for Ground Zero": ©*The New York Times*

12.12.03
"Master Planner or Master Builder?": ©*The New York Times*

Permissions for Previously Published Material

New York Daily News
"Brave New World" (cover)
December 19, 2002
Reprinted with permission from the *New York Daily News*

The Wall Street Journal
Bravin, Jess
"Ground Zero Finalist's Past Draws Questions"
February 26, 2003
Reprinted with permission from *The Wall Street Journal*

New York Daily News
Meier, Richard
"Let Culture Soar at Ground Zero"
February 26, 2003
Reprinted with permission from Richard Meier

Architecture Today
Viñoly, Rafael
"My Kind of Town"
May 1, 2002
Reprinted with permission from *Architecture Today*

The following items are reprinted with permission
from *The New York Times*:

The New York Times (page-one)
February 27, 2003

The New York Times Magazine (cover)
September 8, 2002

Bagli, Charles
"Visions For Ground Zero: The Debate; Architects' Proposals
May Be Bold, But They Probably Won't Be Built"
December 19, 2002

Finn, Robin
"A Visionary of the Skyline With 3 Pairs of Glasses"
January 22, 2003

Gordon, Alastair
"At Home With: Frederic Schwartz; The Man Who Dared the
City to Think Again"
September 19, 2002

Muschamp, Herbert
"Designers' Dreams, Tempered by Reality"
February 26, 2003

Viñoly, Rafael
"Master Planner or Master Builder?"
December 12, 2003
Reprinted with permission from Rafael Viñoly

Wyatt, Edward
"Panel Supports 2 Tall Towers at Disaster Site"
February 26, 2003

Wyatt, Edward
"Two Finalists Are Selected For the Void at Ground Zero"
February 5, 2003

Published in Australia in 2006 by
The Images Publishing Group Pty Ltd
ABN 89 059 734 431
6 Bastow Place, Mulgrave, Victoria 3170, Australia
Tel: +61 3 9561 5544 Fax: +61 3 9561 4860
books@images.com.au
www.imagespublishing.com

National Library of Australia Cataloguing-in-Publication entry:

Lewis, Hilary.
Think New York: a ground zero diary.

ISBN 1 920744 74 6.

1. World Trade Center Site (New York, N.Y.) – Planning.
2. City planning – New York (State) – New York.
3. Urban renewal – New York (State) – New York – Planning.
4. September 11 terrorist attacks, 2001.
I. Viñoly, Román. II. Title.

711.4097471

Coordinating editor: Robyn Beaver ·

Designed by Pure+Applied, New York
www.pureandapplied.com

Film by Mission Productions Limited

Printed by Everbest Printing Co. Ltd., in Hong Kong/China

IMAGES has included on its website a page for special
notices in relation to this and our other publications.
Please visit www.imagespublishing.com